Racism and anti-racism in
American popular culture

For Nicholas

WITHDRAWN

Racism and anti-racism in American popular culture

Portrayals of African-Americans in fiction and film

Catherine Silk *and* John Silk

Manchester University Press

Manchester and New York

Distributed exclusively in the USA and Canada by St. Martin's Press

Published by Manchester University Press
Oxford Road, Manchester M13 9PL, UK
and Room 400, 175 Fifth Avenue,
New York, NY 10010, USA

Distributed exclusively in the USA and Canada
by St. Martin's Press, Inc.,
175 Fifth Avenue, New York, NY 10010, USA

British Library cataloguing in publication data
Silk, Catherine
        Racism and anti-racism in American popular culture:
        portrayals of African-Americans in fiction and film.
        1. Fiction in English. American writers. Special
        subjects: United States. Black persons   2. American
        cinema films, history. Special subjects: United
        States. Black persons
        I. Title   II. Silk, John
        791.43'09'3520396073

Library of Congress cataloging in publication data
Silk, Catherine, 1946–
        Racism and anti-racism in American popular culture: portrayals of
        African-Americans in fiction and film / Catherine Silk, John Silk.
        p.   cm.
        Includes index.
        ISBN 0-7190-3070-6
        1. Afro-Americans in mass media – United States.   2. United States-
        Popular culture – History – 20th century.   I. Silk, John, 1942–
        II. Title.
        P94.5.A372U57 1990
        813.009'3520396073 – dc20   89-12627

ISBN 0 7190 3070 6 *hardback*

Typeset in Great Britain
by Williams Graphics, Llanddulas, N. Wales

Printed in Great Britain
by Courier International, Tiptree, Essex

Contents

	Acknowledgements	vi
	Introduction	vii
Part One	**Literary reactions to the Civil War and Reconstruction**	**1**
1	From colonial days to the Civil War	3
2	Joel Chandler Harris: *Uncle Remus: His Songs and Sayings* (1880)	13
3	Albion Tourgee: *Bricks Without Straw* (1880)	26
4	Charles Chesnutt: *The Conjure Woman* (1899)	38
5	Thomas Dixon: *The Clansman* (1905)	48
Part Two	**Literary reactions to the Second World War and the Second Reconstruction**	**59**
6	From Jim Crow to the Second Reconstruction	61
7	Howard Fast: *Freedom Road* (1944)	72
8	Ann Petry: *The Street* (1946)	84
9	William Styron: *The Confessions of Nat Turner* (1967)	95
10	Alice Walker: *Meridian* (1977)	106
Part Three	**Portrayals on film**	**119**
11	*Birth of a Nation* and silent film	121
12	Hollywood's Golden Age and *Gone with the Wind*	134
13	'The Death of Uncle Tom' (1941–1969)	148
14	From Blaxploitation to *The Color Purple*	163
	Index	177
	Filmography	184

Acknowledgements

We would like to thank the following people for their help. The American Embassy in London, the Research Board and the Department of Geography at the University of Reading assisted with grants towards visiting the United States in 1985. Staff at the Mississippi Department of Archives and History in Jackson, Mississippi and at the library of Louisiana State University in Baton Rouge were extremely helpful in allowing us to use their resources. Don and Carrie Vermeer showed us great hospitality and were unfailingly kind to us during our visit to Louisiana State University, also in 1985.

We would also like to thank those friends, colleagues and students who have been so encouraging to us while we have been working on this project.

Introduction

The history of African-Americans is a centuries-long one of struggle against oppression and discrimination. Between the sixteenth and the nineteenth century probably nine and a half million Africans were forcibly removed from their homes, their families and their cultures, and taken to the New World. In the United States they were used as slave labour in order to build up the society and economy of a new country. Speaking different languages, sold away from their families, they gradually developed a culture which helped them to survive in these appalling conditions. Religion, music and oral tales were significant elements in an evolving and rich counter-culture.

When finally freed in 1863 they were subjected to horrendous violence, discrimination and economic exploitation, particularly, but not only, in the Southern States. By the twentieth century a system of segregation and discrimination so rigid and pervasive had been set up in the South that the average white would not come across a black person unless s/he was his servant or employee.

Not until the so-called Second Reconstruction of the nineteen-fifties and sixties did African-Americans even come close to sharing in the American democratic system, to which they had contributed so much.

In this book we have traced the changing racist ideas and practices of American society from the Civil War to the nineteen-eighties, and looked at the ways in which such ideas are embodied in popular culture, in particular in fiction and film.

There is currently an ongoing debate about race and the definition of racism (see for example Banton (1977), van den Berghe (1978), Lawrence (1982), Jackson (1987)). We have taken a racial group to be one which has been socially defined. In terms of the natural division of humankind, it is possible to argue that there is no such thing.

For those determined to define race, criteria have varied from real or imaginary innate physical characteristics to presumed behavioural differences. Skin pigmentation, shape of head and even shape of eyes or feet have been used by some to define racial groups. Racist beliefs and practices can be defined as those which use these definitions to justify and explain the exploitation and oppression of one 'racial group' by another.

In the United States we believe racism evolved as an attempt to justify slavery, segregation, discrimination and the economic exploitation of black people. These practices came to be based on ideas of racial inferiority which were elaborated into pseudo-scientific theories.

These and ideas and practices associated with them changed throughout the period at which we are looking. To give one example, the elaborate racism which was used to justify slavery stressed both the inferiority and docility of black people. Blacks were, it was explained, almost subhuman and were suitable only for hard physical labour. It followed that they were therefore happy under slavery where they were forced to work hard and had no decisions to make. After the Civil War racists still stressed the inferiority of blacks, but now it appeared they were no longer naturally docile but extremely aggressive, and could only be controlled if kept strictly segregated and forced to do mostly menial work. Black men were also discovered to be sexually aggressive, and were said to be naturally attracted to white women as the women of a 'superior race'. More subtle racism also developed; in the twenties for instance many liberals believed that black people were exotic primitives, more in tune with natural rhythms than whites. He have therefore treated racism as a dynamic ideology and traced changes as elaborated in and reflected in the popular culture of the time.

We have also stressed the constant thread of anti-racism, both in the practices of society at large, and in popular culture. At all times in America there have been those, both black and white, who have been prepared to question the basic assumptions of racism and to fight them.

Popular culture is also a term under constant debate (e.g. Hall and Jefferson (1976), Bennett *et al.* (1981), Silk (1984)). The term is sometimes used to refer to the ways in which the working class and other non-dominant groups express themselves culturally. More frequently, popular culture refers to culture produced for consumption by the masses. This is usually viewed in derogatory terms. Media research has shown the ways in which the press, cinema and radio have considerable power to shape opinions and can actively influence behaviour. In the

nineteen-thirties, cultural critics from both left and right in the political
spectrum deplored the effects, as they saw it, of the mass media in
destroying traditional culture (e.g. Twelve Southerners (1977); Leavis
(1932)), or reducing the working class to a resigned and passive mass
(Adorno and Horkheimer (1979); see also Swingewood (1977)). Later
research cast doubt on these views. Mass communications research for
example in America in the early forties showed that any power that
media exercised depended upon their location within existing structures
of social relationships and systems of culture and belief (McQuail, 1977,
p. 73). Recognition of other influences is taken into account. The role
of financial backers, of the government, the role of censors, publishing
houses and film companies must all be examined. It is within this complicated nexus of relationships that people directly involved in producing
books or films must work.

For our purposes popular culture can be defined as works of fiction
or movies which were produced at important moments in the development of racist and anti-racist ideas, and which at the time had, or were
aimed at, a large audience. We have taken into account whether the
audience was black or white, middle or working class, Northern or
Southern, and also the ways in which audiences themselves changed
over time. We have looked closely at the ways in which particular
aesthetic and ideological devices within texts help to reinforce ideas in
society. For example, the use of the first person narrative by writers like
Harris and Styron, who put their words into the mouths of stereotypic
black characters, is an extremely effective aesthetic and ideological
device.

By studying these works in their historical, aesthetic and political
context, including the economic, political and social context in which
they were produced, it becomes possible to examine racism as a
changing ideology. It is also then possible to look at its relationship to
society, ideas and practices at particular times in African-American
history. We can look too at the effects of popular culture on the various
audiences who consume it.

Although the effects of popular culture can be exaggerated, our work
shows that the persistent portrayal of racist ideas in works which reach
wide audiences exacerbates the problems of racism and discrimination,
which themselves provided the climate in which these particular works
were produced. For those writers and film-makers who were always prepared to go 'against the grain' we have nothing but admiration, and we
hope that we have shown how important such 'cultural struggle' can be.

References

Adorno, T. W. and Horkheimer, M. (1979) 'The culture industry: enlighten-
ment as mass deception', in Adorno, T. W. and Horkheimer, M. (eds),
Dialectic of Enlightment, Verso, London

Banton, M. (1977) *The Idea of Race*, Tavistock, London

Bennett, T., Martin, G., Mercer, C. and Woollacott, J. (eds) (1981) *Culture,
Ideology and Social Process: A Reader*, Batsford Academic and Educational Ltd/
The Open University Press, London

Hall, S. and Jefferson, T. (eds) (1976) *Resistance Through Rituals: Youth Subcultures
in Post War Britain*, Hutchinson, London

Jackson, P. (ed) (1987) *Race and Racism: Essays in Social Geography*, Unwin
Hyman, London

Lawrence, E. (1982) 'Just plain common sense: the "roots" of racism' in
Centre for Contemporary Cultural Studies (eds), *The Empire Strikes Back:
Race and Racism in 70s Britain*, Hutchinson, London

Leavis, F. R. (1932) 'Under which king, Bezonian?', *Scrutiny*, 20, pp. 1–24

McQuail, D. (1977) 'The influence and effects of mass media', in Curran, J.,
Gurevitch, M. and Woollacott, J. (eds) *Mass Communication and Society*,
Arnold, London, pp. 70–94

Silk, J. A. (1984) 'Beyond geography and literature', *Environment and Planning D*
(Society and Space), 2, pp. 151–78

Swingewood, A. (1977) *The Myth of Mass Culture*, Macmillan, London

Twelve Southerners (1977) *I'll Take My Stand*, Louisiana State University Press,
Baton Rouge and London (originally published in 1930)

van den Berghe, P. L. (1978) *Race and Racism: A Comparative Perspective*, New
York, Wiley (2nd edition)

PART ONE

Literary reactions to the Civil War and Reconstruction

1

From colonial days to the Civil War

The early American colonists found themselves in a vast new land full of natural resources waiting to be exploited but they had available very little labour-power, and it was this combination of factors which led to the early use of indentured servants in New England and Virginia. In Virginia they were used for tobacco cultivation, and such labour was used in the new colonies, particularly in New England throughout the seventeenth century. Indentured labour was based on a mutually binding agreement: the indentured servant agreed to work a company's land for seven years, at the end of which time he received some land himself and became free. The first blacks taken to Virginia in 1619 were such servants, and Franklin (1974, p. 56), points out that as late as 1651 blacks whose period of service had expired were being given land.

However, indentured labour was soon found to be unsuitable. There were not enough people willing to come as indentured servants, and those that came often ran away, leaving the labour needs of the new colonies unmet. Slavery was already being used off the American coast in the sugar plantations of the Caribbean, and it was an easy step to enslave the black labourers of the new colonies, and begin to import more. Arguments which were used to justify slavery were the fact that blacks would be easier to spot if they ran away, and that harsh punishments to discipline them would be justified because most blacks were not Christians. (Harsh punishments did not of course stop when most blacks had become Christian; other justifications were rapidly found.) In 1661 came statutory recognition of slavery in Virginia. The growth of the United States was therefore built on a most unstable foundation: the use of slavery as a source of the accumulation of capital in a developing nation-state.

The economic successes of Virginia and Maryland led to the use of slavery in the Carolinas. By the middle of the eighteenth century the institution of slavery was a necessary fundamental part of the developing American economic system. In 1664 in Maryland, inherited slave status was recognised,and union between the races was prohibited, because 'divers free born *English* women, forgetful of their free condition, and to the disgrace of our nation, do intermarry with Negro slaves' (Degler, 1984, p. 34).

The ideology of racism was further strengthened by the use of slave codes; instituted to deter rebellion and to get the most work possible from slaves, they also helped to underline notions of the superiority of whites, and the inferiority of blacks. Treated consistently as inferior, not allowed to learn to read or write or to 'better themselves' in any way, blacks were then castigated for being naturally inferior. The Virginia Slave Code was heavily influenced by slave codes previously used in the Caribbean, and itself was to later influence the slave codes of other Southern States. Slaves were not permitted to leave the plantation without written permission of their masters; for 'petty' offences they could be whipped, branded or maimed, for 'serious' ones they could be killed. It is difficult with hindsight to believe that the people who framed these laws could believe themselves to be morally superior to the people whom they were exploiting. As Franklin says (1974, p. 58):

The docility of the slaves, about which many masters boasted, was thus achieved through the enactment of a comprehensive code containing provisions for punishment designed to break even the most irascible blacks in the colony. With the sheriffs, the courts, and even the slaveless whites on their side, the masters should have experienced no difficulty in maintaining peace among their slaves.

The contradiction between slavery as an economic system and the development of a new state based on ideas of freedom and individual liberty, surfaced as an issue during the American War of Independence. During this period, colonists often referred to the injustices of both slavery and of their colonial status *vis-à-vis* England. When the British Army declared free all blacks who fought with them, George Washington rescinded his earlier decision that no blacks were to be allowed into the American army. Many slaves ran away during the war years, understanding clearly the significance for themselves of this fight for freedom. It is estimated that in 1778, 30,000 slaves ran away in Virginia. The Declaration of Independence, however, remained silent on the issue of slavery, so that the very document which summed up the ideology of American individual liberty allowed the continuation of slavery – the freedom of the individual was to mean the freedom, if that person were white, to own another person.

The Constitutional Convention of 1787, meeting in Philadelphia to frame a Constitution and to decide the basis of representation to the new Congress, found itself under great pressure from the Southern States. This, coupled with the necessity the Convention felt to repress the upsurge of feeling among ordinary people for greater rights ensured that they were willing to accommodate. Independence had led to widespread demands for real democracy among ordinary Americans, and the anti-slavery movement was seen as an integral part of this generalised unrest. For every five slaves therefore, it was decided that white Southerners were allowed three votes. The uneasy and unstable collaboration between two economic systems continued, and would not be resolved until the Civil War. This compromise was to postpone the inevitable conflict between North and South for seventy-five years.

The anti-slavery movement however continued after the war and a victory appeared to have been gained in the 1787 addition to the Northwest Ordinance passed by Congress, which stated that in the territory covered by the Ordinance, there should be no slavery.

By the end of the eighteenth century, slavery was dying out in New England. In 1781, for example, Massachusetts declared slavery to be illegal. During the economic recession of that period, it appeared for a time that slavery would die a 'natural' death.

What rejuvenated the institution was the invention of the cotton gin, and the enormous demand for cotton from countries like Britain, which was rapidly industrialising. Cotton cultivation required little capital, and with the new cotton gin slave labour increased the production of the crop enormously. England, in particular, paid high prices for as much cotton as the Southern States could produce, and continued to do so for many years.

The movement West, which gathered pace after the peace of 1815 and the entry of new states into the Union – Louisiana in 1815, Mississippi in 1817, and Alabama in 1819 – was to lead to the South's deeper economic and ideological investment in slavery. The white South became united in its defence of slavery; any Southerners who disagreed left the South. Vociferously it called for slavery to be an integral part of the new lands – while the economic and political interests of the North opposed it. Slavery had become a barrier to America's economic development, but for the South slavery was its source of wealth, and ideologically it was seen as the basis of the region's special and unique 'culture'. In this way, the frontier, and the concomitant notion of manifest destiny, became, for the South, intrinsically bound up with its right to hold slaves. Many Southern spokesmen began calling for the annexation of new lands as a means of safeguarding slavery.

The attacks on slavery by the Anti-Slavery League and others were to lead, especially after the War of 1812, to the South's determined defence of slavery. It was during this ante-bellum debate that many of the classic racist ideas which still permeate American society originated, and as the conflict grew nearer, the white South felt less and less inclined to apologise for slavery. Indeed part of its justification came to be that slavery was a positive good and was a system under which the slaves themselves were content. This notion of slavery was closely related to the elaboration of the idea that black people were inferior to whites. Educators and ministers in the South now joined the debate and based their defence of slavery on the same arguments. 'Ethnological writers such as Richard Colfax, Samuel Cartwright, and Josiah Nott detailed the physical deficiencies of the Negro, his cranial characteristics, his facial angles, and concluded that intellectually the Negro was incapable of being the equal of whites'(Christian, 1980, p. 9). Slavery brought civilisation and religion to people who would otherwise know neither; it was an efficient method of creating wealth and a leisure class whose culture would be impossible without it, and the manifest destiny of the American people moving West was dependent upon it. By the last decade of the ante-bellum period such arguments were increasingly dressed up in pseudo-scientific language.

At the same time, anti-slavery feeling was growing in the North and had become quite militant by 1830. In 1831 the New England Anti-Slavery Society was formed. The abolitionists argued that slavery was against the teachings of Christianity and contrary to the fundamental principles of American democracy. They also argued, more pragmatically, that it was an uneconomic and wasteful system. The abolitionists attempted, as part of their struggle, to counter the images put forward by the pro-slavery advocates. Black abolitionists like Frederick Douglass were particularly effective in putting forward positive images, for their very existence, intelligence and skills refuted the arguments of those who wished them to remain slaves. Slave narratives were a constant reminder of the lies being told by those whose interests were served by the continuation of slavery, and black abolitionist speakers had a great impact in the North.

The supposed contentment and docility of black people under slavery was undermined not only by the work of free black abolitionists in the North, but also by the endemic resistance of blacks under slavery. Special tools had to be made for slaves as they destroyed ordinary farm implements; self-mutilation and suicide were the desperate resort of many who felt they could not live under such a system, and the murder of their children by women whose children were to be sold away from them was not uncommon:

we may better understand now a Margaret Garner, fugitive slave, who, when trapped near Cincinnati, killed her own daughter and tried to kill herself. She rejoiced that the girl was dead – 'now she would never know what a woman suffers as a slave.' and pleaded to be tried for murder. 'I will go singing to the gallows rather than be returned to slavery.' (Aptheker, quoted in Angela Davis, 1982, p.21)

Southern newspapers of the time show that overseers and masters were regularly killed by slaves in the woods or in the fields. The slave also 'burned forests, barns, and homes to the extent that members of the patrol were frequently fearful of leaving home lest they be visited with revenge in the form of the destruction of their property by fire' (Franklin, 1974, p. 157.)

Although it is true that slave revolts were infrequent, they took place regularly enough to cause great concern among the white population. In 1811 in New Orleans about 500 slaves were involved in an uprising. In the Vesey uprising of 1822 in South Carolina many thousands of blacks were involved, and in 1831 perhaps the most famous uprising of all took place in Virginia when the mystic Nat Turner led a revolt. There also existed, throughout slavery, communities of Maroons all over the South – black people who had escaped slavery, and lived and worked together, often with Native Americans. These groups of free blacks were a source of fear to the white slave-owning classes, and represented the inability of their group to destroy rebelliousness within the slave community.

The debate between pro- and anti-slavery factions helped to shape the literature produced in the ante-bellum South, and itself illustrates the fact that there has always been a struggle between racist and anti-racist ideas in the United States. During the early period of slavery, many, though not all, white people appeared willing to believe in the inferiority of black people. There were periods, however, for example during the War of Independence, when the contradictions in these ideas began to surface. During the ante-bellum period, particularly between 1830 and the outbreak of the Civil War, many white people, particularly in the North, began increasingly to question these ideas and to oppose them; the fundamental conflict of interest between North and South was to mean that these anti-slavery ideas gained more influence. Their time had come. The enormous popularity of novels like *Uncle Tom's Cabin* is but one illustration of this.

The idea of a distinctive Southern literature was a product of this conflict between North and South as Southern writers increasingly saw their role as spokesmen for the South. This necessarily entailed defending the South against attacks upon it and upon slavery. Most literature in the South was produced by upper middle-class white men, who used their work to defend their way of life. Influenced primarily by English writers like Sir Walter Scott, they often found the historical novel a useful vehicle for putting forward their point of view. This was a device which was to continue and to gain a much larger audience after the Civil War. The first major work in the plantation tradition is Kennedy's *Swallow Barn* published in 1832.

Kennedy populates his Old Dominion with comic eccentrics, cultured gentlemen, gracious ladies, and contented childlike slaves .... Far more significant as cultural myth than as aesthetic creation, *Swallow Barn* can be seen legitimately as the first major statement in the literary battle over the image of slavery that includes works as disparate as *Uncle Tom's Cabin, Uncle Remus, His Songs and Sayings, The Conjure Woman, The Clansman, Gone With the Wind*, and *Roots*. (Werner, 1985, pp. 90–1)

Local-colour humorous sketches published in local newspapers were extremely popular and also remained influential in the post Civil War period; Joel Chandler Harris's sketches of Uncle Remus first appeared as newspaper sketches for example. Meanwhile, most slave culture, apart from the slave narratives of escaped blacks, was both oral and counter-cultural, a method of survival as well as a means of making sense of an absurd and cruel world.

During the eighteen-fifties the conflict between North and South came to a head. There was increased controversy over slavery in the newly acquired territory in the South-west. By the 1850 agreement, California was declared free, but slaveholders were protected by the stringent Fugitive Law. Neither section was really committed to this compromise. In 1852 *Uncle Tom's Cabin* was published and sold 300,000 copies in its first year. Its dramatisation on the stage increased its popularity and ensured that it reached an even wider audience. The 1854 Kansas–Nebraska Act inflamed the situation as both North and South struggled for control of the territories, which by the act could decide on the issue of slavery through their own territorial legislatures.

By the late eighteen-fififties the situation between North and South was such that the raid on Harper's Ferry by John Brown and his followers and the Republican victory in 1860 made war between the two inevitable.

Behind the secession of the South from the Union, after Lincoln was elected President in the fall of 1860 as candidate of the new Republican party, was a long series of policy clashes between South and North. The clash was not over slavery as a moral institution – most northerners did not care enough about slavery to make sacrifices for it, certainly not the sacrifice of war. It was not a clash of peoples ... but of elites. The northern elite wanted economic expansion – free land, free labor, a free market, a high protective tariff for manufacturers, a bank of the United States. The slave interests opposed all that; they saw Lincoln and the Republicans as making continuation of their pleasant prosperous way of life impossible in the future. (Zinn, 1987, p. 184)

It can be seen therefore that slavery was used in the days when the United States was first being settled as a primitive method of ensuring the accumulation of capital necessary for the young country to expand and make use of its economic resources. Blacks were enslaved rather than whites, initially for reasons of expedience, and once treated consistently as inferior human beings, a whole panoply of racist ideas evolved in order to justify this inhuman treatment. Eventually slavery was no longer necessary for the economy of America as a whole; in fact it was holding back its untrammelled industrialisation. However, it was more entrenched than ever in the Southern States whose whole white way of life depended upon its continuance. The struggle between North and South was to culminate in the Civil War, but it was a struggle which had long and deep roots, and which manifested itself not only in political and economic disagreements, but in a long ideological battle over slavery and its racist images.

References

Aptheker, H. (1968) *American Negro Slave Revolts*, International Publishers, New York

Blassingame, J. W. (1973) *The Slave Community: Plantation Life in the Antebellum South*, Oxford University Press, Oxford and New York

Brock, W. (1973) *Conflict and Transformation: The United States, 1844–1877*, Penguin, Harmondsworth

Camejo, P. (1976) *Racism, Revolution, Reaction, 1861–1877: The Rise and Fall of Radical Reconstruction*, Monad Press, New York

Camejo, P. (1978) *Who Killed Jim Crow? The Story of the Civil Rights Movement and its Lessons for Today*, Pathfinder Press, Inc., New York

Christian, B. (1980), *Black Women Novelists: The Development of a Tradition, 1892–1976*, Greenwood Press, Westport, Conn.

Current, R. N. (ed) (1969) *Reconstruction in Retrospect: Views From the Turn of the Century*, Louisiana State University Press, Baton Rouge

Davis, A. (1982), *Women, Race and Class*, Women's Press, London

Degler, C. (1970) *Out of Our Past: The Forces that Shaped Modern America*, Harper & Row, New York, Cambridge and London (3rd edition)

Du Bois, W. E. B. (1971) *The Autobiography of W. E. B. Du Bois*, International Publishers, New York

Elkins, S. M. (1976) *Slavery: A Problem in American Institutional and Intellectual Life*, University of Chicago Press, Chicago and London

Foner, P. S. (1976) *Organized Labor and the Black Worker, 1619–1973*, International Publishers, New York

Franklin, J. H. (1974) *From Slavery to Freedom: A History of Negro Americans*, Alfred A. Knopf, New York (4th edition)

Gaston, P. M. (1970) *The New South Creed: A Study in Southern Mythmaking*, Louisiana State University Press, Baton Rouge and London

Genovese, E. D. (1967) *The Political Economy of Slavery: Studies in the Economy and Society of the Slave South*, Vintage Books, New York

Gramsci, A. (1971) *Selections from the Prison Notebooks*, Lawrence & Wishart, London

Gramsci, A. (1979) *Letters from Prison*, Quartet Books Ltd, London

Gutman, H. (1976) *The Black Family in Slavery and Freedom, 1750–1925*, Pantheon, New York

Harding, V. (1983) *There is a River: The Black Struggle for Freedom in America*, Vintage Books, New York

Heffner, R. D. (1976) *A Documentary History of the United States*, New American Library, New York and Scarborough, Ont.

Hobson, F. (1983) *Tell About the South: The Southern Rage to Explain*, Louisiana State University Press, Baton Rouge and London

Jordan, W. (1968) *White Over Black: American Attitudes Toward the Negro, 1550–1812*, University of North Carolina Press, Chapel Hill

Kiernan, V. G. (1980) *America: The New Imperialism: From White Settlement to World Hegemony*, Zed Press, London

Lindenmeyer, O. (1970) *Black History: Lost, Stolen, Or Strayed*, Avon Books, New York

Logan, R. W. (1970) *The Negro in the United States. Volume I: A History to 1945 – From Slavery to Second-class Citizenship*, Van Nostrand Reinhold, New York

McPherson, J. M. (1965) *The Negro's Civil War*, Vintage Books, New York

Marable, M. (1983) *How Capitalism Underdeveloped Black America*, Pluto Press, London

Marable, M. (1985) *Black American Politics: From the Washington Marches to Jesse Jackson*, Verso Books, London

Marx, K., and Engels, F. (1974) *The Civil War in the U.S.*, International Publishers, New York

Novack, G. (1980) *Understanding History: Marxist Essays*, Pathfinder Press, New York

Paskoff, P. F., and Wilson, D. J. (eds) (1982) *The Cause of the South: Selections from De Bow's Review, 1846–1867*, Louisiana State University Press, Baton Rouge and London

Phillips, U. B. (1966) *American Negro Slavery: A Survey of the Supply, Employment and Control of Negro Labor as Determined by the Plantation Regime*, Louisiana State University Press, Baton Rouge

Reed, J. S. (1982) *One South: An Ethnic Approach to Regional Culture*, Louisiana State University Press, Baton Rouge

Rose, W. L. (1982) *Slavery and Freedom: Four Episodes in Popular Culture*, Oxford University Press, Oxford and New York

Rubin, L. D. Jr, Jackson, B. J., Moore, R. S., Simpson, L. P., and Young, T. D. (eds) (1986) *The History of Southern Literature*, Louisiana State University Press, Baton Rouge and London

Scott, J. A. (1974) *Hard Trials on my Way: Slavery and the Struggle against it 1800–1860*, New American Library, New York and Scarborough, Ont.

Stampp, K. M. (1965) *The Era of Reconstruction, 1865–1877*, Vintage Books, New York

Thornbrough, E. L. (ed) (1972) *Black Reconstructionists*, Prentice-Hall, Inc., Englewood Cliffs, NJ

Tindall, G. B. (1976) *The Ethnic Southerners*, Louisiana State University Press, Baton Rouge

Washington, Booker T. (1967) *Up From Slavery*, Airmont Publishing Company, Inc., New York

Werner, C. (1985) 'The Old South', in Rubin, L. D. Jr *et al.* (eds), pp. 81–91

White, J. (1985) *Black Leadership in America, 1895–1968*, Longman, London and New York

Williams, E. (1975) *Capitalism and Slavery*, André Deutsch, London

Williams, J. (1986) *Eyes on the Prize: America's Civil Rights Years, 1954–1965*, Viking, New York

Woodward, C. Vann (1966) *Reunion and Reaction: The Compromise of 1877 and the End of Reconstruction*, Little, Brown & Co., Boston

Woodward, C. Vann (1971) *American Counterpoint: Slavery and Racism in the North-South Dialogue*, Little, Brown & Co., Boston

Woodward. C. Vann, *Origins of the New South, 1877–1913*, Louisiana State University Press, Baton Rouge

Woodward, C. Vann (1974) *The Strange Career of Jim Crow*, Oxford University Press, Oxford and New York

Zinn, H. (1987) *A People's History of the United States*, Longman, London and New York

2

Joel Chandler Harris: *Uncle Remus: His Songs and Sayings* (1880)

When *Uncle Remus* first appeared in book form in 1880, it was destined to become one of the most influential of the highly popular 'local-colour' novels of the eighteen-eighties. In the Southern version of the local-colour novel, writers portrayed an idyllic, usually ante-bellum South, one in which black and white, rich and poor, lived amicably together under the paternal eye of the white plantation-owner. Many critics have seen the enormous popularity of these novels as an ideological victory for the Southern States, one which, as it were, compensated Southern whites for the rather more concrete defeat at Appomattox.

It was the local-colour writers of the eighties, like Harris, Page and Nelson, who created the enduring plantation stereotypes of contented slave, southern belle, courtly planter, 'moonlight and magnolias'. As we have argued elsewhere, this literature had an important function in effecting reconciliation between the ruling classes of North and South after the devastation of the Civil War. Northern magazines were extremely anxious to publish such work, and so-called 'unreconstructed' material was edited out. Southern writers were quick to learn; Harris himself for example, changed his short story, 'A Story of the War'. When first published in the newspaper, *Atlanta Constitution* Uncle Remus kills a Union soldier, but in the version published in *Songs and Sayings* he merely wounds him, then helps to nurse him back to health, and is finally seen loyally working for him after he has married the local Southern belle!

Such reconciliation, of course, was at the expense of the Southern working classes, both black and white. It was the eighteen-nineties in particular which were to see a determined onslaught upon the rights of black people in the South. The work of Harris and of others in the previous decade was to begin to forge acceptance for racist ideas.

What is particularly interesting about the 'Uncle Remus' tales is the complexity of the relationship between the author's ideology, the tales, and the ways in which various audiences have read them.

One device which Harris and later other Southern writers were to use to great effect, was to place their philosophy of race relations into the mouths of black characters. Apologies for racism proved to be far more effective when its victims, like Uncle Remus himself, were made to plead its cause. The original character of Uncle Remus, created by Harris for his humorous sketches in *Atlanta Constitution* played this role. Voicing both the fears and the beliefs of the white population of Atlanta, the shuffling figure of Uncle Remus is portrayed as a regular visitor to the newspaper office in which Harris worked. Here he begs from the white employees while simultaneously giving voice to his contempt for the 'new' i.e. free blacks, who, he says, are lazy, greedy, and good for nothing but the chain gang. What particularly infuriates Uncle Remus is that they appear to forget how lucky and how happy they were when they lived under slavery. Harris's description of Uncle Remus's conversation with a friendly white policeman about the perils of education for blacks is a good example. The white man is told that since Remus's daughter has begun school, he and his wife can do nothing with her; she has begun to have ideas above her station:

'Look at my gal. De ole 'oman sont 'er ter school las' year, and'now dassent hardly ax 'er ter kyar de washin' home. She done got beyant 'er bizness. I 'aint larnt nuthin' in books, 'en yit I kin count all de money I gits. No use talkin', boss. Put a spellin' book in a nigger's han's, en right den en dar' you loozes a plow-hand. I done had de spe'unce un it.' (Harris, 1982, p. 216)

This tale contains many ideological and aesthetic devices which were at the time very effective. The white policeman and Uncle Remus are both native Southerners, from the same small town, but the policeman talks in standard English, whereas Uncle Remus speaks in broad dialect. He is thus 'placed' as a character, slightly humorous, quaint, and by extension typical of many black people. Uncle Remus himself, always portrayed as a stereotypical 'sympathetic old darky' condemns his own people for their ingratitude to whites and for their desire for education. Thus the condemnation appears more 'true' and Harris's attempt to reverse a reality which so obviously frightened him as a white man is given a credence which was to find a sympathetic audience among white Northern liberals.

A black character argues that education only spoils blacks for work, while a white Southern policeman, a potent symbol of the white oppression of black people, is portrayed as not only a sympathetic character, but as more liberal than Uncle Remus.

Such obviously crude methods disappear in the section 'Legends of the Old Plantation' in which appear many of the Brer Rabbit stories. In the Uncle Remus figure of these tales is created one of the most powerful and pervasive racist stereotypes in American culture; Aunt Jemima and Uncle Ben are only the most obvious descendants. Kindly, asexual, unthreatening to whites or to their power, Uncle Remus fulfils almost primal longings for love and attention on the part of whites. He obviously represents for Harris, at one level, the kindly father-figure he never knew in real life. It can be seen as an especially ironic aspect of Southern popular culture that having once successfully established a white hegemony, the need for unqualified love and approval was often projected onto selected blacks..Through such black characters Southerners could also implicitly ask how can we be oppressing black people – look how they love us.

It is this particular ideological myth which Alice Walker subverts so effectively in her novel *The Color Purple*. Miss Eleanor Jane, the white girl whom Sofia was forced to raise at the expense of her own children, brings her baby son to see Sofia. She persists in attempting to get her to say how much she, Sofia, really loves Eleanor Jane's baby:

'Just a sweet, smart, cute, *innocent* little baby boy, say miss Eleanor Jane, Don't you just love him? she ast Sofia point blank.
No ma'am, say Sofia. I do not love Reynolds Stanley Earl. Now. That's what you been trying to find out ever since he was born. And now you know.
... Eleanor Jane start to cry. 'I love children, say Sofia. But all the colored women that say they love yours is lying. They don't love Reynolds Stanley any more than I do. But if you so badly raise as to ast 'em, what you expect them to say? Some colored people so scared of white folks they claim to love the cotton gin.'
(Walker, 1983, pp. 223–5)

The Uncle Remus character is certainly one such figure; he shows throughout the tales not only how much he loves white folks, but particularly how much he loves white children. It is in fact the relationship between Uncle Remus and the little white boy to whom he tells the tales that is central to Harris's success. Through the telling of the tales uncle Remus is seen to help initiate the boy into the mysteries and codes of a white racist society. The warm firelit cabin, in which Uncle Remus affectionately cuddles the child functions as a microcosm of the ideal world of paternalistic race relations that Harris so fervently wanted to believe in.

Each tale is 'framed' by a description of Uncle Remus and the little white boy settling down in the cabin for a story-telling session. In the same way after the story-telling, the child and the old man discuss the tale. There is a tension between this framework and the content of the tales themselves which has been interpreted in various ways. The stories themselves, which most critics accept as genuine black folklore, and which functioned under slavery as an important counter culture among slaves, have been co-opted by a white writer and used simply as another local-colour device. At the same time the 'framework' is used to put forward a racist stereotype – the avuncular Uncle Remus. The many blacks who were to reject the Harris version of Brer Rabbit stories, were simply recognising this.

On the other hand there are interpretations which stress the potentially subversive effect of the inherent contradiction between framework and tale. The world which is described in the tales is far from idyllic; it is rather one in which survival is the only victory, in which nothing is what it seems, and where everyday conversation masks power struggles and the predatory designs of the animals concerned. The trickster figure of the rabbit represents the black male attempting to survive under slavery; Harris himself was clear about this. While Uncle Remus therefore is apparently educating the boy into the precepts of a white racist society the tales are simultaneously telling him a very different story!

As each tale begins, the little white boy from the big house goes down to the cabin where Uncle Remus lives in order to hear one of his stories about the animal world. In this warm, cosy place where the firelight constantly flickers Harris has created what seems to be a child's retreat from the real world. Both the boy, because of his youth, and Uncle Remus because of his great age are 'displaced' from the harsh social relationships which really existed in the post-bellum South. This displacement is further stressed by the description of their relationship in the 'limbo' of the old man's cabin. The relationship itself is contradictory: sometimes idyllic, at other times strangely ambivalent. Usually Uncle Remus is loving and affectionate towards the boy, a totally unthreatening father-figure who appears to exist quite literally only to love and amuse the child. His language reflects this; he calls the boy 'honey' and is shown cradling him and stroking his hair affectionately. At the same time, he is shown to have some authority over the child, an authority in which he consciously identifies with Miss Sally, the little boy's mother, '"en w'at yo' gran'ma wouldn't er stood me en jyo' ma ain't gwineter sta' nudder."' (Harris, 1982, p. 130). In this way the ex-slave and the ex-slave-owner are shown to have a common interest in socialising white middle-class children. Many later Southern novels and films were to show such black servants, usually women, more concerned with middle-class mores than were their charges, for example the character played by Hattie McDaniel in *Gone With the Wind*.

The fundamental irony, which has been pointed out by most critics, is the contrast between this essentially harmonious frame and the genuine black folklore of the stories. In many of the frames, Uncle Remus begins by reprimanding the little boy for his bad behaviour, and it is through these conversations that the 'code' in which Joel Chandler Harris believed becomes clear. In this code people care for one another, they don't lie, and paternalistic characters in positions of responsibility look after weaker people. That this code is a reflection of Harris's solution to the problems of the South need hardly be stressed; race relations would no longer be a problem if blacks trusted whites and if whites took their paternalistic role seriously. In 'Mr. Fox is Again Victimized', for example, Uncle Remus at first refuses to tell the child a story at all, '"I ain't tellin' no tales ter bad chilluns," said Uncle Remus' (Harris, 1982, p. 70), and it is only after he has been bribed by a gift of some cakes that he consents.

Sometimes, the tales are specifically used to comment on the child's behaviour and are in effect, an extended reprimand, as in 'The Awful Fate of Mr. Wolf' in which the wolf is scalded to death as a punishment for harassing the rabbit. In case the point is missed, Uncle Remus introduces the story by saying:

'olks w'at's allers pesterin' people, and bodderin' 'longer dat w'at ain't dern, don't never come ter no dood end. Dar wuz Brer Worl; stidder mindin' un his own bizness, he hatter take an go in pardnerships wid Brer Fox, and day want skacely a minnit in de day dat he want atter Brer Rabbit.' (Harris, 1982, p. 89)

In this way, Uncle Remus uses the tales as morality lessons for the boy. However, the world that is presented within the tales is in direct conflict with everything that Uncle Remus preaches, and here lies the irony. In his conscientious refusal to 'cook' the black folklore tales which are the basis of his book, Harris effectively allows this contradiction to emerge quite starkly. For the world of the tales, the world of Brer Rabbit, is a nightmare where to survive by one's wits, to be physically

alive at the end of the day is the greatest victory possible. At the end
of 'Miss Cow Falls a Victim to Mr. Rabbit' we are told: 'e bleedzd ter
laff. Fox atter 'im, en Cow atter 'im, and dey ain't kotch 'im yit'
(Harris, 1982, p. 80).

Critics have pointed out that the world of Brer Rabbit is the world
of slavery as experienced by black males. For many, Brer Rabbit is the
southern black male, ancestor of the blues trickster figure; a very
American confidence man, using his wits in order to survive. Brer
Rabbit's most typical trick is to turn the tables on an animal more
powerful than himself, thus surviving their attempts to destroy, kill, eat
or torture him. Many struggles take place around food and, to a lesser
extent, sex. The obsession with food and with hunger clearly reflects
a world in which slaves were chronically underfed and had little or no
control over what and when they ate.

It is also a world without any semblance of justice; and Brer Rabbit
is shown to have no principles, only the desire and the will to survive.
In 'Mr. Rabbit Nibbles Up The Butter' we first see the animals in a
rare display of co-operation repairing a roof, but Rabbit keeps sneaking
off to eat the butter that is meant to later be their meal. When the theft
is discovered, he frames the possum, who is killed attempting to jump
over a fire in order to prove his innocence. Interestingly enough, Uncle
Remus refuses to reassure the little boy who is clearly puzzled by the
injustice of the possum's fate, saying:

'Dat w'at make I say w'at I duz, honey. In dis worril, lots er fokes gotter suffer
fer udder fokes sins. Look like hit's might on-wrong; but hit's des dat away.
Tribulashun seem like she's a waitin' roun de cornder fer ter ketch one en all
un us, honey.' (Harris, 1982, p. 107)

Later, commenting on the story 'Jacky My Lantern'. he says: '"Hit
may be wrong er't may be right, but dat's w'at I years"' (Harris, 1982,
p. 150). Just as Harris insisted that he never 'cooked' the stories, so
Uncle Remus abdicates all responsibility for the content of the tales.
Ironically, Uncle Remus the story-teller justifies this attitude by saying
to the boy: '"I don't wanter tell you no stories."' In this way the
moralising Uncle Remus can allow the tales to undermine the overt
advice which he is constantly giving him, and when this disturbs him,
Uncle Remus simply denies responsibility.

The relationship betwen old man and child is itself however not quite
as idyllic as at first appears. For Uncle Remus is also shown to be
pathetically dependent upon the little boy for crumbs from the white

folk's table. Food is overtly used by the little boy to placate and to please Uncle Remus: ' "Please, Uncle Remus, if you will tell me, I'll run to the house and bring you some tea-cakes" ' (Harris, 1982, p. 71). These are considered to be such a treat that Uncle Remus eats only some, putting the rest by until another day.

Even when Uncle Remus is specifically disciplining the child, the use of dialect functions to subvert any authority Uncle Remus may have; the boy, however young, is placed as a member of a 'superior' class by his use of standard English. During the tale of 'The Awful Fate of Mr. Wolf', when Uncle Remus attempts to reprimand the boy 'the child laughed, and playfully shook his fist in the simple, serious face of the venerable old darkey, but said no more' (Harris, 1982, pp. 88–90).

The uneasy relationship between appearance and reality, itself an integral part of the slave's world, is underlined by these contradictory levels of story-telling. The reader is being told a story about a man telling stories in which characters consistently lie in order to survive or to prey upon one another, and then these stories themselves are presented as true. The way in which Uncle Remus *acts* occasionally intensifies this effect; at one point we are told that Uncle Remus 'allowed his venerable head to drop forward until his whole *appearance* was suggestive of the deepest dejection; and this was intensified by a groan that *seemed* to be the result of great mental agony' (Harris, 1982, p. 124; emphasis added). Later he is described as 'sitting in his door, with his elbows on his knees and his face buried in his hands, and he *appeared* to be in great trouble'' (Harris, 1982, p. 142).

It is true to say, however, that however ironic and multi-layered are the potential meanings of the tales their enormous popularity has usually been based on rather more crude readings. In practice, they were a part of that ideological and political onslaught against blacks in the latter part of the nineteenth century. Their readers were primarily white, Northern and middle-class, and increasingly open both to racist ideas and to the necessity of reconciliation between Northern and Southern whites. 'Harris's tales began to appear just at the moment when interest in the Negroes was rapidly rising' (Downs, 1977, p. 160). As many of them saw it, the idyllic relationship between Uncle Remus and the little boy reflected a South in which the North increasingly wanted to believe. The tales also told them that, left alone, the white South could be trusted to solve the race problem. Ex-slaves, like Uncle Remus obviously bore no resentment toward white ex-slave-owners. In the Introduction to the tales Harris addresses these Northern readers:

If the reader not familiar with plantation life will imagine that the myth-stories of Uncle Remus are told night after night to a little boy by an old negro who appears to be venerable enough to have lived during the period which he describes – who has nothing but pleasant memories of the discipline of slavery – and who has all the prejudices of caste and pride of family that were the natural results of the system. (Harris, 1982, pp. 46 – 7)

It is the old black man himself who is used to reassure Northern whites about the stability of the South, while the tales themselves were enjoyed primarily for their local colour and use of dialect and the childlike animal stories. For many whites, including in later years Roosevelt's wife, they were seen as ideal bedtime stories for children. The impact of the work of Harris and other Southern local-colourists was enormous:

For better or for worse Page, Harris, Allen, and their associates of the South, with the aid of Northern editors, critics, magazines, publishing houses, and theaters, had driven completely from the Northern mind the unfriendly picture of the South implanted there in the days of strife.' (Buck, 1937, p. 235)

The gentle local-colour stories of Harris and other Southern writers constituted part of a new wave of racism after the Civil War. Initially, after the upheavals of both the Civil War and of Radical Reconstruction in the South, the stories of Joel Chandler Harris served to reassure their Northern white audience about the situation in the South. From these tales they learnt that black people in the South were contented if only paternalistic white Southerners were allowed control over them. It seemed increasingly true to the white North that the South had been right all along about blacks and the 'problem' of race. This in turn meant that they need no longer feel guilty about the South; white Southerners could be trusted to take care of any problems. The knowledge and patronising affection with which writers like Harris portrayed characters like Uncle Remus seemed to prove both the childlike inferiority of black people and the responsibility of whites like Harris. In Hemenway's view, (1982, pp. 21 – 2):

Harris reinforced a historical theory of slavery that began with the premise, widespread in his generation, that the human relationships of the peculiar institution had been close and mutually supporting. Remus's dialect especially supports this fantasy. The standard English used by the author to frame the tales contrast with the vivid dialect in the stories themselves, suggesting that black language is colorful but ignorant, that black people are picturesque but intellectually limited.

This 'gentle' racism was in fact to lay the groundwork for a whole new set of racist ideas, that were to become widely accepted by the early part of the twentieth century. For example the later myth of the black rapist was based on the concept of the childlike nature of the black man, whose powerful instincts, if not kept in control by whites, could easily turn him into a mindless beast. Local-colour stories dovetailed neatly into the new theories of Social Darwinism and biological determinism. With the rise of imperialism in the latter part of the nineteenth century, racism was to become shriller and more violent. The disfranchisement of blacks and the enormous increase in the numbers of lynchings were only a part of the attack on blacks' civil, political and economic rights. The novels of Thomas Dixon are more typical of this later phase of racism than the work of Harris. But in Harris's stories can be seen the basis of later racist ideas, which others were to take to their logical conclusion.

In his book, *Race, the History of an Idea in America* Gossett (1975) traces the ways in which racist ideas changed in order to justify both the treatment of blacks in the South and also those people brought into the American orbit through imperialism. Racism became more and more respectable, and social scientists were enthusiastic in their desire to 'prove' the inferiority of black people. In particular, the popular arguments of Social Darwinism, which to many social scientists were scientific ideas were used to show the evolutionary and hereditary inferiority of black and working class people. In both popular and academic works black people were described as inherently inferior to the 'Anglo-Saxon' race, and indeed, for many social scientists it was simply a matter of time before black people died out. These ideas were themselves backed up by simplistic ideas of the relationship between environment and racial characteristics. For example, the Anglo-Saxon race was superior because it came from colder climates and was therefore inherently more intellectual and adventurous. Black people on the other hand, coming from tropical climates, were suited only to physical labour. Anthropologists spent much time collecting folklore and other information about 'backward' people.

Popular novelists and writers like Frank Norris, Jack London and Owen Wister helped to publicise race theories in their novels and to glorify the Anglo-Saxon race. (Gossett, 1975, p. 286). The same commentator in fact says that 'American thought of the period 1886 – 1921 generally lacks any perception of the Negro as a human being with potentialities for improvement.' However, the Uncle Remus stories were read by more than one audience. White Southerners for example read the tales, and not only felt a sense of justification *vis-à-vis*

race relations in the South, but also identified with the character of Brer
Rabbit, seeing him not as a black character but as representing the weak
and beaten South outwitting the stronger North, and surviving on its
own terms:

White southerners could read his books and find justification for the way of life
they had gone to war to defend. White northerners could read his books and
believe that the white southerners were thoroughly reconstructed and should
be given control over their own affairs, particularly the affairs that related to
the future of the black man in the South. But black men could also read Harris'
books, as Charles Chesnutt read them to his children, and could find in them
not just stereotypes of the contented darky and faithful black family retainer
but also, as Rubin points out, black characters who 'in their humanity and
strength strike at the very foundations of race prejudice'. (L. H. MacKethan,
1980, p. 63)

All these meanings can, and have been, read into the tales, but what
of course is most significant is how *most* people read them at the time.
It was of little comfort to black people who were being oppressed,
lynched and disfranchised, to understand the ironic and subversive
meanings of many of the tales. Whatever Harris's conscous or unconscious intentions, it appears that his audience did not read the stories
as subversive. At the time the tales seemed to confirm the stereotype
of the contented 'darky' and to glorify life on the old plantation (Rubin,
1975, p. 103).

The later history of the book illustrates this relationship further.
As audiences changed, and particularly as the real world in which
they were living changed, so too did the apparent meanings of the
stories. As late as the nineteen-thirties (Hemenway, 1982, p. 8),
the image of the smiling, menial, black servant figure was firmly
rooted in the American popular imagination, and the character of
Uncle Remus was in fact being used to sell Coca Cola. However the
Second World War was a watershed for American blacks and for race
relations within the USA. Contradictions between dominant ideology
and the reality of American society were no longer so easily masked.
The US government's fight for the 'four freedoms' and against fascism
was carried out using a segregated army with American black soldiers,
many of whom were living under Jim Crow in the South. The emergence of new African countries, soon to be represented in the U.N.
together with a marked migration of Southern black to Northern states,
and increased unrest among them, led to embarrassing pressure upon
the American government.

This conflict was to surface in popular culture after the Second World War. There was, for example, a debate among black artists about the role of blacks in movies. Many black actors were becoming more determined not to portray stereotypic roles in films. They recognised that these stereotypes both reflected white fears of blacks and helped to reinforce their inferior status in society. Significantly, when Walt Disney began to make a movie version of Harris's Brer Rabbit stories, *Song of the South* (1946), the black actor Leon Hardwick refused the role of Uncle Remus, deciding 'it would make him a traitor to the race' (Cripps, 1977, p. 384). When the movie finally came out blacks and white liberals picketed performances of it, while Hollywood awarded James Baskette, who played Uncle Remus in the film, a posthumous Oscar. In the late sixties, at the height of the Civil Rights movement, the film was removed from circulation, as its racist message had become more obvious to a wider audience, and it was now considered controversial. But in the nineteen-eighties, it is not only again in circulation, but more popular than ever. (Hemenway, 1982, p. 8.) 'The centennial of Uncle Remus's first appearance, fall 1980, found black and white parents, kids in tow, waiting in long lines to view the reissued movie once again.'

Today, critical scholarship tends to look not only at the figure of Uncle Remus, but at the tales themselves, their structure and their probable relationship to genuine black folklore. The pride in a black cultural heritage, first manifested on a genuinely wide scale in the nineteen-sixties, shows itself in pride in the complex and satisfying tales of Brer Rabbit, ironically saved for posterity by a white Southerner, who is now increasingly seen less as a creative writer himself, and more as a caretaker and transmitter of black folklore. Different audiences still read the tales, and watch the movie, and they still receive different messages, but it is increasingly difficult to interpret them as they once were; the times have changed and with them the tales.

References

Baer, F. E. (1981) 'Joel Chandler Harris: An "Accidental Folklorist"', in Bickley (ed.), pp. 185 – 96
Bain, R., Flora, J. M. and Rubin, L. D. Jr (eds) (1980) *Southern Writers: A Biographical Dictionary*, Louisiana State University Press, Baton Rouge and London
Bickley, R. B. Jr. (ed.) (1981) *Critical Essays on Joel Chandler Harris*, G. K. Hall & Co., Boston

Bickley, R.B. Jr. (1978) *Joel Chandler Harris*, Twayne Publishers, New York

Bier, J. (1981) 'Duplicity and Cynicism in Harris's Humor', in Bickley, pp. 98–103

Bone, R. (ed.) (1981) 'The Oral Tradition', in Bickley, pp. 130–46

Boskin, J. (1986) *Sambo; The Rise and Demise of An American Jester*, Oxford University Press, Oxford and New York

Brookes, S.B. (1950) *Joel Chandler Harris; Folklorist,* University of Georgia Press, Athens

Brown, S. (1937) *The Negro in American Fiction*, Associates in Negro Folk Education, Washington, DC

Buck, P.H. (1937) *The Road To Reunion*, Little, Brown and Co., Boston

Butcher, M.J. (1956) *The Negro in American Culture,* New American Library, New York

Cousins, P.M. (1968) *Joel Chandler Harris: A Biography*, Louisiana State University Press, Baton Rouge

Cripps, T.S. (1977) *Slow Fade to Black*, Oxford University Press, New York

Davis, A. (1982) *Women, Race and Class*, The Women's Press, London

Downs, R.B. (1977) *Books That Changed the South*, University of North Carolina Press, Chapel Hill, NC

Ellison, M. (1985) 'Black perceptions and red images – indian and black literary links', *Phylon*, 44, part 1, pp. 44–55

Flusche, M. 'Underlying Despair in the Fiction of Joel Chandler Harris', in Bickley, pp. 174–85

Franklin, J.H. (1974) *From Slavery to Freedom, A History of Negro Americans*, Alfred A. Knopf, New York

Fredrickson, G.M. (1971) *The Black Image in the White Mind*, Harper and Row, New York

Gaston, P.M. (1970) *The New South Creed*, Louisiana State University Press, Baton Rouge and London

Gossett, T. (1975) *Race: The History of an Idea in America*, Southern Methodist University Press, Dallas, Tex.

Griska, Joseph M. Jr. (1978) '"In Stead of a Gift of Gab"', Some New Perspectives on Joel Chandler Harris Biography', in Bickley, pp. 210–27

Harris, J.C. (1982) *Uncle Remus: His Songs and His Sayings,* Penguin, London

Hedin, R. (1982) 'Uncle Remus: puttin' on ole massa's son', *Southern Literary Journal*, 15, part 1, pp. 83–90

Hemenway, R. (1982) 'Introduction: Author, Teller, and Hero', in Harris, pp. 7-33

Higgs, R.J. (1984) 'Southern humor – the light and the dark', *Thalia, Studies in Literary Humor*, 6, part 2, pp. 17–27

Jones, A. H. (1983) 'J. C. Harris: tales of Uncle Remus – animal wisdom reconciles a nation', *Journal of American History Illustrated*, 18 (3), pp. 34–9

Keenan, H. T. (1984) 'Twisted tales: propaganda in the tar-baby stories', *Southern Quarterly*, 22, part 2, pp. 54–69

Light, K. (1981) 'Uncle Remus and the Folklorists', in Bickley (ed), pp. 146–58

MacKethan, L. H. (1980) 'Joel Chandler Harris: Speculating on the Past', in *The Dream of Arcady: Place and Time in Southern Literature*, Louisiana State University Press, Baton Rouge

MacKethan, L. H. (1980) 'Joel Chandler Harris', in Bain *et al.* (eds), pp. 208–11

Martin, J. (1981) 'Joel Chandler Harris and the Cornfield Journalist', in Bickley (ed), pp. 92–8

Rubin, L. B. (1975) 'Uncle Remus and the Ubiquitous Rabbit', in *William Elliot Shoots a Bear: Essays on the Southern Literary Imagination*, Louisiana State University Press, Baton Rouge

Smith, J. D. (1984) 'The unveiling of slave folk culture, 1865–1920', *Journal of Folklore*, 21 (1), pp. 47–62

Williamson, J. (1986) *A Rage for Order: Black-White Relations in the American South since Emancipation*, Oxford University Press, Oxford and New York

Wolfe, B. (1981) 'Uncle Remus and the Malevolent Rabbit: "Takes a Limber-Toe Gemmun fer ter Jump Jim Crow"', in Bickley (ed), pp. 70–85

3

Albion Tourgee: *Bricks Without Straw* (1880)

As we have already seen, when *Bricks Without Straw* (1880) was first published, a new ideology of racism was emerging in the United States, but it was not yet firmly established. The immediate post Civil War period was one of revolutionary uncertainty, a time when many ideas were thrown into the melting pot, and the balance of forces in terms of class, race, region, and political party appeared to be particularly fluid. During the most crucial period of this struggle, 1865 – 1879, Tourgee, a white, liberal Northerner, lived and worked in North Carolina. It was his experiences during this time which led him to write his novels. His avowed aim was to explain to the North what was really happening in the South, and in particular the ways in which black people were being forced into a new kind of economic peonage, which was rapidly replacing slavery as a new form of social control. It can be seen therefore that Tourgee was a writer who was consciously attempting to stem, through his work, the tide of the new ideology of racism. He believed strongly in the moral purpose of art and in the power of cultural intervention to change radically people's ideas about the world they live in.

By the mid eighteen-eighties, however, the vogue of local-colour novels, most of them Southern in origin and subject matter, had become enormously popular. With their nostalgia for mythical ante-bellum days, their genteel racism was in harmony with current ideas and was helping to pave the way for the shriller and more overt racism of the late nineteenth century. Tourgee's work therefore is particularly significant. It is consciously oppositional at a time of growing racism, and an analysis of his novels helps to clarify the ways in which such popular novels are produced and, even more crucially, received during such a period.

Born on a farm in Ohio, in the then Western Reserve, Tourgee was brought up to believe strongly in the ideology of individualism, and of moral responsibility for one's own actions. Particularly characteristic of his upbringing was an emphasis on the necessity of open and free debate on all subjects. He grew up with the native and naïve optimism of many such nineteenth-century Americans; the American Way was the way forward for all. He came to believe that the racism of the Southern States was holding back the development of true American values.

His actions and experiences during the Civil War confirmed his view of the world. Discharged after only several weeks in the Union army, because of injuries to his back, he spent his year of convalescence recruiting others to the cause. Re-enlisting, he was wounded again and for some months was a prisoner of war in several Southern prisons. Generally, Tourgee found army discipline hard to accept and was constantly in trouble for insubordination. Once, he was arrested for refusing to give up a black man who, he claimed, had helped to save his regiment. The meaning of the Civil War and subsequent events in the South, as he saw and interpreted them, were to dominate his views for the rest of his life.

Accepting that they were now irrevocably part of the Union and that the institution of slavery was abolished forever, white Southerners of the ruling classes reacted to defeat by attempting to rebuild a society identical in all other respects to the ante-bellum world they had fought to preserve. In particular, they were determined that blacks would continue to be slaves in all but name.

The first step in this process was the establishment of the so-called 'Black Codes'. In North Carolina these were written into law in 1866 by a presidentially reconstructed state legislature which was 'chosen in essentially the same way that unreconstructed legislatures had been chosen for thirty years' (McKee Evans, 1967, p. 66). Through these laws blacks could be arrested for a score of minor 'offences' such as 'intending' to steal livestock. Once imprisoned they were liable to be hired out as labourers at the courts' whim.

Vigilante groups, militias of ex-Confederates, sprang up everywhere in the South, ensuring that black people understood their place in society now they were 'free'. At this stage however, the South was seen by the incensed radical Congress in Washington to be overreaching itself and the result was the passing of the two Reconstruction Acts of 1867. These made the return of any state to the Union dependent upon the writing of universal manhood suffrage into their state constitution.

The years between the Reconstruction Acts and the Hayes – Tilden compromise of 1876, when the last federal troops were removed from the South, witnessed a persistent power struggle between various groups. The Conservatives proved to be willing to use any method to recreate a racist society in which the blacks would be the 'mud-sills'. Republican and black opposition was left to rely on increasingly inconsistent and feeble support from the federal government. The Ku Klux Klan and other para-military gangs became, in effect, the extra-legal arm of the Democratic Party. In most of the South, including much of North Carolina, Republicans found themselves unable to cope with the organised violence of the opposition: 'In the face of implacable white resistance they proved unable to preserve law and order or their own existence, against attempts at violent overthrow. In certain parts of the South the authorities were almost paralyzed by organized lawlessness' (Trelease, 1972, p.xxxiv). Recognising that they would not always be able to count upon the support of Federal troops, the Republicans in North Carolina determined to set up a state militia, but in their determination that it should be politically neutral, they weakened it before it was even formed: 'in a belt across the middle of North Carolina, this had meant a Conservative militia, led by former Confederate officers. Lacking force, the civil authority had degenerated into empty pronouncements and bluster' (McKee Evans, 1967, p. 45).

This pattern, on one side the deliberate and cynical use of violence, and on the other a half-hearted attempt to oppose it, continued throughout this period. It has been pointed out by historians like Trelease and McKee Evans, that in those areas where there was a majority of blacks, or where there was a more determined opposition to the Klan and other similar groups, the paramilitaries were usually defeated. Significantly, however, even during those brief periods when there was a Republican state government in North Carolina, most local governments, the courts, and very importantly, the media, were always controlled by the Democrats.

In 1871, the federal government finally passed the Ku Klux and Federal Election Acts in order to protect non-Democrats and to attempt to hold fair elections. But for North Carolina, as for much of the South, such help came too late:

Having seized control of the decisive branch of the state government, the legislature, the Conservatives were now in a position to employ legal rather than extralegal methods to extend their power; so, following some convictions under the Ku Klux Act, they allowed their shady auxiliary to fall into disuse. (McKee Evans, 1967, p. 148)

Tourgee not only lived in North Carolina throughout this period, but he was actively involved in the political struggle which was going on. In 1867 he became a leading member of the new Republican Party in North Carolina, and was a delegate to the North Carolina constitutional convention of 1868. Later, as an elected superior court judge, he was to witness the destruction of Reconstruction by the armed gangs of the Ku Klux Klan and others. His own judicial circuit was the scene of 'an undeniable reign of terror [which] continued until at least fifteen murders and hundreds of lesser atrocities had been committed by the Klan' (Olsen, 1969, p. x). Tourgee's fearlessness in the face of the constant threat of violence, coupled with his determination to stand up for the freedman, became legendary. He came to represent for many North Carolinians the epitome of the so-called 'carpetbagger'.

Moving to the South partly for health reasons and partly to begin a new life, Tourgee brought with him his own ideas about what was necessary to reunite North and South into a free nation. It was this almost missionary zeal which irritated many white Southerners. Accepting that they had lost the war had not affected their sense of righteousness, or their belief in the Southern system. The South was to be again irritated by what it saw as Northern 'do-gooders' in the Civil Rights movement of the nineteen-sixties almost a century later.

Tourgee was incensed by what he saw in North Carolina:

Technical emancipation simply had not destroyed the behaviour and belief of generations, and Tourgee found himself constantly irritated by a conspicuous racial oppression that ranged from milder requirements for black subservience, to expressions of vicious racism and a denial of civil equality, to callous manhandling and even murder. (Olsen, 1969, p. ix)

The development of his ideas in response to these events can be seen most clearly in his novels. He came to recognise the tenacious hold of ideologies upon people even when the world in which they live has been changed forever. The defeat of the Civil War was a fact which had to be recognised, but racist ideas were simply modified to suit the new conditions. Instead of ante-bellum slave patrols, there was now the Ku Klux Klan, instead of slavery there was economic peonage and the convict lease system.

Unlike Howard Fast, Tourgee was not led by his recognition of these facts to a belief in the necessity of force to ensure real democracy in the

South. Instead, he came to believe that the fight against racist ideology should be waged through culture and education. It was necessary to convince people that racism was wrong, and to do this the artist should aim to show his audience the true nature of social relations in the South. Ironically, Tourgee's emphasis on the power of ideas led him to have some sympathy with white Southerners and with the way they felt about race. Both North and South were, he believed, imprisoned in old ideologies which they did not control:

> ... not only did Tourgee come to see that the policies of the government were mistaken: he came to realize that – given the exclusion from government of the former governing classes in the South and their fear of being governed by the Negroes – the creation of the Klan was inevitable; he even came in certain respects to admire it. (Wilson, 1962, p. 536)

He was also sympathetic to the literary tradition of the South. He was out of touch with, and later openly antagonistic to, the new realism which was emerging and which was to dominate American literature in the late nineteenth century. In particular, he objected to the subject-matter of many contemporary novels and, as he believed, their obsession with the unpleasant side of life. Later he was to despise what he saw of the immorality of many realist writers who portrayed humans as victims of a harsh environment over which they had no control.

Like Page and Harris, Tourgee was brought up to admire the work of Cooper and Scott, and Cooper remained for him the model of a great novelist. Believing that art should serve a moral and didactic purpose, the *content* of a work of art was always considered by him to be more important than its form. Historical events like Reconstruction should be used to teach a lesson. He wrote of the novelist Charles Reade: 'He recognised the underlying truth of all artistic production, that its highest purpose is to teach a noble lesson' (Gross, 1963, p. 145). These beliefs led to Tourgee taking 'structural liberties with the form at a time when more serious novelists were attempting to devise some sort of technical standards' (Gross, 1963, p. 521).

In every sense, then, Tourgee was writing against the grain. By the time that *Bricks* appeared, the Republican party had all but ceased to exist in the South, and blacks had been abandoned to their fate. An increasingly sympathetic white Northern audience were devouring the local-colour novels of the South. So hungry were they for genteel racist fiction that Northern magazines sent talent scouts South to discover more writers:

For better or for worse, Page, Harris, Allen, and their associates of the South, with the aid of Northern editors, critics, magazines, publishing houses, and theaters, had driven completely from the Northern mind the unfriendly picture of the South implanted there in the days of strife. In place of the discarded image they had fixed a far more friendly conception of a land basically American and loyal to the best traditions of the nation, where men and women had lived noble lives and had made heroic sacrifices to great ideals, where Negroes loved 'de white folks,' where magnolias and roses blossomed over hospitable homes that sheltered lovely maids and brave cadets, where romance of the past still lived, a land where, in short, the nostalgic Northerner could escape the wear and tear of expanding industry and growing cities and dwell in a Dixie of the storybooks which had become the Arcady of American tradition. (Buck, 1937, p. 235)

Tourgee's first novel *A Fool's Errand* had been a best-seller, and the initial success of *Bricks Without Straw* (50,000 copies sold in the first few months after publication) indicates that there was still a Northern audience willing to listen to anti-racist views. Other liberal writers, like Cable and Twain, were also having some success at this time. Para-doxically, however, one reason for the success of *Bricks* was probably its more moderate tone, for 'Its educational remedy corresponded to and encouraged the growing popularity of a moderate approach to the problem of race' (Olsen, 1969, p. xv).

Tourgee's avowed aim in *Bricks Without Straw* was to tell the story of Reconstruction from the point of view of the freedman. At this stage the ideological debate about racism was among white people. For obvious reasons there were as yet few black writers, (for a summary of the black autobiographical tradition see Chapter 7) and black people were to become used to hearing a white philosophy of racism put into the mouths of black characters. We have already seen one example of this in the 'Uncle Remus' stories. Although Tourgee's sympathies were with the freedman, his radicalism is that of a white reformer with a missionary zeal to convert other whites to his point of view. Because of this, although meant to be written from the point of view of the freedmen, *Bricks* remains a novel written as it were 'from the outside' and its narrative embodies a contradictory, patronising attitude towards black people.

Tourgee uses several effective methods in order to get over his message. First, he attempts to refute the ideological stereotypes which were emerging at this time. In particular he attacks the notion that the freedman was lazy, criminal, and unable to cope with a freedom which he didn't really want. He uses the character of Nimbus Ware to show that it is precisely the freedman who works hard and attempts to succeed, who is likely to be victimised by the Klan. This remained true in the twentieth century. Black writing (the autobiographies of Malcolm X and Richard Wright for example) constantly illustrates how blacks who became 'too successful' were either killed by the Klan or driven out of their home towns. Tourgee based the character of Nimbus Ware on freedmen he had known. The sense of immediacy and urgency which he achieves in this book is largely because he constantly uses events he has recently witnessed and incorporates them into the narrative.

Nimbus is deliberately described to us as an anti-sterotype:

His face was rather heavy – grave, it would have been called if he had been white – and his whole figure and appearance showed an earnest and thoughtful temperament. He was as far from the volatile type, which, through the mimicry of burnt-cork minstrels and the exaggerations of caricaturists, as well as the works of less disinterested portrayers of the race, have come to represent the negro to the unfamiliar mind, and as the typical Englishman is from the Punch-and-Judy figures which amuse him. The slave Nimbus in a white skin would have been considered a man of great physical power and endurance, earnest purpose, and quiet, self-reliant character. Such, in truth, he was. (Tourgee, 1969, p. 20)

Throughout the first part of the book, Ware begins to build up his own business, and it is this success which begins to anger the whites of the town. Of Nimbus, the white sheriff says:

'There'll be trouble with that nigger yet. He's too sassy. You'll see.'
'How so?' asked the chairman. 'I thought you said he was industrious, thrifty, and honest.'
'Oh, yes,' was the reply, 'there ain't a nigger in the county got a better character for honesty and hard work than he, but he's too important – has got the big head, as we call it.' (Tourgee, 1969, p. 39)

Nimbus's greatest mistake is shown to be that he believes in the reality of his new legal freedom and acts on this basis. He even stands up to his old owner after being insulted by him:

Strangely enough, the colored man did not quail. His army life had taught him to stand his ground, even against a white man, and he had not yet learned how necessary it was to unlearn the lesson of liberty and assume again the role of the slave. The white man was astounded. Here was a 'sassy nigger' indeed! This was what freedom did for them! (Tourgee, 1969, p. 89)

Nimbus's subsequent career is based upon the experiences of black people whom Tourgee knew. Similarly, his description of the Klan and its activities is based on his own detailed knowledge of the organisation. To make his point, he uses types, rather than carefully individualised characters, very much as he believed his hero Cooper did. These character types are then placed in a dynamic narrative structure. A good story-teller, Tourgee succeeds brilliantly in giving the reader an eye-witness account of a turbulent period, constantly engaging our interest in what will happen next. Criticised for his lack of a sophisticated aesthetic approach, he is often grudgingly praised by critics for his skills as a narrator. Gross, for example, while criticising the fact that 'the narrator is often replaced by the expositor' also refers to the 'burning intensity' of his novels (Gross, 1963, p. 577).

The stereotype of the poor white is also attacked by Tourgee. As Fast was to do later, in his novel *Freedom Road*, Tourgee shows that the KKK was primarily composed at this time of members of the Southern ruling classes and not of disgruntled and jealous poor whites. Of the KKK Berry tells Nimbus, ' "Dey wuzall good men. I seed de hosses, when dey mounted ter go 'way. I tell ye dey wuz good 'uns! No pore white trash dar; no lame hosses ner blind mules ner wukked down crap-critters. Jes sleek gentlemen's hosses, all on 'em" ' (Tourgee, 1969, pp. 229–30.)

His most powerful rebuttal of the poor-white stereotype is the creation of Jackson, who is shown attempting to work with blacks on a basis of equality, but is finally forced to leave the South. This character is probably based on John W. Stephens, a poor white who lived in Caswell County, North Carolina, after the Civil War. Ill-educated and poverty-stricken, he was an early member of the Republican Party and con-sistently worked with black people. After receiving many threats to his life he wrote to Governor Holden in a desperate attempt to get help, 'I can look to know source but the Republican party if thaire is any thing that you can do for me in this hour of kneed pleas let me know what it is' (quoted in Trelease, 1972, p. 213). Trelease also tells us that, because of his willingness to work with black people, Stephens was expelled from his church and socially ostracised. He was to be brutally murdered by the Klan, his pleas for help from the Republican party unheeded. The fictional character of Jackson fares a little better, escaping to the North. As under slavery, this journey North often remained for blacks and sympathetic whites the only hope of survival.

Technically, Jackson's story is used by Tourgee as a device by which Hesden, his white Southern hero, gradually learns to recognise the truth about the South. Jackson is an ex-Union officer who bitterly recognised the truth of the saying common during the Civil War that it was 'the rich man's war and the poor man's fight' (Tourgee, 1969, p. 300). Seeing Reconstruction as an opportunity for both black and white,

'He freely gave expression to these ideas, and, as he traded very largely with the colored people, soon came to be regarded by them as a leader, and by "the good people of Horsfor" as a low-down white nigger, for whom no epithet was too vile' (Tourgee, 1969, p. 301). He makes, in other words, precisely the same mistake as Ware. He believes that finally it is possible to make the American Dream of true equality possible. However, whipped by the KKK and threatened with death, living a life of constant fear, he finally decides to flee North, and his explanation of his reasons to Hesden helps to convince him that something is wrong in his native state. His words also prefigure what was to become the reality of the Solid South in later years:

'I'm as white as anybody, and hain't no more reason to stand up for niggers than any of the rest of the white people – no, nor half as much as most of 'em, for, as fur as I know, I hain't got no relations among 'em. But I do say that if the white folks of the South can't stand up to a fair fight with the niggers at the polls, without cuttin' and murderin', and burnin', and shootin', and whippin', and Ku Kluxin', and cheatin', and swindlin', they are a damned no 'count people, and don't deserve no sort of show in the world – no more than a mean, sneakin', venomous moccasin-snake – there!'(Tourgee, 1969, p. 301)

This use of anti-stereotypes by Tourgee is one of his most effective methods of using character to put forward his interpretation of Reconstruction. However, it is through the central romantic relationship between Hesden, a Southern aristocrat, and Mollie, a Northern white missionary school-teacher, together with Hesden's gradual conversion to the author's own views, that he primarily works. The structural centrality of the Hesden – Mollie relationship is both a strength and weakness of the novel. As an exciting 'love-story' it successfully enables Tourgee to embody his ideas in his narrative while maintaining the interest of the reader. However, the emphasis on the relationship between Southern and Northern white, implies, however liberally, that race-relations are a problem to be solved between whites. The emphasis within the narrative on these two characters serves to push the experiences of the black characters to the periphery; they become, however sympathetically portrayed, minor characters in the central drama of the lives of white people.

Thematically, of course, this enables the novel to have a happy ending in the idyllic marriage of the white couple, with whom we are encouraged to identify, while simultaneously allowing Tourgee to use the narrative to show the appalling treatment suffered by blacks under Reconstruction. If the novel had concentrated primarily upon the black characters, Nimbus, Lugena and Eliab, the reader would have been left feeling distinctly uneasy. The narrative structure thus allows the reader to 'enjoy' the book at the level of romance and melodramatic plot, absorbing Tourgee's message in the process. However, the ideological and aesthetic effect of structuring the novel in this way is to draw the reader into a primary identification with the white characters, at the expense of the blacks. Once this implicit assumption is written into the narrative, a patronising attitude towards black people is allowed to surface at other points in the text, thus weakening the explicit aim of the novel – to give the freedman's point of view and experience of Reconstruction.

For example, when the black voters wish to use her school as a polling station, Mollie objects in case this inflames local opinion. She threatens to resign if they use the building, 'when the people have once lost confidence in me, and I am required to give up my own deliberate judgment to a whimsical desire for parade, I can do no more good here, and will leave at once' (Tourgee, 1969, p. 129). Mollie's attitude is consistently that of the missionary, come to help an inferior people. It is stressed that her only relationship with black people is an authoritative one; she never socialises with them for

Her work had not grown uninteresting, nor had she lost any of her zeal for the unfortunate race she had striven to uplift; but her heart was sick of the terrible isolation that her position forced upon her. She had never once thought of making companions, in the ordinary sense, of those for whom she labored. They had been so entirely foreign to her early life that, while she labored unremittingly for their advancement and entertained for many of them the most affectionate regard, there was never any inclination to that friendly intimacy which would have been sure to arise if her pupils had been of the same race as herself. She recognized their right most fully to careful and polite consideration; she had striven to cultivate among them gentility of deportment; but she had longed with a hungry yearning for friendly white faces, and the warm hands and hearts of friendly associates. (Tourgee, 1969, pp. 189 – 90)

Interest in the relationship between Mollie and Hesden is maintained through the unwinding of the melodramatic plot with its misunderstandings and coincidences. This serves both to delay the eventual union between Hesden and Mollie, and symbolically North and South, and also to foreground their romantic relationship as the primary thematic preoccupation. In contrast, the relationship between Nimbus and Lugena is an unproblematic 'given'. The plot is constantly manipulated in order to maintain this structure and thus the marginalisation of the black characters. Mollie, for example, is conveniently absent when the

KKK come to Red Wing and, staying at Hesden's for some weeks after-
wards, is not involved in the consequences of the raid. Had she been
present, the incident would have served to draw the experiences of blacks
into the centre of the novel. At one point an implicit criticism of its own
structure surfaces within the narrative. When Mollie is finally returning
to Red Wing, full of romantic thoughts of Hesden, she mishears
Nimbus's cry for help for the voice of love:

She had forgotten Red Wing and all that pertained to it. The new song her lips
had been taught to sing had made thin and weak every melody of the past. Shall
care cumber the heart of the bride? She knew vaguely that she was going to Red
Wing. She recognized the road, but it seemed glorified since she travelled it
before. Once, she thought she heard her name called. The tone was full of
beseeching. She smiled, for she thought that love had cheated her, and syllabled
the cry of that heart which would not be still until she came again. She did not
see the dark, pleading face which gazed after her as her horse bore her swiftly
beyond his ken. (Tourgee, 1969, p. 284)

This is not to deny that by the standards of the day Tourgee's novel
was a radical one. Even as he wrote it, racism was being strengthened
nationally, and the tide of feeling was moving against blacks. The North
in particular was losing what little sympathy it had had in the immediate
aftermath of the Civil War, and the books of Harris and others were
telling them what they wanted to hear. Tourgee was attempting to tell
the North the truth about the South and its treatment of black people
just as they were becoming more and more unwilling to listen. Tourgee
quite literally lost his audience; by the mid eighteen-eighties 'he was
addressing a minority of Northerners in magazines and newspapers
which did not represent the attitude of the general public'(Gross, 1963,
p. 142). He believed that the answer was education, and this novel was
a part of his attempt to persuade the North to help provide this.
However, this brave attempt to counter the ideological onslaught against
black people was itself modified by Tourgee's own ideas. He believed
the answer to racism lay in attempting to change the ideas of the white
South through persuasion. As McKee Evans writes, 'against the
barbarians from outer darkness, one must be prepared to use violence'
(1967, p. 83).

The message of the novel becomes therefore a contradictory one.
Tourgee successfully shows the exploitation and oppression of black people, and he emphasises the way in which naked and open force was used
both to maintain this oppression and to destroy any democratic
opposition. However, he poses the problem concretely only to 'solve'

it at another level. The solution is to educate both exploiters and exploited and Hesden's conversion is meant to embody this. The conversion is achieved primarily through the eventual resolution of the romantic relationship between Mollie and Hesden; thus the future is shown to lie in their hands, and the relationships, activities and ideas of white people predominate. Economic exploitation and organised violence are textually resolved through the romantic love of two white individuals.

When the novel was eventually republished in 1969 after the Civil Rights movement of the fifties and sixties, its meaning had itself been reconstructed by a new generation. Ironically, the history of his novel in itself refutes Tourgee's thesis. It was not books like his that helped to change the South. It was only after the determined fight by blacks and whites during the 'Second Reconstruction' that books like Tourgee's finally found their audience.

References

Buck, P. H. (1937) *The Road to Reunion, 1865–1900*, Little, Brown & Co., Boston

Butcher, M. J. (1956) *The Negro in American Culture*, New American Library, New York

Cowie, A. (1948) *The Rise of the American Novel*, American Book Co., New York

Evans, W. McKee (1967) *Ballots and Fence Rails: Reconstruction on the Lower Cape Fear*, University of North Carolina Press, Chapel Hill

Franklin, J. H. (1961) 'Introduction', in Tourgee (1961), pp. i–vii

Franklin, J. H. (1974) *From Slavery to Freedom: A History of Negro Americans*, Alfred A. Knopf, New York (4th edition)

Gross, T. L. (1963) *Albion W. Tourgee*, Twayne Publishers, New York

Jeans, D. N. (1984) 'Fiction and the small town in the United States: a contribution to the study of urbanisation', *Australian Geographical Studies*, 22, pp. 261–74

Olsen, O. H. (1965) *Carpetbagger's Crusade: The Life of Albion Winegar Tourgee*, The Johns Hopkins University Press, Baltimore, Md

Olsen, O. H. (1969) 'Introduction', in Tourgee (1961)

Tourgee, A. W. (1961) *A Fool's Errand*, The Belknap Press of Harvard University Press, Cambridge, Mass.

Tourgee, A. W. (1969) *Bricks without Straw*, Louisiana State University Press, Baton Rouge

Trelease, A. W. (1972) *White Terror: The Ku Klux Klan Conspiracy and Southern Reconstruction*, Secker & Warburg, London

Wilson, E, (1962), *Patriotic Gore*, André Deutsch, London

4

Charles Chesnutt: *The Conjure Woman* (1899)

Charles Chesnutt's book of short stories, *The Conjure Woman*, is another example of a writer consciously working in opposition to what was becoming the dominant ideology of racism – the extremely virulent and vicious racism of late nineteenth-century America. The stories are written by a 'black' who chose not to 'pass' for white, and, like Tourgee's novel, they are primarily addressed to a Northern white liberal audience. In many ways they serve to illustrate the limitations of oppositional art in an advanced capitalist society.

Charles Chesnutt was born in Cleveland, Ohio, in 1858, but spent most of his childhood in Fayetteville, North Carolina. In 1884 he was to move with his family back to Cleveland, where he spent the rest of his life. He had however spent his childhood and young adulthood in the Reconstruction and post-Reconstruction South.

He witnessed and personally experienced the deteriorating position of black people in the US, both North and South. In 1877, the Hayes – Tilden compromise led to the presidential abandonment of Reconstruction, as 'Economic interests in the two sections especially insisted upon a compromise. The North was growing increasingly weary of the sectional division resulting from the "Negro question"' (Logan, 1970, p. 37). Gradually the Supreme Court revoked the protection it had given blacks in the post Civil War period. For example, in 1883 the Civil Rights Act of 1875 was declared unconstitutional. Segregation was becoming established. In 1887 Tennessee passed the first 'Jim Crow' law instituting segregation on public transport.

For a while it appeared that the short-lived Populist movement held out a hope of united black – white action:

Radical leaders like Tom Watson of Georgia told the poor whites and Negroes that they were being deliberately kept apart and fleeced. He called on them to stand together and work for their common good. Along with other leaders, he was at the time opposed to Negro disfranchisement and looked forward to a coalition of Negro and white farmers to drive the Bourbons from power. (Franklin, 1974, p. 270)

Through violence, fraud and intimidation however the Democratic party succeeded in using the black vote to defeat the Populist party at the polls. This defeat, and fear that poor whites might be disfranchised, led to a reversal of Populist policy and support for black disfranchisement.

At the same time lynching was becoming a common method of controlling and of terrorising the black population. There were at least 2,500 lynchings in the last sixteen years of the nineteenth century (Franklin, 1974, p. 322). Most of these took place in the deep South. Between 1900 and 1914 at least 1,100 blacks were lynched, mostly, though not always in the Southern states.

Politically disfranchised, socially segregated, subject to uncontrolled violence, blacks were also exploited economically. Not allowed to take skilled work in the new industries, which were springing up in the South, not allowed to become members of most trade unions, many blacks were driven into economic peonage through the sharecropping and the convict lease system.

The destruction of slavery leading to the unification of ruling-class interests, together with the exploitation, oppression and disfranchisement of black people, laid the basis for the emergence of a new nationalism in the late nineteenth century. It was a nationalism which soon became associated with the expansion of American imperialism. A new virulent form of racism was used both to justify increased oppression of black people at home, and the denial of civil rights to those areas being taken over by American interests:

One of the most salient features of the American imperial problem was that the United States, unlike the other imperial powers, had a color problem at home and therefore had to pursue a policy with regard to race that would not upset the racial equilibrium within the United States. (Franklin, 1974, p. 313)

Southern racist myths were given more credence by the new concept of the 'white man's burden'. History, literature and the new disciplines of the social sciences all rushed to put forward a view of black people as inherently inferior to whites. As discussed earlier, Social Darwinism was used to justify second class citizenship at home and imperialism abroad, for it explained how inferior races were not yet ready to stand on their own two feet, but needed the guidance of the superior race.

Like Tourgee, Chesnutt believed firmly in the American Dream. He
was in many ways a natural conservative. In the Gilded Age 'when
material success was a sign of virtue' (Degler, 1984, p. 279), and when
self-help and hard work were seen as essential American virtues,
Chesnutt could have stood as a model for an Horatio Alger character.
He always showed a great awareness of the value of money, turning
down the job of personal secretary to George Washington Cable in 1889
because it would have meant a drop in income. A workaholic, who
devoured popular self-help manuals and organised every moment of his
day, he was in the very best tradition of the late nineteenth-century
middle-class man who was determined to succeed. 'In the tradition of
rugged American individualism, he had conducted his business and
literary affairs according to his faith that "talent, wealth, and genius"
could attain "social standing and distinction" in the American scheme
of things' (Andrews, 1980, p. 75).

Largely self-educated, setting up and running a very successful court-
reporting firm in Cleveland, Chesnutt would appear to be the very
epitome of the self-made businessman. But he found himself in a
contradictory position; he was black, and his conventional belief in
individual progress in American society conflicted with his experience
and knowledge of racial oppression. He was to find that he could never
separate his desire for personal success within the American way of life
from his desire to improve the situation for all black people: 'personal
advancement socially, economically and even politically seemed hollow
and unproductive to Chesnutt unless it created directly or indirectly
improved opportunity for similar advancement for other Afro-
Americans' (Andrews, 1980, p. 86).

Chesnutt's ambition was to become a successful writer while also
putting forward the case for better race relations in America. In his first
published book of short stories *The Conjure Woman* (1899), which brought
together many stories published previously in various Northern
magazines, we can see the ways in which Chesnutt attempted to put
his ideas into practice. Of the book, Chesnutt himself told an inter-
viewer, 'those dialect stories, while written primarily to amuse, have
each of them a moral, which, while not forced upon the reader, is none
the less apparent to those who read thoughtfully' (Andrews, 1980, p. 39).

Chesnutt began his career by choosing to write in a genre comfortably
familiar to his readers – the local-colour story. The tales themselves
are set in the post-Reconstruction South, with the central character
being an old black ex-slave reminiscing about the days of slavery.

In fact the first cover of the book featured a picture of an avuncular black man with a white rabbit: readers were being lulled into expecting another Uncle Remus. Uncle Julius, like Uncle Remus, tells his tales to a white character, one already made familiar from countless local-colour stories with a reconciliation theme – the Northerner who goes South after the Civil War. He has gone South to improve his wife's poor health in the warmer and more tranquil climate, and also to set up his own business.

Having set up this conventional, if not stereotypical framework, Chesnutt then attempts to subvert it. He hoped, by so doing, to entertain the reader with a familiar format, while drawing him/her into sympathy with the plight of blacks. The assumption is, as with Harris and Tourgee, that the audience to be swayed is a liberal, white and primarily Northern one: 'with hardly a cursory glance his prospective reader would dismiss his work as biased if they suspected his intent' (Render, 1980, p. 34). As we have already seen, Tourgee had discovered many years before that Northern liberals were tired of being told about the 'race problem'. What Chesnutt was attempting was to tell them about it surreptitiously as it were, gaining their sympathy without apparently asking for it.

For this purpose he used three main techniques – the presentation of Uncle Julius, the presentation and content of the tales, and the divided response to the tales of the two white listeners, Uncle Julius's employer and his wife.

At first Uncle Julius appears to be a stereotype. When the Northern couple first meet him, he is eating grapes on the land they are thinking of buying:

One end of the log was already occupied by a venerable-looking colored man. He held on his knees a hat full of grapes, over which he was smacking his lips with great gusto, and a pile of grapeskins near him indicated that the performance was no new thing. We approached him at an angle from the rear, and were close to him before he perceived us. He respectfully rose as we drew near, and was moving away, when I begged him to keep his seat. (Chesnutt, 1969, p. 9)

Uncle Julius then 'entertains' the couple with a story about how the plantation of grapevines they are planning to buy and cultivate is 'goophered' or bewitched. An apparently innocent story based on a naïve old black's belief in the supernatural, the story in fact functions in two ways. The real motive of Uncle Julius in telling the tale is to attempt to dissuade the couple from buying the land, and thus

interfering with his untrammelled use of it. The reader will find that
Uncle Julius always has an ulterior motive in this book; none of his tales
are the innocent entertainment which they at first appear to be. In this
way, while enjoying the picturesque dialect and the tales of the supernatural, the reader is simultaneously being presented with another
figure, who subverts the by now extremely familiar stereotype. For
Uncle Julius quite clearly uses his knowledge of what whites have come
to expect of Southern blacks, and his own knowledge of history, in a
constant attempt to get his own way.

Ostensibly a local-colour story about the supernatural, it leads the
reader imperceptibly into a tale of slavery in which the dehumanisation
of black people is shown, through their supernatural transformation into
things. This is a device used in most of the stories in the collection. In
this first tale, 'The Goophered Grapevine', Uncle Julius tells the story
of how the vineyard came to be bewitched. The pre-war owner Dugal
McAdoo, noticing that his slaves were eating the grapes, asks Aunt
Peggy, a free black and a conjure woman to help him. She 'goophers'
the vineyard so that any black person who eats the grapes will die; several
slaves who unwittingly eat them die mysteriously. When a new slave,
a very old man, is brought to the plantation and eats some grapes, the
other slaves tell him what his fate will be. He asks Aunt Peggy for help
and she gives him some conjure medicine. He does not die but his life
becomes grotesquely entwined with the life of the grapevines. His health
fluctuates with the seasonal changes of the vineyard. 'Befo' dat, Henry
had tol'able good ha'r 'round' de aidges, but soon ez de young grapes
begun ter come, Henry's ha'r begun to quirl all up in little balls, des
like dis yer reg'lar grapy ha'r, en by de time de grapes got ripe his head
look des like a bunch er grapes' (Chesnutt, 1969, p. 22). Out of season,
he almost dies. McAdoo decides to make money out of this
phenomenon, selling him when fit, and buying him back for almost
nothing when he is ill. When the grapevine finally fails one year, Henry
dies.

Many of the tales present similar themes – the attempts by slaves
to retain their humanity in the face of a system which treats them as
things. Indeed, sometimes they actually become things. Significantly,
when his vines fail, 'Mars Dugal' tuk on might'ly 'bout losin' his vimes
en his nigger in de same year' (Chesnutt, 1969, p. 32). To the white man
grapes and slaves are no more than things which he owns.

In other stories, the supernatural becomes something used by slaves
to defeat their enemies. In these stories metamorphosis in particular

becomes a method of survival while still functioning as a symbol of extreme alienation. For example in 'Po' Sandy' Sandy, as a slave, has the misfortune to be such an efficient worker that when his owner's children married 'dey all un 'em wanted dey daddy fer ter gin 'em Sandy fer a weddin' present' (Chesnutt, 1969, p. 41). To be fair(!) therefore, his owner *lends* him periodically to all of them until 'it got so Sandy did n' hardly knowed whar he wuz gwine ter stay fum one week's een' ter der yuther' (Chesnutt, 1969, p. 42). His owner meanwhile sells Sandy's wife to a speculator, giving Sandy a dollar in compensation. When Sandy remarries, they are so in love their only wish is to be together, but Sandy is still being lent out and they are constantly separated. Finally, he tells Tenie, his wife, 'I wisht I wuz a tree, er a stump, er a rock, er sump'n w'at could stay on de plantation fer a w'ile' (Chesnutt, 1969, p. 45). Tenie, a conjure woman, is persuaded to transform him into a tree, so that he can stay on the plantation and be near her. The only way that they can remain together is for Sandy to become a 'thing'.

However, one day when she is absent, Sandy is cut down and made into a new kitchen, as an improvement to his master's property. Tenie goes mad with grief and dies:

'Dere did n' 'pear ter be nuffin pertickler de matter wid her, – she had des grieve' herse'f ter def fer her Sandy. Mars Marrabo did n' shed no tears. He thought Tenie wuz crazy, en dey ain' much room in dis worl' fer crazy w'ite folks, let 'lone a crazy nigger.' (Chesnutt, 1969, p. 59)

Within a grotesque and alienating system, only supernatural powers can give black people any semblance of control over their own lives.

Metamorphosis works differently in 'Mars Jeems's Nightmare' in which the cruel Mars Jeems is himself turned by Aunt Peggy into a slave. Through this searing experience he finally learns to be kinder to his slaves. In this tale again, slaves, feeling themselves to be almost totally helpless in a hostile system, turn to the supernatural. The wish-fulfilment of such stories, while unrealistic, is also extremely satisfying for the reader, both aesthetically and emotionally.

Belief in a greater justice somewhere is a necessary one for groups who find themselves with almost no power in a repressive society. In her book of essays *In Search of Our Mothers' Gardens*, Alice Walker tells of how her mother in the poverty-stricken days of the thirties, walked one day into town to get free flour from the Red Cross. Receiving on the same day a new dress from one of her sisters living in the North she wears it. The white woman at the distribution centre refuses to give her the flour saying, 'Anybody dressed up as good as you don't need to come here begging for food' (Walker, 1983, p. 16). Later this same white woman becomes crippled with arthritis. The satisfaction with which she tells her daughter of this leads Walker to say, 'And I knew she was thinking, though she never said it: Here I am today, my eight children healthy and grown and three of them in college and me with hardly a sick day for years. Ain' Jesus wonderful?' (Walker, 1983, p. 16).

It is not only the content of the tales which Chesnutt uses to attempt to win the reader's sympathy and to subvert current ideas. The character of Uncle Julius is also important. Every tale is used by him to try to get his own way over some issue, and he is often successful. After telling of Po' Sandy's metamorphosis, his employer's wife will not use the lumber from the old school room for her new kitchen, and her husband is forced to buy new wood. We learn later from the white narrator Uncle Julius's real motive for telling the tale:

I bought the new lumber, though not without grumbling. A week or two later I was called away from home on business. On my return, after an absence of several days, my wife remarked to me:
'John, there has been a split in the Sandy Run Colored Baptist Church on the temperance question. About half the members have come out from the main body, and set up for themselves. Uncle Julius is one of the seceders, and he came to me yesterday and asked if they might not hold their meetings in the old schoolhouse for the present'.
'I hope you didn't let the old rascal have it,' I returned, with some warmth. I had just received a bill for the new lumber I had bought. 'Well,' she replied, 'I coud n't refuse him the use of the house for so good a purpose.' (Chesnutt, 1969, p. 62)

Each fantastic story is framed by the narration of the white North-erner who is actually reporting the tales. This realistic framework and the comments of the white narrator are undercut by the content of the tales, which deny his brash common sense and his inability to see anything but local-colour in the stories. In the two characters of the white employer and his wife Annie, Chesnutt embodies within the text two contradictory responses to his work. The white narrator's incomprehension is what he fears; the ability of the woman to perceive more in the tales is what he hopes for. After the story about Po' Sandy, Annie remarks, 'What a system it was ... under which such things were possible' (Chesnutt, 1969, p. 60). Her rational husband replies:

'What things? ... Are you seriously considering the possibility of a man's being turned into a tree?'

'Oh, no,' she replied quickly, 'not that;' and then she murmured absently, and with a dim look in her fine eyes, 'Poor Tenie!' (Chesnutt, 1969, pp. 60–1)

The devices used by Chesnutt have been much admired by recent critics. Andrews, for example, discusses how the reader is first encouraged to identify with the white narrator and then, 'Chesnutt, janus-faced, turns to the reader behind the mask of Uncle Julius and leads him unexpectedly into the strange and disquieting world of the Old South' (1980, p. 44). Or as Render says, 'in a format already pleasantly familiar to the public, [he] presents slave life from the victims' more traumatized point of view' (1980, p. 37).

Unfortunately, however, the majority of readers at the time the book was published missed the irony. The subtlety of Chesnutt's devices was in fact too great for them. Most readers interpreted *The Conjure Woman* as enjoyable local-colour stories, featuring a quaint and superstitious old darky on the lines of Uncle Remus. In the first month after publication the book sold over 1,000 copies and the publishers were quite satisfied. The majority of critics 'received Chesnutt as a promising new regionalist who had mined a delightful new vein of literary ore which would provide "a relief from the serious fiction of the day"' (Andrews, 1980, quoting from the *St Paul Minn Dispatch*, 1899).

Later in his career Chesnutt, encouraged by the moderate success of *The Conjure Woman*, attempted to be more overt in his criticisms of racism. In *Rena Walden* he wrote a realistic story examining the problems of being a mulatto in a racist society. 'But finding a publisher for the story introduced the author to a problem which he had not yet encountered in his budding career – the problem of white editorial resistance to new departures in literary realism dealing with Afro-Americans' (Andrews, 1980, p. 24). Chesnutt was to write to his publishers in the early nineteen-hundreds, 'I am beginning to suspect that the public as a rule does not care for books in which the principal characters are colored people, or with a striking sympathy for that race' (Render, 1980, p. 146). Although in 1904 the National Cyclopedia of American Biography ranked Chesnutt as 'one of the foremost storytellers of the time' (Render, 1980, p. 146), his publisher would not publish *The Colonel's Dream* because his other two novels attempting to deal seriously with race had been unpopular. When, through the influence of his friend Walter Hines Page, it was finally published, it was a financial failure.

Tourgee's overt attempt to stem the growing tide of racism failed as the liberal, Northern audience he addressed disappeared, turning instead to the comfortable and genteel racism of writers like Harris, who not only entertained them and offered them a comfortable escapism, but made them feel better about themselves and their own racism. Chesnutt tried more subtle methods; it is now acknowledged by many critics that he wrote marvellously complex tales whose ironic multi-layered structure repays careful analysis. But his work shows clearly that ideological messages only reach those people who are willing to listen. Only when a later audience became receptive to what he was saying, could his tales be really appreciated.

References

Andrews, W. L. (1980) *The Literary Career of Charles Chesnutt*, Louisiana State University Press, Baton Rouge
Bone, R. A. (1965) *The Negro Novel in America*, Yale University Press, New Haven and London
Buck, P. H. (1937) *The Road to Reunion, 1865–1900*, Little, Brown & Co., Boston
Cash, W. J. (1968) *The Mind of the South*, Alfred A. Knopf, New York
Chapman, A. (ed) (1968) *Black Voices*, New American Library, New York
Chesnutt, C. (1969) *The Conjure Woman*, University of Michigan Press, Ann Arbor
Degler, C. N. (1984) *Out of Our Past: the Forces That Shaped Modern America*, Harper & Row, New York, Cambridge and London
Franklin J. H. (1974) *From Slavery to Freedom: A History of Negro Americans*, Alfred A. Knopf, New York (4th edition)
Gibson, D. B. (1981) *The Politics of Literary Expression: A Study of Major Black Writers*, Greenwood Press, Westport, Conn.
Gross, S. L., and Hardy, J. E. (eds) (1966) *Images of the Negro in American Literature*, University of Chicago Press, Chicago
Heermance, J. N. (1974) *Charles W. Chesnutt*, Archon Books, New York
Hughes, C. M. (1970) *The Negro Novelist, 1940–1980*, Citadel Press, New York
Logan, R. W. (1970) *The Negro in the United States. Volume I: A History to 1945 – From Slavery to Second-class Citizenship*, Van Nostrand Reinhold, New York
MacKethan, L. H. (1980) *The Dream of Arcady: Place and Time in Southern Literature*, Louisiana State University Press, Baton Rouge
MacKethan, L. H. (1985) 'Plantation Fiction, 1865–1900', in Rubin *et al.* (eds), pp. 209–9
Martin, J. (1967) *Harvests of Change: American Literature, 1865–1914*, Prentice-Hall, Englewood Cliffs, NJ
Meier, A. (1973) *Negro Thought in America, 1880–1915*, University of Michigan Press, Ann Arbor

Render, S. L. (1980) *Charles W. Chesnutt*, Twayne Publishers, New York

Rhode, R. D. (1975) *Setting in the American Short Story of Local Color*, Mouton, The Hague

Rubin, L. D. Jr, Jackson, B. J., Moore, R. S., Simpson. L. P. and Young, T. D. (eds) (1985) *The History of Southern Literature*, Louisiana State University Press, Baton Rouge

Walker, A. (1983) *In Search of Our Mothers' Gardens*, Harcourt Brace Jovanovich, San Diego, New York and London

5

Thomas Dixon: *The Clansman* (1905)

Dixon's novel appeared as the 'new racism', developed since the Civil War and the defeat of Radical Reconstruction, had become widely accepted. The book was produced when anti-black propaganda had become respectable. Dixon used the already existing racist climate in order to write a best-seller which pandered to current racist ideas about black people, particularly about black men. He also, however, helped to reinforce these ideas through the immense popularity of his book, and later the film based on his books, *The Birth of a Nation* (see Chapter 11).

During the Civil War, while most white men were away at the war, most of the economic activity was carried on by the women who had been left behind and by those slaves, both male and female, who had not managed to escape to fight with the Union Army. There was not, as Angela Davis has pointed out, one reported case of a white woman being raped by a black man during this time, and there is no evidence that such a possibility even occurred to the absent white soldiers.

In the post-war South of Radical Reconstruction black people, and poor whites, were unable to achieve economic independence. Southern commercial and landowning interests totally opposed any such moves; their economic and, eventually, their political power triumphed. Federal reluctance to take the necessary military and political action was equally important, and did little to counter the activities of illegal patrol groups which sprang up in the South. After 'Redemption', these extra-legal activities continued, and were extremely effective in the disfranchisement campaign against blacks. Groups like the Ku Klux Klan and the Knights of the White Camellia needed a justification, particularly for Northern consumption, for their appalling atrocities against black people. At first they used the fear of black uprisings against whites, but as this explanation became less and less believable, they turned to the myth of the black rapist.

Ideologically, the ground had been well prepared for such ideas, as we have already seen. The local-colour novels of the eighteen-eighties, so popular in the North, had consistently stressed the inferiority and the docility of the black man. Portrayed as a pathetic figure unable to cope without the white man's help, he was simultaneously shown as capable of reverting to his natural state of savagery without that control. By the turn of the century Uncle Remus had become the Negro as Beast (the title of one book by a Southern racist). The new stereotype now dominated Southern literature, and its acceptance by many people helped to justify the large numbers of lynchings of black men at this time. Lynchings, and the uncontrolled use of violent mob rule against black people, helped to maintain the super-exploitation of blacks in the South which drove some into an economic peonage only a little better than slavery.

There were, of course, other reasons why the North was more open to extreme racist ideas at this time. The growth of American imperialism, and the absorption of what the Nation called 'inferior' races, refused the right to vote or to become citizens, could only help the cause of the South. Articles on the theme of the 'white man's burden' became common in popular magazines, and it appeared to many Northern whites, including liberals, that the white South had been shouldering such a burden for some time. The manifest destiny of the Anglo-Saxon race was to push forward to new frontiers, bringing civilisation and Christianity to the 'darker peoples' of the world, while never forgetting the genetic inferiority, neatly explained by the new social sciences, of these people.

The myth of the black rapist was an extremely important idea in this context. It helped to justify terrorising and oppressing black people, particularly in the South. The justification for lynching was the ever present danger of white women being raped by uncontrollable black men. White women were only safe if they allowed themselves to be protected by white men.

The significance of Dixon's badly written and sensational novel lies in its ability to put forward concretely and dramatically an extreme version of this racist philosophy. Its immense popularity, and the even greater popularity of the film *Birth of a Nation*, helped to make these ideas respectable.

Dixon, like Tourgee, had no ambition to be a great writer. He was interested, as he himself candidly claimed, in only two things. He wanted to make a great deal of money, and he wanted to convert people to racist ideas. Tourgee had seen himself as a missionary taking ideas of American democracy and equality to the South. The white South, however, had remained unconvinced. Dixon also saw himself as converting the unbeliever, in this case the white North. He believed that the white North and South should combine against the blacks and protect their 'Anglo-Saxon' heritage. By the time that *The Clansman* appeared many Northerners already agreed with much of this, and Dixon was to find an extremely receptive audience. Dixon too believed in the American Dream, but his version of it was a white one, in which the Anglo-Saxon descendants of the old clansmen of Scotland and Ireland would rule the world.

The Clansman then puts forward this racist version of the American Dream, which was to dominate American thinking for many years. In a melodramatic pot-pourri, he mixes together the confused racist thinking of the time. Notions of Anglo-Saxon superiority and the shared traditions of white people, both North and South, predominate. The threat of black domination and rape are portrayed as threats to white civilisation, which also explain the historical necessity of the Ku Klux Klan. The Klan will protect civilisation from the barbarians, in particular it will protect 'the race' by protecting white women, whose main function, as in all right-wing ideologies, is to reproduce the superior race. To read Dixon's novel is like looking through a camera obscura at an inverted image of the real world, and it is a measure of the strength of racist ideology at this time that it is in this inverted world that many Americans had come to believe.

The novel is structured around two white families, one Northern and one Southern, who become by the novel's close, one family through intermarriage. In this way the novel reverses the liberal notion of America as one big family, the melting pot of different races and cultures, by stressing that the true American family is the white Anglo-Saxon one; other groups remain 'outside'. It is the attempt of the newly freed blacks to become part of the family that has to be squashed once and for all. It is through the myth of the black rapist that Dixon gathers together the disparate threads of his ideological message. This allows him to create the new white family in the face of the threat of 'black domination', and simultaneously to stress the place of women within this family.

Each member of the Northern family, the Stonemans, is initially structurally linked with a member of the Southern family, the Camerons. Finally, the Northern characters become converted to the Southern point of view, and are absorbed into the Southern family. The daughters, Elsie Stoneman and Margaret Cameron, are shown as almost mirror opposites as the novel opens.

It is through the portrait of Margaret that we are shown what the true Southern woman is like:

She had not a pin or brooch or piece of jewelry. Everything about her was plain and smooth, graceful and gracious. Her face was large – the lovely oval type – and her luxuriant hair, parted in the middle, fell downward in two great waves. Tall, stately, handsome, her dark rare Southern beauty full of subtle languor and indolent grace, she was to Phil a revelation. (Dixon, 1970, p. 62)

Later in the novel when Phil proposes to her, she shows that her ideas are also those of Dixon's perfect woman,' "And you won't be disappointed in my simple ideal that finds its all within a home?"' (Dixon, 1970, p. 282). Phil kindly accepts her subordination, and in his reply recognises the relationship between these ideas and his acceptance of racism:

'No. I love the old-fashioned dream of the South. Maybe you have enchanted me, but I love these green hills and mountains, these rivers musical with cascade and fall, these solemn forests – but for the Black Curse, the South would be to-day the garden of the World!' 'And you will help our people lift this curse?' softly asked the girl, nestling closer to his side.

By contrast, when Ben Cameron and Elsie fall in love, she at first resists his attempts to dominate her. It is not until she moves to the South that she will begin to change. While still living in the North she says:

'I don't care to be absorbed by a mere man.' 'Don't wish to be protected, sheltered, and cared for?'
'I dream of a life that shall be larger than the four walls of a home. I have never gone into hysterics over the idea of becoming a cook and housekeeper without wages, and snuffing my life out while another grows, expands, and claims the lordship of the world. I can sing. My voice is to me what eloquence is to man. My ideal is an intellectual companion who will inspire and lead me to develop all that I feel within to its highest reach.' (Dixon, 1970, p. 127)

Fighting words! But after living in the South for some time, her instinctive racism, which Dixon shows all good whites share, coupled with her experience of and growing fear about black people, leads her to gradually realise the necessity for that protection from a strong man that she formerly scorned. We see most clearly in the developing relationship of Ben and Elsie the ways in which the myth of the black rapist functioned. By the end of the novel it is not only blacks who have been defeated: Elsie and other white women have also found themselves subjugated. Only through the Klan, we are told, can white womanhood be protected. Elsie finally understands this as she sobs to Mrs Cameron, while Ben is out lynching black people, ' "If he dies, I shall never forgive myself for not surrendering without reserve and fighting his battles with him" ' (Dixon, 1970, p. 363). She has become more than willing to reject her earlier self when she tells Ben, ' "When I first met you – it seems now ages and ages ago – I was a vain, self-willed, pert little thing" ' (Dixon, 1970, p. 333).

Phil Stoneman's conversion to the Southern way of life is an easier one, for as a white man he has to give up nothing to become a true Southerner. Portrayed throughout the novel as brothers under the skin through their shared Anglo-Saxon superiority, at one point Phil actually takes on the identity of Ben in order to save his life. In Margaret Phil has an adoring Southern belle for a wife, and through his marriage to her he becomes Ben's brother in fact. But his real conversion takes place in a man's world of work and business. Unlike many other Southern writers Dixon did not see a conflict between the Old and the New South in terms of industrial expansion. He welcomed Northern industrial penetration into the South so long as the South could continue to have complete control over black people without any interference from the North. Phil's conversion mirrors that of many Northern businessmen who were to find racism in the South a useful phenomenon. It meant not only a divided Southern working class but also unlimited supplies of cheap labour for their new factories and railroad building.

His combination of entrepreneurial energy and acceptance of racism makes Phil Stoneman an acceptable member of Dixon's Anglo-Saxon family. The difference in fortune between the two families will be overcome as Southern and Northern whites learn to work and to live together. At first, Phil's energy and success only serve to stress the poverty of the South:

While the Camerons were growing, each day, poorer, Phil was becoming rich. His genius, skill, and enterprise had been quick to see the possibilities of the water-power. The old Eagle cotton mills had been burned during the war. Phil organised the Eagle and Phoenix Company, interested Northern capitalists, bought the falls, and erected two great mills, the dim hum of whose spindles added a new note to the river's music. (Dixon, 1970, p. 278)

The natural beauty of North Carolina and the noise and hum of Northern enterprise are shown as harmonious, especially as Phil has become one with the South on the subject of race, 'the laziness and incapacity of the Negro had been more than he could endure ... Phil would employ only white men in any capacity' (Dixon, 1970, p. 277). The name of his company symbolically unites North and South in the eagle as symbol of the USA and the phoenix as the South rising proudly from the ashes of defeat.

The two fathers, Dr Cameron and Mr Stoneman, are also schematically linked: Dr Cameron, the humiliated Southern patriarch, whose power will be restored through the defeat of black people, and Stoneman, the hard-hearted Northerner, who himself will be converted through the Klan's rescue of his son. As Dr Cameron grows in stature, Stoneman is constantly humiliated, until he recognises that it is the Klan which has kept his family together and rescued his son. The true father becomes the one who can protect his family from the black threat.

Mrs Cameron is contrasted with Lydia, sinister mulatto and housekeeper mistress of Stoneman, whose only desire is to enter and to destroy the pure white family. The descriptions of Lydia Brown rely, as do those of many of the black characters in the book, on the use of animal imagery, in an attempt to stress their sub-human status: 'Lydia Brown was a mulatto, a woman of extraordinary animal beauty and the fiery temper of a leopardess' (Dixon, 1970, p. 57). Stoneman only believes in equal rights for blacks because he is attended 'by a strange brown woman of sinister animal beauty and the restless eyes of a leopardess' (Dixon, 1970, p. 79).

As Stoneman's mistress, Lydia is potentially a step-mother to Phil and Elsie. This, combined with the attentions of Lynch, mulatto governor of South Carolina, towards Elsie, seriously threatens the integrity of the superior Anglo-Saxon family. Elsie instinctively recognises the dangers of her father's politics; she repulses Lynch's sexual advances, and when her father is ill, 'She installed an army nurse, took charge of the place, and ignored the existence of the brown woman, refusing to speak to her or permit her to enter her father's room' (Dixon, 1970, p. 167).

Mrs Cameron, on the other hand, is portrayed as a surrogate mother, and eventually mother-in-law to Elsie, a relationship to which she is inherently suited because of her Anglo-Saxon heritage:

The heritage of centuries of heroic blood from the martyrs of old Scotland began to flash its inspiration from the past. Her heart beat with the unconscious life of men and women who had stood in the stocks, and walked in chains to the stake with songs on their lips. (Dixon, 1970, p. 101)

In a later description of Mrs Cameron, seen comforting Elsie, she is portrayed as more divine than human, a natural mother, and justification for the Klan:

Never had he seen his mother so beautiful – her face calm, intelligent and vital, crowned with a halo of gray. She stood, flushed and dignified, softly smoothing the golden hair of the sobbing girl whom she had learned to love as her daughter. Her whole being reflected the years of homage she had inspired in husband, children, and neighbours. What a woman! She had made war inevitable, fought it to the bitter end; and in the despair of a Negro reign of terror, still the prophetess and high priestess of a people, serene, undismayed and defiant, she had fitted the uniform of a Grand Dragon on her last son, and sewed in secret day and night to equip his men. And through it all she was without affectation, her sweet motherly ways, gentle manner and bearing always resistless to those who came within her influence. (Dixon, 1970, p. 362)

As with Lydia Brown, black characters are described throughout the novel in terms of animal imagery. The only explanations given for their behaviour are their inherent savagery and sexual lust. Their thoughts, fears and feelings are never described. Dixon clearly understood that racial hatred depends upon this ability to dehumanise those people who are being victimised. The murder of Gus is therefore portrayed as the killing of a thing or an animal, not of a sentient human being. In this way Dixon can justify killing and lynching as something necessary to preserve a higher civilisation which is personified in the white female characters.

However, blacks had lived in the South as slaves for hundreds of years without Southern whites apparently noticing their savagery and sexual obsessions. This was explained by Dixon and others as being a result of white control; it was only after black men were foolishly given their freedom that these characteristics became apparent. Most Southern racists wished black people to remain in the South as cheap labour; in fact they made it extremely difficult for them to leave. White writers like Harris stressed how foolish were those black people who attempted to go North and leave their white Southern protectors. The racism which developed in the South stressed that there would be no race problem, if whites were allowed complete control over black people. The Klan was a necessary step in regaining such control, and Dixon believed that once racism was fully established, the Klan had served its purpose.

To emphasise their point, Southern writers described life before the war as idyllic. Blacks were childlike, lazy, but very happy and not at all dangerous. In fact, reading many white accounts of the ante-bellum South, it becomes difficult to understand how any work at all got done. Typically, Mrs Lenoir tells Mrs Cameron, ' "You know, the farm was my dowry with the dozen slaves Papa gave us on our wedding-day. The negroes did as they pleased, yet we managed to live and were very happy" ' (Dixon, 1970, p. 189). Once they have gained their freedom, blacks remain lazy, but are also now sexually threatening and 'insolent' to white people. All freedom really means to them, stresses Dixon, was the chance to marry white women.

In the early part of the novel, we meet very few black characters. It is through dialogue between white characters that we learn of their ungrateful behaviour now that they have gained their freedom. Once the white characters have all moved South to North Carolina, more and more blacks are brought in and are portrayed as a constant threat to the Southern way of life. In the film version of the book, this is shown quite clearly in the images of the main street of the Southern town in which the Camerons live. Initially, before the war, the street is bustling with carriages, white people, and happy, smiling 'darkies.' Gradually, after the war, the street is taken over by 'insolent' and threatening black men, while white characters are literally pushed back into their homes, hiding from the black threat. This 'insolence' reaches its height in the rape of Marion. After this the Klan is formed; portrayed as the cavalry were later shown in Westerns, they come riding into town where they soon put blacks back into their place – in terms of the main street they are literally removed once again to the periphery. They have been successfully expelled.

The climax of the book is the violent overthrow of Reconstruction by the Ku Klux Klan. The fact that the role of the Klan in both the book and the film prefigures later popular Westerns which climaxed with a cavalry charge against groups of Native Americans is not chance. The function of the Klan in Dixon's book is intimately linked to popular racist notions of the frontier and also of contemporary American imperialism, popularly presented at the time as a new frontier. Dixon draws constantly upon current racist ideas of how America had been settled, and popular conceptions of contemporary imperialist expansion. Both Southern and Northern pioneers were Anglo-Saxon refugees from oppression bravely settling a new land. The Klan are portrayed as direct inheritors of these early pioneers and are also taking on the 'white man's burden'.

Dr Cameron, Southern patriarch, is Dixon's spokesman when he tells Stoneman, in an hysterical outburst:

'we are great because of the genius of the race of pioneer white freemen who settled this continent, dared the might of kings, and made a wilderness the home of Freedom. Our future depends on the purity of this racial stock. The grant of the ballot to these millions of semi-savages and the riot of debauchery which has followed are crimes against human progress.' (Dixon, 1970, p. 291)

At this time the US 'had to pursue a policy with regard to race that would not upset the racial equilibrium within the United States' (Franklin, 1974, p. 313). Therefore:

The immunity with which the Klan were to be allowed to lynch and to terrorise blacks was clearly linked to imperialist ideology. Few regarded these manifestations of violence as an inherent part of the industrial imperialism to which America was committed, although to be sure, an integral part of that imperialist ideology was the subjection of the black man to caste control and wage slavery. (Franklin, 1974, p. 322)

The KKK, like America itself, has a sacred mission, appealing to 'Chivalry, Humanity, Mercy, and Patriotism' (Dixon, 1970, p. 320). The Klan will lynch and terrorise black people 'for their God, their native land, and the womanhood of the South' (Dixon, 1970, p. 338). Inheritors of the Scottish Clansmen, the Klan too will fight for freedom – freedom from black domination!

Dixon effectively turns the world upside down. Oppressed blacks become brutal conquerors; the violent, raping Klan become freedom fighters and the chivalrous protectors of white womanhood. Every character, every event in the novel is used to deliver this message. Such virulent racism was to become less necessary and less popular as racist ideas entered the mainstream of American thought. Later novelists, like Margaret Mitchell, were able to assume a consensus among their white readers about the implicitly assumed characteristics of the black stereotypes in their novels. The work of Dixon and others had been done.

References

Auken, S. van (1941) 'The Southern historical novel in the early twentieth century', *Journal of Southern History*, XIV, pp. 157–91

Buck, P. H. (1937) *The Road to Reunion, 1865–1900*, Little, Brown & Co., Boston

Camejo, P. (1976) *Racism, Revolution, Reaction, 1861–1867: The Rise and Fall of Radical Reconstruction*, Monad Press, New York

Cash, W.J. (1968) *The Mind of the South*, Alfred A. Knopf, New York

Cook, R.A. (1974) *Thomas Dixon*, Twayne Publishers, New York

Cripps, T.S. (1977) *Slow Fade to Black: The Negro in American Film, 1900–1947*, Oxford University Press, New York

Current, R.N. (1986) 'Fiction as history: a review essay', *Journal of Southern History*, 52, pp. 77–90

Davenport, F.G. Jr (1979) 'Thomas Dixon's mythology of Southern history', *Journal of Southern History*, 36, pp. 350–67

Davis, A. (1982) *Women, Race and Class*, Women's Press, London

Degler, C.N. (1984) *Out of Our Past: The Forces that Shaped Modern America*, Harper & Row, New York, Cambridge and London

Dixon, T. Jr (1970) *The Clansman: An Historical Romance of the Ku Klux Klan*, University Press of Kentucky, Lexington

Downs, R.B. (1977) *Books that Changed the South*, University of North Carolina Press, Chapel Hill

Evans, W. McKee (1967) *Ballots and Fence Rails: Reconstruction on the Lower Cape Fear*, University of North Carolina Press, Chapel Hill

Faulkner, H. (1984) 'Homespun justice: the lynching in American fiction', *South Dakota Review*, 22, pp. 104–19

Franklin, J.H. (1974) *From Slavery to Freedom: A History of Negro Americans*, Alfred A. Knopf, New York (4th edition)

Fredrickson, G.M. (1971) *The Black Image in the White Mind*, Harper and Row, New York

Gaston, P.M. (1970) *The New South Creed: A Study in Southern Mythmaking*, Louisiana State University Press, Baton Rouge and London

Gossett, T.F. (1975) *Race: The History of an Idea in America*, Southern Methodist University Press, Dallas, Tex.

Hernton, C.C. (1970) *Sex and Racism*, Paladin, London

Hobson, F. (1983) *Tell About the South: The Southern Rage to Explain*, Louisiana State University Press, Baton Rouge and London

Hofstadter, R. (1955) *Social Darwinism in American Thought*, Beacon Press, Boston

Jones, H.J. (1982) 'Images of state legislative reconstruction participants in fiction', *Journal of Negro History*, 67, pp. 318–27

Kiernan, V.G. (1980) *America: The New Imperialism: From White Settlement to World Hegemony*, Zed Press, London

Kirby, J.T. (1986) *Media-Made Dixie: The South in the American Imagination*, Louisiana State University Press, Baton Rouge and London (revised edition)

Logan, R.W. (1954) *The Negro in American Life and Thought: The Nadir, 1877–1901*, Dial Press, Toronto and New York

Meier, A. (1973) *Negro Thought in America, 1880–1915*, University of Michigan Press, Ann Arbor

Rogin, M. (1985) 'The sword became a flashing vision: D.W. Griffiths' *The Birth of a Nation*', *Representations*, Winter 1985, pp. 150–95

Rollins, P. C. (ed) (1983) *Hollywood as Historian: American Film in a Cultural Context*, University Press of Kentucky, Lexington

Rose, W. L. (1987) *Slavery and Freedom: Four Episodes in Popular Culture*, Oxford University Press, Oxford and New York

Scott, A. F. (1970) *The Southern Lady: From Pedestal to Politics, 1830–1930*, University of Chicago Press, Chicago

Sorlin, P. (1980) *The Film in History: Restaging the Past*, Blackwell, Oxford

Tindall, G. B. (1976) *The Ethnic Southerners*, Louisiana State University Press, Baton Rouge and London

Trelease, A. W. (1972) *White Terror: The Ku Klux Klan Conspiracy and Southern Reconstruction*, Secker and Warburg, London

Wallace, M. (1979) *Black Macho and the Myth of the Superwoman*, John Calder, London

White, J. (1984) *Black Leadership in America, 1895–1968*, Longman, London and New York

Williamson, J. (1986) *A Rage for Order: Black-White Relations in the American South Since Emancipation*, Oxford University Press, Oxford and New York

Woodward, C. Vann (1974) *The Strange Career of Jim Crow*, Oxford University Press, Oxford and New York

PART TWO

Literary reactions to the Second World War and the Second Reconstruction

6

From Jim Crow to the Second Reconstruction

The period from 1906 to the end of the First World War was one of the worst of times for African-Americans; Logan (1970) calls it the 'nadir'. America was a changing society during this period, but not for blacks. It was the period of the Progressive movement, when groups as diverse as labour unions, the churches, utopian novelists, and farmers pressed for change. In 1912 Eugene Debs, the Socialist Party candidate, polled 900,000 votes. But blacks could have been forgiven for despairing; a stultifying consensus on race appeared to have been reached; strengthened by imperialist ideas, racism appeared unshakeable.

In 1910 the National Association for the Advancement of Colored People (NAACP) was formally founded; as an integrated organisation it would fight throughout this period for an end to segregation and discrimination and to achieve equal rights for black people. The election of Woodrow Wilson in 1912 was to lead to the institution of segregation among federal employees in rest rooms and restaurants. Himself a Southerner, Wilson and his government were to be dominated by white Southerners.

When America finally entered the First World War, black Americans were nevertheless keen to enlist and serve their country. Wartime experiences, however, embittered many of them. It was some time before Congress even agreed to set up a segregated camp for black officers, and while wearing uniform black soldiers were to struggle against discrimination in the North, where they were often denied service in restaurants and admission to theatres, as well as in the South.

On the home front hundreds of thousands of blacks migrated during the war from the South to the North in search of work. Lynchings continued and in 1915 the Ku Klux Klan re-emerged, partly as a response to the notorious film *The Birth of a Nation* (see Chapter 11).

It was still possible for lynchings to take place in public in the South (Franklin, 1974, p. 351). Blacks would find the Klan also in the North, where there were many willing recruits among white Southerners who had themselves migrated North in search of better jobs.

By April 1919 most black soldiers were back in America, many hoping for a better future. In May 1919, the editorial of the black newspaper, *Crisis*, announced: 'Make way for Democracy! We saved it in France, and by the Great Jehovah, we will save it in the U.S.A. or know the reason why' (Franklin, 1974, p. 355).

Such enthusiasm was soon to be dampened. Race riots increased so that by 1919 at least twenty-five had occurred, and the disturbances in Chicago became known as the 'Red Summer'. Law and order broke down in the city completely, and thirty-eight people were killed.

During the nineteen-twenties, the NAACP and other inter-racial organisations continued fighting through the courts for civil rights, but for many working-class blacks, especially those living in appalling conditions in large Northern cities, much of this seemed irrelevant. To some extent, this explains the attraction of the 'Garvey Movement' to working-class blacks. Although rarely convinced by Garvey's 'Back to Africa' philosophy, these groups were impressed by his emphasis on black pride, and Garveyism became a mass movement for a time in the twenties.

When depression came at the end of the twenties black people were hardest hit, and were also discriminated against when they tried to obtain relief. Some religious and charitable organisations, in the North as well as the South, excluded African-Americans from the soup kitchens they operated to relieve the suffering. However, the new Democratic administration of 1932, led by Franklin Roosevelt, tried to provide jobs as well as dole to both blacks and whites. Such 'New Deal' policies reinforced an important development in black politics from the late nineteen-twenties – Northern blacks' willingness to vote for Democratic candidates, reversing their former allegiance to the party associated with Lincoln, freedom and emancipation.

In 1936, the majority of blacks voted for Roosevelt. The number of blacks in the administration tripled in the thirties. However, gains for blacks were limited – resentment over poverty and discrimination broke out in the Harlem riots of 1935, and Roosevelt himself did not support an anti-lynching bill.

'New Deal' politics helped to stabilise American society in the nineteen-thirties but it would be war that created new employment.

Without state intervention the American system was under severe threat. Though accused of communism by those Americans incensed by the amount of State intervention he introduced, Roosevelt was clear about his role, 'I am fighting communism, Huey Longism, Coughlinism, Townsendism, I want to save our system, the Capitalist system' (quoted in Carroll and Noble, 1980, p. 342).

Culturally, two important developments occurred during the interwar period: a new sympathy on the part of some white writers towards the plight of black people and towards black culture; and even more importantly the explosion of black voices and talents which emerged in the Harlem Renaissance.

More sympathetic portrayals of blacks by whites like Eugene O'Neill, Sinclair Lewis and Paul Green were an important step forward in the presentation of blacks in popular culture, and there were 'not only more novels by and about Negroes, but also a consistently more realistic treatment of the Negro as a human being rather than as a symbol or type' (Butcher, 1971, p. 132). In 1920 Clement Wood's sociological novel *Nigger* was published, the same year as Stribling's *Birthright*.

However, the new literature had significant limitations; much culture produced by sympathetic whites still contained racist ideas, however subtle, and the great best-seller of the thirties was to be *Gone With the Wind*, complete with black stereotypes and totally unreconstructed white characters. One problem was that some white artists looking at black culture saw 'exoticism' and 'primitivism' which they both praised and assumed were characteristically black attributes. The same approach had been evident in attitudes in the late nineteenth century to 'primitive' peoples discovered by anthropologists and painted by painters like Gauguin.

It is in the work of black artists that the real interest of the period lies. At last they were finding a voice of their own. The enormous migration North by blacks and their concentration in urban areas laid the basis for the development of an intellectual and artistic class. Furthermore, a shared past based on oppression during and after slavery had promoted the idea of a distinct and authentic cultural community (Franklin, 1974, p. 374). In 1917 James Weldon Johnson published *Fifty Years and Other Poems*, in 1922 *The Book of American Negro Poetry*, and he helped to edit several books of Negro spirituals. Other significant poets included Claude McKay, Jean Toomer, Countee Cullen, and Langston Hughes.

Generally, however, the situation for black Americans on the eve of the Second World War was still bleak. Unemployment stood at nine million and affected blacks disproportionately. But there had been massive changes in the lives of many African-Americans. Large numbers had migrated North to work in new industries; they used their votes to make small but concrete gains in representation. Culturally, there had been an enormous upheaval with African-Americans beginning to enter the mainstream of American popular culture in ways previously unthinkable (movies remained a particularly difficult area; see Chapter 12), and legally the NAACP had continued its battle in the courts achieving modest but significant gains which would be built upon after the war.

But the war against fascism was to be fought by segregated armies. Initially, blacks were not allowed to enlist at all in the Marines or Air Corps. Within the Army they were rigidly segregated, and usually given only the most menial tasks. Black officers in charge of black units served under white officers, and the government was to allow the Red Cross to segregate blood to be used for transfusion.

The contradiction between the war for freedom and against fascism and the treatment of black Americans, caused great bitterness. Blacks were not prepared to fight for their country under these conditions, and struggled throughout the war to better them. The campaign to admit blacks to the Air Corps for example was successful, and the eventual enlistment of blacks into the Marine Corps was another important breakthrough. Blacks were segregated within these organisations, but at least they were now allowed to join them!

At home, it was not until A. Philip Randolph threatened a huge march by blacks upon Washington, that Roosevelt issued an executive order banning discrimination in defence industries and in the federal government.

When the war ended it was clear that things must change; blacks themselves had shown that they were unwilling any longer to accept second-class citizenship. In America, as in countries like Britain, the Second World War had inaugurated enormous changes and unemployment appeared to be a thing of the past. New African nations would soon be winning their independence and claiming places at the United Nations; discrimination against black Americans could only embarrass the American government at the UN.

Black migration continued throughout the forties, with another million African-Americans moving North, and the NAACP prepared themselves for further legal struggles. Political representation increased, with over twenty-four blacks in state legislatures, and blacks generally participated enthusiastically in electoral politics. Even in the South, the number of blacks registered to vote increased from 2% in 1940 to 12% in 1947 (Marable, 1984, p. 15). Successful legal action was taken by black teachers in some areas to obtain equal pay; more blacks were going to college and university, and the average income of black workers rose steadily.

By the early fifties the momentum of change had slowed. There were several reasons for this, but most important were the resistance of the South to change and the impact of the Cold War climate upon the movement for Civil Rights. In 1947 the Taft–Hartley Act required union officials to declare themselves not to be Communists or Communist sympathisers and the CIO did not fight this requirement. The US Chamber of Commerce called for a bar on Communists in many jobs in both public and private sectors (Carroll and Noble, 1980, p. 358); the activities of the House Un-American Activities Committee (HUAC) led to the blacklisting of four hundred actors, writers, and directors in the movie industry. By the late forties and early fifties anti-Communism had reached hysterical proportions in America, the McCarthyite witch-hunt being only the most visible manifestation of a wide-spread paranoia.

The effect on the emerging Civil Rights movement was particularly damaging. Many black and liberal leaders put their energies into rebutting charges of Communist sympathies, and even the NAACP were willing to expel any members accused of Communism.

At the same time, Supreme Court decisions in favour of civil rights had little impact as in practice they were virtually ignored. The Court decided in 1950 that separate but equal facilities constituted discrimination, and in 1954 finally ruled against segregation in schools. Many school districts in the border states quickly desegregated, but then the momentum stopped, as most of the Deep South simply ignored the ruling.

Suburbanisation was leading to increased segregation in housing, as zoning laws were deliberately used to keep out blacks. It was clear to black Americans that earlier optimism about rapid change had been misplaced. It was at this point that the Civil Rights movement suddenly emerged with new strength and determination in the South among the most oppressed blacks in the country. Their fight led to the momentous struggle for equal rights in the fifties and sixties, and to what many commentators, harking back to the upheavals of the nineteenth century, now call the 'Second Reconstruction'.

The incident triggering off the events of the next decade is now famous. In 1955, Mrs Rosa Parks, a forty-three year old black seamstress and active member of the local NAACP, refused to give up her seat to a white person on a bus in Montgomery, Alabama and was arrested. The NAACP and the black community in Montgomery were prepared to act.

For almost a year, Montgomery's black community refused to ride the buses. Martin Luther King and his followers stressed non-violent, Christian methods of opposing violence, segregation and oppression. The Montgomery boycott was successful; in November 1956 the Supreme Court found that segregation on the buses in Montgomery was unconstitutional.

The boycott also led to the founding of the Southern Christian Leadership Conference (SCLC) in the South. Unfortunately it led also to a white backlash. The crisis at Little Rock, Arkansas over the attempt to desegregate the local high school, showed the viciousness of this reaction, as pictures of violent, chanting whites were flashed all over the world on people's television screens. This media attention was to be an important aspect of the Civil Rights movement, as many liberals, not just in America, but throughout the world, became increasingly sickened by pictures of policemen and dogs setting upon black people, including children (Sitkoff, 1981, p. 66).

In 1960 the Student Nonviolent Coordinating Committee (SNCC) was set up in North Carolina and the Congress of Racial Equality (CORE) was re-activated and began the 'Freedom Rides' into the South. The first 'sit-in' occurred in Greensboro, North Carolina in a five-and-dime store, and was quickly followed by others. Six months later, Greensboro desegregated its stores and for the first time in history 'Greensboro blacks could sit down at a lunch counter and be served a cup of coffee' (Sitkoff, 1982, p. 72). By the end of 1961 nearly two hundred cities had begun to desegregate, but the Deep South, in particular Mississippi, had hardly been touched.

The determination of young blacks, many from the South, to end segregation by their own direct actions, ended for ever one of the most pernicious and deep-seated stereotypes of American culture – that of the docile and contented negro. White Southerners were amazed at the determination and bravery shown by black people, and could no longer pretend to the world that they 'knew the negro' and how to handle him.

The Freedom Rides continued and helped to draw many recruits, both black and white, into the movement. Activists expanded their role as 'freedom workers' to include voter registration. They overtly rejected Martin Luther King's emphasis on reconciliation. The backlash of violence by whites against the freedom workers meant that they became cynical about non-violence, and about the federal government's willingness to act on their behalf. In the Mississippi Freedom Summer of 1964, thirty homes and thirty-five churches were burned, at least eighty people beaten, thirty shot, and at least six killed (Sitkoff, 1982, p. 123). Civil Rights activities led to severe disruption of normal business activity in cities like Birmingham, Alabama, and political and business leaders at local and national level realised that segregation must end.

In 1963 200,000 people, black and white, marched on Washington demanding civil rights for blacks, and in the following two years important Civil Rights legislation was pushed through Congress by President Johnson. The Civil Rights Act of 1964 banned racial discrimination and segregation, and the Voting Rights Act of 1965 ended age-old devices like literacy tests which had been used to stop blacks from voting. 'The deepest of Deep South states saw the most dramatic changes, with the percentage of registered blacks increasing from 19 to 61 in Alabama, from 7 to 67 in Mississippi, and from 27 to 60 in Georgia' (Polenberg, 1983, p. 192).

The Civil Rights movement had therefore made concrete gains, but at enormous cost to those who took part. Many were beaten or imprisoned; some murdered. Large numbers suffered stress-related illnesses – ulcers, migraines, nervous breakdowns. Stress and the ever-increasing white backlash of violence led to splits and tensions within the Civil Rights movement itself: black against white, male against female. There had been resentment for some time among black activists at the knowledge that whites could return to good jobs or to universities after their stint of working in the South; among white men there was much uneasiness about rumours that black men were forcing white women to sleep with them, accusing them of racism if they did not. In 1966, feeling had become so strong that whites were expelled from CORE whose new leaders stressed, not integration, but 'black power'.

In the North, the influence of the Civil Rights movement upon urban blacks during this period had been enormous. 'As the civil rights united front gradually came unstuck, the only original voice which articulated an alternative vision for black Americans was that of Malcolm X' (Marable, 1984, p. 96). Malcolm X appealed to race pride, to separatism, to the right of blacks to practise self-defence. Known for his controversial comments – 'the only thing I like integrated is my

coffee' – and charismatic speaking ability, he won the hearts of
millions of urban blacks. The cry of 'Black Power' frightened whites
and liberals. The Black Power movement was not, however, just a
political movement; it was also a cultural one. It 'legitimized African-
American values and life-styles, food and fashions, poetry and prose,
theater and dance, dialect and music' (Polenberg, 1983, p. 233).
Blacks took African surnames, demanded black studies courses at
colleges and universities, wore their hair in an 'Afro' style; they
emphasised their own long-suppressed culture. Similar motivations
underpinned the development of a 'Black Aesthetic', in which black
artists of the sixties aimed at 'the destruction of the white thing,
the destruction of white ideas, and white ways of looking at the world'
(Neal, 1968).

Poverty, a growing disillusionment with the Vietnam War in which a
disproportionate number of blacks were sent to fight, and a frustrated
belief in black power led to explosions in northern ghettos in the
nineteen-sixties. In 1964 there was ghetto rioting in New York City, and
in 1965 in the Los Angeles ghetto of Watts. There was rioting also in
Florida, Cleveland, Rochester, Jersey City, Chicago and Philadelphia.
This wave of riots would continue intermittently for years. It was only
through a strong military and police presence that the rioting was finally
stopped. Sixty thousand soldiers and national guardsmen were called
out in 1968. The assassinations of both Malcolm X and Martin Luther
King seemed to many young urban blacks proof that violence was
necessary to meet violence. Books like Malcolm X's autobiography,
Eldridge Cleaver's *Soul on Ice* and James Baldwin's *The Fire Next Time*
became the bibles of urban young blacks. The revolutionary Black
Panther Party was founded in 1966; their acceptance of the need for
violence in American society in order to bring about change terrified
white liberals.

The aggressive reaction of blacks led in turn to a white backlash in
the Northern States. In 1968 more than 9.9 million people voted for
the Southern racist candidate George Wallace, and the right-wing
Richard Nixon was elected President. In California Ronald Reagan was
voted in as Governor. Nixon himself made it clear that he was against
enforcing integration by busing for racial balance.

Meanwhile, the Supreme Court began a series of decisions which
halted much of the momentum towards civil rights. In 1974 they
found against the necessity for interdistrict busing to stop segregation
in schools. The 1978 Bakke decision, which declared the use of quotas

for racial minorities at the University of California unconstitutional, made the use of positive discrimination to help blacks less likely.

The achievements of the Civil Rights movement therefore can only be understood if the differences between North and South are taken into account. The Civil Rights movement began in the South, and that is where its most important victories were gained. It was a movement which sprang out of the culture of the South, profoundly influenced by Southern black rural culture, history, and religion.

Its gains were impressive, and should not be underestimated. Blacks can now vote, and there are many black office-holders and officials, 2,500 in 1980, compared with less than one hundred in 1965. In 1979 George Wallace attended the inauguration of Birmingham's first black mayor. By 1980, Mississippi, once the most notoriously racist state in America was proudly claiming more black officeholders than any other state (Sitkoff, 1981, p. 229), and the Civil Rights movement has itself now become enshrined in the South as a part of its history. Most significantly of all, blacks began returning to live in the South after more than a hundred years of migration North. In 1978, the black magazine *Ebony* said of Atlanta, Georgia:

The fact that Blacks control Atlanta's government, its police and fire departments and the city's school system is a strong recommendation for Blacks who are planning to move to this clean, fast-growing and young city. In particular, professional advancement opportunities make the city attractive. (Polenberg, 1983, p. 279)

During the Reagan administration, it appeared to many blacks and liberals, that the clock had been successfully turned back in terms both of civil rights and economics. Inflation had increased from 0.2 per cent to 4.7 per cent, mortgage rates from 2 to 4.7 per cent also, and real farm incomes had fallen in just three years up to 1984 by fifty per cent. All this hit the poor and the black community disproportionately (Marable, 1985, p. 300).

But even in the North, there were positive changes which were due to the Civil Rights movement. The 'Rainbow Coalition' campaign of Jesse Jackson is an important indication of how much things have changed. Jesse Jackson's campaign in the nineteen-eighties is significant not only because for the first time blacks had a black Presidential candidate for whom to vote, but also because Jackson appealed to a wide spectrum of voters opposed to Reagan's right-wing political and economic policies, including blue-collar and unemployed whites and white small farmers. The heir to Martin Luther King, Jackson is a Southerner in the tradition of great religious and political leaders from the South. He uses liberation theology and liberal politics in the context of black Southern culture (Marable, 1985, p. 273).

The political map of the United States is beginning to be redrawn in ways that would have been impossible in the days before the Civil Rights movement, and blacks have shown that they are prepared to continue their centuries-long fight for full participation in the American system – politically, culturally and economically. In terms of popular culture and ideology, although racism is still deep-rooted in American society, certain stereotypes have disappeared for good; no-one would now attempt to justify discrimination by pointing to the contentment of blacks with the status quo.

The literary and cultural renaissance thrown up by the Civil Rights movement continues today in all areas, particularly in the amazing phenomenon of black women's writing, and the constant rediscovery of previously ignored black literature such as the works of Ann Petry and Zora Neale Hurston. A new generation of black artists is now also at work, trying to retain the integrity of the more nationalistic cultural movement based on the struggles of the fifties and sixties, while moving away from portrayals of blacks which they consider uncritical and overly sentimental. They include the writers Terry MacMillan (*Mama* (1987)) and Trey Ellis (*Platitudes* (1986)), and film-makers Spike Lee and Neema Barnett.

Much still remains to be done; but politically, socially and culturally African-Americans are making their voices heard, and have shown that they still hope one day to play their full part in the American Democratic system. 'The struggle to complete the unfinished business of American democracy will endure until its fulfillment' (Sitkoff, 1981, p. 237).

References

Aptheker, H. (1978) *American Negro Slave Revolts*, International Publishers, New York

Bain, R., Flora, J. M., and Rubin, L. D. Jr. (eds) (1979) *Southern Writers. A Biographical Dictionary*, Louisiana State University Press, Baton Rouge and London

Blassingame, J. (1978) *The Slave Community. Plantation Life in the Antebellum South*, Oxford University Press, New York and London

Butcher, M.J. (1956) *The Negro in American Culture*. New American Library, New York

Carroll P., and Noble, D. (1980) *The Free and the Unfree: A New History of the United States*, Penguin Books, Harmondsworth

Christian, B. (1980) *Black Women Novelists*, Greenwood Press, Westport, Conn.

Davis, A. (1982) *Women, Race and Class*, The Women's Press, London

Degler, C. N. (1984) *Out of Our Past: The Forces That Shaped Modern America*, Harper and Row, New York, Cambridge and London

Elkins, S. M. (1976) *Slavery. A Problem in American Institutional and Intellectual Life*, University of Chicago Press, Chicago and London

Ellis, T. (1986) *Platitudes*, Vintage Books, New York

Franklin, J. H. (1974) *From Slavery to Freedom: A History of Negro Americans*, Alfred A. Knopf, New York

Genovese, E. D. (1967) *The Political Economy of Slavery. Studies in the Economy and Society of the Slave South*, Vintage Books, New York

Kiernan, V. G. (1980) *America: The New Imperialism. From White Settlement to World Hegemony*, Zed Press, London

Logan, R. W. (1970) *The Negro in the United States, Vol. I: A History to 1945*, Van Nostrand Reinhold, New York

MacMillan, T. (1987) *Mama*, Jonathan Cape, London

McPherson, J. M. (1965) *The Negro's Civil War*, Vintage Books, New York

Marable, M. (1984) *Race, Reform and Rebellion: The Second Reconstruction in Black America, 1945–1982*, Macmillan, London

Polenberg, R. (1981) *One Nation Divisible: Class, Race and Ethnicity in the United States since 1938*, Penguin, Harmondsworth

Rose, W. L. (1982) *Slavery and Freedom: Four Episodes in Popular Culture*, Oxford University Press, Oxford and New York

Rubin, L. D. Jr, Jackson, B.J., Moore, R.S., Simpson, L.P. and Young, T.D. (eds) (1985) *The History of Southern Literature*, Louisiana State University Press, Baton Rouge and London

Scott, J. A. (1978) *Hard Trials on My Way: Slavery and the Struggle Against It, 1800–1860*, New American Library, New York

Sitkoff, H. (1981) *The Struggle for Black Equality 1954–1980*, Hill and Wang, New York

Tindall, G. B. (1976) *The Ethnic Southerners*, Louisiana State University Press, Baton Rouge and London

Williamson, J. (1986) *A Rage for Order: Black–White Relations in the American South since Emancipation*, Oxford University Press, New York and Oxford

Woodward, C. Vann (1971) *American Counterpoint: Slavery and Racism in the North-South Dialogue*, Little, Brown & Co., Boston and Toronto

X, Malcolm (1970) *Autobiography*, Penguin, Harmondsworth

Zinn, H. (1987) *A People's History of the United States*, Longman, London and New York

7

Howard Fast: *Freedom Road* (1944)

We have seen how new racist ideas evolved in the US after the Civil War, and how they were used to justify the continued oppression of black people, both at home and in the new American neo-colonies. By the turn of the century many of these ideas had been accepted, even by white people who considered themselves to be liberals. A system of legal segregation, almost total disfranchisement and economic super-exploitation of African-Americans now existed in the South, and *de facto* segregation and discrimination in the North. Ideologically, politically and economically it was well and truly the 'Solid South', and it was not until after the Second World War that the South was to find its system under concerted attack.

By the nineteen-twenties, another more subtle racist image had emerged to complement the earlier stereotypes, that of the primitive exotic who was naturally musical and passionate. Official school textbooks, used both in the North and the South, portrayed the slave 'either as a totally dependent creature anxious to please the white folks, as a crippled and defenceless shell, or an irrepressibly buoyant and carefree bundle of rhythmic energy. He is invariably suckled from womb to tomb, nursed from cradle to grave' (Lindenmeyer, 1970, p. 16). Texts of this kind were still being approved by the New York Board of Education in 1950.

Nevertheless, individuals and groups continually challenged racism throughout this period – the NAACP worked through the courts for example, fighting for equal rights for black people. In the late nineteenth century, as we have seen, there were always writers, like Chesnutt, Cable and Tourgee, who continued to question in their work the racist assumptions prevalent in literature. They challenged powerful vested interests in 'writing against the grain', attempting to put an alternative

view of race relations and of the history of Reconstruction in the South
in their stories and novels. They were however isolated liberal individuals appealing to an increasingly shrinking liberal audience at a time
of increasing racism.

Fast, however, was writing self-consciously within a radical tradition
at a moment when race relations in America were about to become an
issue once again. But now it would be racist ideas which would be
challenged. The audience he addressed was no longer a white, Northern
liberal audience, whom he hoped to convert, but 'ordinary people'.

Rideout argues convincingly that what he calls the radical novel in
America emerged in two great waves in American literature, and that
these waves were themselves a product of the emergence of firstly the
Socialist Party and later the CPUSA, (Communist Party of the USA),
of which Fast was a member when he wrote *Freedom Road*. The development of the radical novel in the pre-First World War period is closely
associated with both the industrial struggles of the working class and
the establishment and relative success of the Socialist Party: 'The
appearance of radical novels in fact parallels fairly closely the fortunes
of the Party' (Rideout, 1956, p. 52).

The late nineteenth century had seen both the consolidation and
expansion of American industrial capital after the defeat of the
slaveocracy, and also the concomitant emergence of oppositional
struggles against the dehumanising effects of capitalist expansion.
Agrarian unrest, the Populist movement, the rise of the People's Party,
and the growing influence of muckraking journalists and novelists were
all indicative of this struggle. Between 1905 and 1915 the number of
overtly Socialist, radical novels which both criticised and questioned
the capitalist system, grew dramatically. Ten were published between
1901 and 1906, and twenty-seven between 1907 and 1913 – enough,
Rideout believes, to form a literary movement. The injustices of
capitalism were highlighted, and many Socialist writers believed that
capitalist society needed to be replaced by a Socialist one. In general,
they tended to believe that this could be achieved peacefully, by
converting as many people as possible to Socialist ideas.

The Socialist Party and its industrial counterpart, the Industrial
Workers of the World (the Wobblies), collapsed after the First World
War, largely because of the repressive legislation passed both during
and after the war. The nineteen-twenties were to see few radical novels
published, for 'in its impulse toward military unity the American state
had crushed, among other elements of dissent, the organizations, the

publications, and the individuals of a Left which had become, as Bourne put it, changing the figure, "like sand in the bearings of the State's great herd-machinery"' (Rideout, 1956, p. 107).

However, the collapse of 1929 was to strengthen yet again oppositional forces within America, and was to see in particular the growth of the CPUSA, which now entered its most influential period, one in which many leading intellectuals and writers were to be attracted to its politics. The emergence of what became known as the 'proletarian novel', owed much to the influence of the CPUSA, in particular through its journal, *New Masses,* and through the John Reed clubs. Richard Wright was to join one of the latter when he first moved to Chicago. There was a great deal of discussion among the writer-members of the CPUSA, and among its sympathisers, about what constituted a genuine 'proletarian novel,' the major dispute being over the relative importance of subject matter and point of view in creating a politically effective novel. Unlike the earlier Socialist novels, which had stressed the necessity for a peaceful transition to socialism, the proletarian novels of the thirties, strongly influenced by the Communist Party, emphasised the need for violent revolutionary change. By 1935 the Year Book Review Digest for the first time listed Proletarian Literature as a distinct classification.

The demise of the proletarian novel as an important cultural form is bound up closely with the fortunes of the CPUSA. The constant U-turns in policies throughout the nineteen-thirties, but especially after 1935, as the CPUSA slavishly followed the latest line from Stalinist Russia, led to demoralisation among party members. For many the 1939 Nazi – Soviet Non-Aggression Pact was the last straw. There were numerous public recantations, including that of the influential Marxist critic, Granville Hicks.

The decade of the nineteen-forties was one of reaction. The CPUSA had been seriously weakened and the disillusionment felt not just by Communists, but also by liberals, was to weaken any effective fightback against the government's determined assault on individual liberties.

The Second World War was used, as had been the first, as a pretext to curtail the rights of individuals:

The decline of liberalism began with the outbreak of the Second World War in Europe, when President Roosevelt announced a policy of expedience which called for the abandonment of social service legislation. The federal government then embarked, not in a systematic way, to be sure, but inevitably just the same, on a decade-long course of curbing individual liberty and tampering with individual belief. The Alien Registration Act was passed in 1940, the first peacetime sedition law in America since 1799. (Eisinger, 1963, p. 95)

The Smith Act of 1941 was used against the tiny American Socialist Workers' Party, and the CPUSA were not displeased to see this act being used against their Trotskyist critics; however it was to be used against them after the war, leading to the imprisonment of many of their leading members. The close of the war saw the Un-American Activities Committee granted permanent status.

Blacks were to face massive discrimination during the Second World War, as they had in the first, both as soldiers and as workers. If they successfully overcame the hurdle of discriminatory drafting procedures and joined up, they then fought the war against fascism in segregated units. Within the army many suffered humiliating treatment; serving black soldiers in the South, for example, were refused food in places which served German POWs. As non-combatants blacks had trouble finding work in industry, including the defence industry, because of discriminatory hiring practices. A threatened march on Washington organised by A. Philip Randolph, President of the Brotherhood of Sleeping Car Porters, embarrassed the federal government, and resulted in an executive order forbidding discrimination in defence industries. Although this had little practical effect, it is an illustration of the nervousness of the federal government, which felt it could not afford to give the enemy the ideological ammunition such a march would create.

There were important differences between the two world wars, however, which were to mean that the Second World War was a watershed in the history of the struggle for black rights, and that the basis for the later struggle for civil rights was also laid. The discrepancy between the ideological offensive of the government, committed to fighting for Roosevelt's 'Four Freedoms', and the reality of the position of blacks within America, was becoming seriously embarrassing. With the setting up of the United Nations and the struggle for freedom of the emerging African countries, many of whom would soon be represented there, the government felt forced to take some minimal action to protect blacks. The migration of black labour from South to North during the War also took place on a massive scale; this suited the need for free mobile labour, and was another factor in the government's realisation that at least a modicum of action should be taken.

In 1944 the War Department forbade racial discrimination in

recreation and transportation facilities. The outcry against this edict in the South was predictable; when the *Montgomery Advertiser,* in answer to the War Department's action wrote 'Army orders, even armies, even bayonets, cannot force impossible and unnatural social race reactions upon us' (Franklin, 1974, p. 448), the struggles of the Reconstruction period were being deliberately evoked.

The fiction produced in the nineteen forties both expressed these factors, and helped to reinforce the overtly reactionary dominant ideology. Most writers turned away from politics and from social protest to the inner world of the individual, and also to the formal aesthetics of literature, seen more and more as supra-historical and thus in themselves a form of escapism. Eisinger points out that Robert Penn Warren's *Night Rider* (1939), Walter Van Tilburg Clark's *The Ox-Bow Incident* (1940), and Carson McCullers' *The Heart is a Lonely Hunter* (1940), 'all bear one meaningful similarity; they turn away from these issues to find their real center in moral-ethical problems, or in what concerns the inward, private being' (Eisinger, 1963 p. 4).

Significantly, it was in 1941 that John Crowe Ransom's *The New Criticism* was published. New Criticism was, and is, enormously influential, stressing the formal aspects of literature, and the personal search for self knowledge in an alienating world. It poses as apolitical, while in its emphasis on formal aesthetic devices, and its implicit assumptions about what constitutes art, it is, as we shall see when examining Fast's novel, extremely political. Formalist criticism is intrinsically reactionary, concentrating on the formal structure and devices of a cultural artefact while largely ignoring substantive content. An example can be found in the critical acclaim of the overtly racist film *Birth of a Nation.* According to Monaco:

It is one of the ugly facts of film history that the landmark 'The Birth of a Nation' (1915) can be generally hailed as a classic despite its essential racism. No amount of technical expertise demonstrated, money invested, or artistic effect should be allowed to outweigh the Birth of a Nation's militantly anti-black political stance, yet we continue in film history as it is presently written to praise the film for its form ignoring, or at best paying lip service to, its disastrous content. (Monaco, 1981, p. 225)

Similarly, it was possible in 1968 for the novel *The Confessions of Nat Turner* to be awarded the Pulitzer Prize despite the fact that in a period of Civil Rights activism, it is a book written by a white Southern liberal rewriting black history in a way many found not only untrue, but racist. Writing at this time Fast was part of the radical tradition already described. But also he was very much writing against the grain of the nineteen-forties – 'turning out a book virtually every year, he did not seem to be aware that Marxism had collapsed in the forties' (Eisinger, 1963, p. 90).

The structure of *Freedom Road*, the language it uses, and its method of characterisation are aesthetic devices which effectively put forward political ideas. This is shown by the overall structure of the novel. It is in two parts; the first and longer section is called 'The Voting', the second much shorter one, 'The Fighting'. 'The Voting' is longer because it evokes a time of change and uncertainty; a time when the future is uncertain and lies in the balance; an unstable period between two social orders. At such a time 'The old is dying and the new cannot be born; in this interregnum there arises a great diversity of morbid symptoms' (Gramsci, 1971 p. 276). One of Fast's achievements is the way in which he concretely evokes the post-bellum period, arguably one of the most significant in American history. He describes events as the new State Convention meets in South Carolina:

And in Charleston, while that happened, the white aristocrats locked their doors, barred their shutters, and waited. Yankee bayonets in the street made them impotent for the time. There was no future and no past in this moment. In the deep strange hole that had been violently scooped in the stream of history something was happening. (Fast, 1972, p. 67)

The language of the novel has been attacked, ostensibly on aesthetic grounds, even by sympathetic critics. However, the language used, the biblical echoes and the 'pseudo-folksy' diction are highly effective aesthetic devices. If the novel is read sympathetically, the effect is movingly cumulative. The biblical language and the folksy idiom in fact have a double function. They emphasise the typicality of the characters, their importance as members of particular social groups, thus moving the emphasis away from the highly charged subjective feelings of a particular realised individual. The effect of creating a folk epic structure is also more subversive than such critics realise. Fast does not simply use implicit parallels in order to convey the universality of people's needs, desires and feelings. By simultaneously evoking the specific nature of the historical mood and emphasising the dynamics of change, both within individuals and in the world they inhabit, the types created never become static symbols, but rather function dynamically. One aesthetic device is thus counterposed by another, allowing the reader to recognise both the 'universality' of people's needs, and their ability to change the world in which they live. On the other hand, for example, in an epic novel like Joyce's *Ulysses* mythic devices, used formally to draw parallels between Bloom's journey through Dublin and the mythic odyssey of Ulysses, dehistoricise and universalise the meaning of Bloom's life.

The theme of constant change is reinforced by the symbol of movement used both in the title and throughout the novel – the road. When Gideon first goes to Charleston he walks there. This stress on the long, hard, physical journey highlights the concrete difficulty of getting from A to B which is an additional struggle for those without money. Secondly, it is a symbolic journey, reminiscent of the long journeys of Hardy's working-class characters, a movement towards freedom and struggle, and in this it contrasts starkly with the use of the road as symbol by writers like Kerouac. Later in the novel while talking with the President, Gideon says ' "when we fought our civil war, we were moving down a proud and shining road, what my people call a hallelujah road" ' (Fast, 1972, p. 160). Yet earlier in the novel, this image is itself ironically undercut when Gideon travels north to Boston, this time by train: 'The train that carried Gideon Jackson through the night, north from Washington D.C., roared into a new world' (Fast, 1972, p. 122). This new world was to offer little to the blacks and poor whites of the South; they would be betrayed by those in whom they put their faith. Gideon's train journey, so much easier than this earlier walk to Charleston, is a deceptive step on the Freedom Road.

Fast's method of characterisation can best be seen in his depiction of Gideon, his central character. Like the other characters, Gideon is portrayed both as a type and as a carefully realised individual. The structure of the novel, the form of the chapter headings used – for example 'How Gideon Jackson ...' – together with the simple and unadorned language stress Gideon's representativeness. But Gideon is not a static figure; he is constantly changing. Events, experience and the power of education lead him to realise the nature of the world in which he lives. The Gideon who is prepared to fight to save his community, the Gideon who believes in the necessity of destroying the ruling class in order to achieve power, is *not* the same Gideon who set off to the State Convention in Charleston with such high hopes. Fast shows us the experiences and events which lead to this change, and through Gideon's increasing awareness the reader is also drawn into this central theme.

Initially, Gideon is shown as confused, groping for answers. He believes goodwill and education are enough:

The chains that bound his people would never be forged again; there was no place for those chains in the sunlight. The rule of the many by the few, the darkest, heaviest evil man had borne in all man's memory, could be pricked like a water-filled bladder, and the content would ooze out the same way. (Fast, 1972, p. 81)

This naïve optimism, with its religious and idealistic overtones is immediately and ironically undercut as Fast juxtaposes a scene in which the white aristocrats of Charleston plan the building of the Ku Klux Klan:

'Gentlemen, we'll play a symphony on that white skin, we'll make it a badge of honor. We'll put a premium on that white skin. We'll dredge the sewers and the swamps for candidates, and we'll give them their white skin – and in return, gentlemen, they will give us back what we lost through this insane war, yes, all of it.' (Fast, 1972, p. 87)

Later in the novel this scene is balanced by another in which Gideon says bitterly:

'I didn't understand that some men are sick, and with their sickness they could contaminate the earth. We all make mistakes, don't we? I think that was the greatest mistake that the men on my side made. When the earth ran with blood during the war, they thought that the evil had been stamped out. But the blood of the sick, the diseased, the debased beyond reason – that blood never ran at all, only the blood of good men, men who had been led and lied to. We let your kind live ...' (Fast, 1972, p. 169–70)

Because of the way in which Gideon is represented, the reader can identify both with him and with the group he represents – working-class blacks and whites. In this way Fast emphasises groups as collections of individuals fighting for group and not simply individual interests. When Gideon is killed his last thoughts are of himself and his family, but as a part of that larger group to which they belong:

Gideon Jackson's last memory as the shell struck, as the shell burst and caused his memory to cease being, was of the strength of these people in his land, the black and the white, the strength that had taken them through a long war, that had enabled them to build, out of the ruin, a promise for the future, a promise that was, in a sense, more wonderful than any the world had ever known. Of that strength, the strange yet simple ingredients were the people, his son, Marcus, his son, Jeff, his wife, Rachel, his daughter, Jenny, the old man who was called Brother Peter, the tall, red-headed white man, Abner Lait, the small and wizened black man, Hannibal Washington – there were so many of them, so many shades and colors, some strong, some weak, some wise, some foolish: yet together they made the whole of the thing that was the last memory of Gideon Jackson, the thing indefinable and unconquerable. (Fast, 1972, p. 244)

Criticism of his work has tended to be political, while masquerading as 'pure' or 'aesthetic'. It assumes implicitly that political and aesthetic criteria are mutually exclusive. Such unspoken assumptions lead to criticism which is unable to analyse the strengths of Fast's work, because he is deliberately writing an unconventional novel, in which the *Angst*-ridden individual of 'high art' is replaced by the individual as part of a social group. However, if the attainment of self-knowledge and the glorification of individual experience is seen as the goal of the arts in general, and of literature in particular, how is a revolutionary novel, concerned with the motives of social groups and the meaning of historical events, to be analysed? Gibson (1981, p. 5) argues that 'if social literature is not entirely denigrated by formalists; then its social character is diminished or destroyed by emphasis on its formal character.' This is particularly true in the case of Fast, whose distinctively political manipulation of aesthetic devices constantly eludes his critics.

For Eisinger, Fast

was aided also by what I might call the typology of communism; all the characters fit into pre-established master categories, so that each character in a book is not more than the fulfilment of a typical figure whose lineaments have been set in a mold. It is a question, of course, whether the dialectical tension of the class struggle, when incorporated into fiction, can yield a satisfying concept of human nature. (Eisinger, 1963, p. 90)

The Southern critic, Hubbell, makes no pretence of attacking Fast on aesthetic grounds:

One of the worst specimens of Northern fiction dealing with Southern life is Howard Fast's Freedom Road ... . The old Abolitionists might be pardoned for their ignorance of Southern history but not a historical novelist of the twentieth century with some pretensions to scholarship. (Hubbell, 1954, p. 851)

One of the most liberal critics, Rideout, recognises that Fast always refused to separate politics and creative writing:

If Sinclair's chief contribution to modern American fiction was to help establish the novel of contemporary history, Fast's has been to show how an already established form, the traditional historical novel, may be used for radical ends. (Rideout, 1956, p. 275)

When dealing specifically with *Freedom Road*, however, he echoes many of the sentiments of other critics:

Gideon Jackson, Fast's Negro hero, is impossibly virtuous, as to a lesser degree are most of the other representatives of the two oppressed groups, and the white planters are unmitigatedly evil. Furthermore, the form of the novel, a spurious kind of folk epic, requires that Jackson be kept rather value as an individual; while the language of the novel, a pseudo-Biblical, 'pseudo-folksy' diction, ends by blurring all the characters rather than illuminating any of them sharply. (Rideout, 1956, p. 278)

What all these critics share is an inability to approach the novel as anything but a failed attempt to write a conventional novel. In such a novel, through the conventional use of aesthetic devices, and the delineation of individual characters, the reader takes on board an ideological message; that individuals and their emotional responses are the central concern of the novel, and by extension should be the central concern of the reader; yet simultaneously the individual stands helpless before the powerful forces of modern capitalism. The superior novelist then becomes the one who can best evoke the feelings of individual alienation felt by the majority of people. Life is seen as more meaningful and stable in a mythical Golden Age of pre-capitalist society in which everyone was content and everyone knew their place. An example of such a mythical society is the portrayal of the 'Old South'. Eisinger himself praises highly Mailer's novel *Barbary Shore* for evoking the feelings of individual helplessness, saying that the novel 'lays communism to rest as a meaningful cultural phenomenon as a way to personal salvation'. It achieves this because it 'records the failure of the social revolutionary in modern society, the victim of nameless terrors and alienation, who cannot make a vital relationship between his ideas and the society he lives' (Eisinger, 1963, p. 93). Since 1945 many novelists have evoked this mood of helpless alienation, the immediate post-war mood of many liberals being epitomised in novels like *The Man in the Grey Flannel Suit*.

Fast, on the other hand, used a popular cultural form, the historical novel, in order to reach a wide audience, and to put forward his belief that individuals were capable of changing for the better the post-war world in which they found themselves. In this he succeeded, for *Freedom Road* had sold over two million copies by the late nineteen-seventies.

Unlike earlier writers we have looked at, Fast was addressing not a white middle-class liberal readership, but those people who are central to his novels – working-class black and white people who do not find their history written in the official text books. It is significant therefore that his books were extremely popular with their readers, but not with the middle class critics who reviewed them. Although writing against the grain, both politically and aesthetically, Fast was also writing at a time when race relations in America were about to be once again 'on the agenda'. Many civil rights activists would later find that an understanding of Reconstruction in American history was essential for an informed debate during what was to become known as the Second Reconstruction. Fast's novel can be seen as one ingredient in the newly emerging questioning of a racism still apparently unassailable in the solid South.

References

Aaron, D. (1965) *Writers on the Left*, Avon, New York
Bowers, C. (1929) *The Tragic Era: The Revolution after Lincoln*, Houghton, Cambridge, Mass.
Buck, P. H. (1937) *The Road to Reunion*, Little, Brown and Co., Boston
Camejo, P. (1976) *Racism, Revolution, Reaction 1861–1877*, Monad, New York
Carroll, P. N. and Noble (1980) *The Free and the Unfree*, Penguin, London
Clark W. van T. (1940) *The Ox-Bow Incident*, New American Library, New York
Dunning, W. A. (1965) *Reconstruction, Political and Economic, 1865–1877*, Harper and Row, New York (first published in 1897)
Eisinger, C. E. (1963) *Fiction of the Forties*, University of Chicago Press, Chicago
Fast, H. (1946) *The Unvanquished*, The World Publishing Company, New York and Cleveland
Fast, H. (1945) *Citizen Tom Paine*, The Bodley Head, London
Fast, H. (1972) *Freedom Road*, Futura, London
Franklin, J. H. (1973) *From Slavery to Freedom*, Alfred A. Knopf, New York
Fredrickson, G. M. (1971) *The Black Image in the White Mind*, Harper and Row, New York
Gibson, D. B. (1981) *The Politics of Literary Expression: A Study of Major Black Writers*, Greenwood Press, Westport, Conn.
Gramsci, A. (1971) *Selections from the Prison Note Books*, Lawrence & Wishart, London
Gurko, L. (1968) *The Angry Decade*, Harper & Row, New York
Hardy, T. (1965) *Tess of the D'Urbervilles*, Washington Square Press, Inc., New York
Hubbell, J. (1954) *The South in American Literature*, Duke University Press, Durham
Joyce, J. (1947) *Ulysses*, Penguin, Harmondsworth
Kerouac J. (1975) *On The Road*, Penguin, Harmonsworth
Kirby, J. T. (1986) *Media Made Dixie, The South in the American Imagination*, Louisiana State University Press, London and Baton Rouge (revised edition)
Lindenmeyer, O. (1970) *Black History: Lost, Stolen or Strayed*, Avon Books, New York
Livingston, D. N. (1984) 'Science and Society: Nathaniel S. Shaler and Racial

Ideology', *Transactions*, Institute of British Geographers (New Series), 9, pp. 181-210

MacCullers, C. (1940) *The Heart is a Lonely Hunter*

MacKethan, L. H. (1980) *The Dream of Arcady*, Louisiana State University Press, Baton Rouge

Marable, M. (1985) *Black American Politics*, Verso, London

Monaco, J. (1981) *How To Read A Film*, Oxford University Press, Oxford and New York

Polenberg, Richard (1983) *One Nation Divisible: Class, Race and Ethnicity in the United States Since 1938*, Penguin, Harmondsworth

Rideout, W. B. (1956) *The Radical Novel in the United States*, Harvard University Press, Cambridge, Mass.

Silk, C. P., and Silk, J. A. (1985) 'Racism, Nationalism and the Creation of A Regional Myth: The Southern States after the American Civil War', in J. A. Burgess and J. R. Gold (eds), *Geography, The Media, and Popular Culture*, Croom Helm, Beckenham, pp. 165-91

Silk, J. A. (1984) 'Beyond Geography and Literature', *Environment and Planning D* (Society and Space), 2, pp. 151-78

Sitkoff, H. (1981) *The Struggle for Black Equality*, Hill and Wang, New York

Stampp, K. M. (1965) *The Era of Reconstruction, 1865-1877*, Vintage Books, New York

Styron, W. (1966) *The Confessions of Nat Turner*, Corgi, London

Wilson, S. (1944) *The Man in the Grey Flannel Suit*, The Reprint Society, London

8

Ann Petry: *The Street* (1946)

In *The Street* Ann Petry examines not only racism, which by this time was so deeply entrenched in American society, but she also looks at the effects that racism has had on the relationships between black men and women. In this she prefigures the work of later African-American women writers like Alice Walker and Toni Morrison, but she also, like Howard Fast, recognises the interplay of class and racial oppression.

The novels already looked at which attempt to put forward an anti-racist philosophy all share a more conventional attitude to sexual relationships and to the portrayal of women in society. Tourgee uses a conventional romantic relationship as the framework of his novel, to such an extent in fact that his primary aim of portraying race relations in the South becomes secondary to the trials and tribulations of the central courtship theme. In the tales of Chesnutt, it is precisely through the attempts of black men and women to achieve lasting relationships that he most effectively evokes the inhumanity of slavery. The conventional relationship between the white plantation owner and his wife is also used to embody an ironic vision within the framework of the tales. Fast's almost allegorical novel set in Reconstruction also accepts implicitly conventional relationships between men and women; the people he describes cannot afford the luxury of questioning such ideas while they are involved in a life and death struggle.

But there is another reason why oppositional novels tended to share basic assumptions about male–female relationships with more mainstream, and even with some racist novels. Under slavery families were forcibly separated: men and women from each other, and both from their children. There were heroic attempts on the part of black men and women to keep together. There is still controversy about how many slave families were forcibly separated by the sale of members of the family but all slaves had to live constantly with the threat: 'Behind the interest of the master in the birth of slave children stood a stark threat to the slave family; the possibility of disruption because of sale' (Degler, 1980, p. 119). There is ample evidence that most slaves maintained deep emotional attachments to their families despite all attempts by slave-owners, and despite the awful conditions under which they lived. Degler quotes from a letter written by a slave Abream Scriven, to his wife in 1858 when he finds out that he is going to be sold:

My dear wife for you and my Children my pen cannot Express the griffe I feel to be parted from you all. Give my love to my father and mother and tell them good Bye for me. And if we shall not meet in this world I hope to meet in Heaven. (quoted in Degler, 1980, p. 120)

This is Frederick Douglass's moving description of his short relationship with his mother:

I never saw my mother, to know her as such, more than four or five times in my life; and each of those times was very short in duration, and at night. She was hired by a Mr. Stewart, who lived about twelve miles from my home. She made her journeys to see me in the night, travelling the whole distance on foot, after the performance of her day's work. She was a field hand, and a whipping is the penalty of not being in the field at sunrise, unless a slave has special permission from his or her master to the contrary – a permission which they seldom get, and one that gives to him that gives it the proud name of being a kind master. I do not recollect of ever seeing my mother by the light of day. She was with me in the night. She would lie down with me, and get me to sleep, but long before I waked she was gone. Very little communication ever took place between us. Death soon ended what little we could have while she lived, and with it her hardships and suffering. She died when I was about seven years old, on one of my master's farms, near Lee's Mill. I was not allowed to be present during her illness, at her death, or burial. (Douglass, 1982, pp. 48–9)

After emancipation, the overriding priority for many freed blacks was to build a family life, to gain some education for their children, and to be economically independent. Many had first to find their families:

The close concern of slave parents for their children was also evident in the public letters and meetings immediately after emancipation in which parents sought to protect their children against mistreatment or indenture service. And as late as the eighteen eighties, one student of blacks in New Orleans has reported, former slaves were still advertising in newspapers, seeking to locate relatives from whom they had been separated during slavery days or in the course of the war. (Degler, 1980, p. 123)

The descriptions of the meetings of the State Convention of South Carolina during Radical Reconstruction by Howard Fast in the novel

Freedom Road are based on historical events and give a good idea of the preoccupations of such assemblies during the short period when freed blacks were allowed to take part in them. There was a great emphasis on the desire for free education for all – for blacks and whites – and particularly there was a desire for what became known as 'forty acres and a mule' some land for freedmen in order that they could begin to support themselves. The refusal of the federal government to support the civil rights of black people, the gradual institution of Jim Crow backed up by the progressively reactionary decisions of the Supreme Court, along with organised terrorism and the calculated use of the sharecropping and convict lease system, ensured that none of these ambitions were realised.

By the end of the nineteenth century racist ideologies and institutions ensured the continued economic exploitation of black people in the South. As discussed earlier in this book, a particularly important part of this ideology was the development of the myth of the black rapist:

In connection with these lynchings and their countless barbarities, the myth of the Black rapist was conjured up. It could only acquire its terrible powers of persuasion within the irrational world of racist ideology. However irrational the myth may be, it was not a spontaneous aberration. On the contrary, the myth of the Black rapist was a distinctly political invention. As Frederick Douglass points out, Black men were not indiscriminately labeled as rapists during slavery. Throughout the entire Civil War, in fact, not a single Black man was publicly accused of raping a white woman ... In the immediate aftermath of the Civil War, the menacing specter of the Black rapist had not yet appeared on the historical scene. But lynchings, reserved during slavery for the white abolitionists, were proving to be a valuable political weapon. Before lynching could be consolidated as a popularly accepted institution, however, its savagery and its horrors had to be convincingly justified. These were the circumstances which spawned the myth of the Black rapist, for the rape charge turned out to be the most powerful of several attempts to justify the lynching of black people. (Davis, 1981, pp. 184–5)

Twentieth century black autobiographies give many examples of black men being lynched. At least two of Malcolm X's male relatives were lynched or 'disappeared' and in the autobiographies of Maya Angelou and Richard Wright we are given moving descriptions of the anxiety and anguish felt by young black men in the South living under the perpetual threat of violence:

The institution of lynching, in turn, complemented by the continued rape of Black women, became an essential ingredient of the postwar strategy of racist terror. In this way the brutal exploitation of Black labor was guaranteed, and after the betrayal of Reconstruction, the political domination of the Black people as a whole was assured. (Davis, 1981, p. 185)

It was impossible for white women in the South to protest as this activity was being carried out in their name. As we have already seen, this organised terrorism worked to 'keep in their place' both black and white women and black men. A concomitant effect of the myth was that of the promiscuous black woman. Black women had been subjected to sexual abuse during slavery, and this continued after freedom.

Together with the economic exploitation to which it was so intimately linked, these ideologies and practices had a devastating effect on the stability of black families. Black men found themselves unable to find work, or as sharecroppers or super-exploited industrial workers, still unable to support their wives and children. Among white people in the South, slavery had served to ensure that manual work and domestic work was denigrated as inferior, and it was always possible for black women to find domestic work in white families. Black families often found themselves therefore relying upon the earnings of black women who were working for white families. As late as 1920 'four-fifths of black married women were employed as domestic servants, farm laborers, or laundresses' (Degler, 1980, p. 391). All these factors were to take a huge toll on relationships between black men and women.

By the time that Ann Petry wrote *The Street* there had already developed a tradition of African-American protest novels, many modelled on Richard Wright's socially determinist book, *Native Son*. However, *Native Son* and other black protest novels continued to portray extremely conventional sexual relations. Like the majority of published African-American literature before the nineteen seventies, it was concerned primarily with the black *man's* relationships with white society and his inability to carve himself a place within it. African-American literature written by women however has often foregrounded relationships between men and women within the black community. White society, though partially responsible for the forms which these relationships take, is not the centre of interest.

In the novels of Zora Neale Hurston for example the white world is of little real significance in comparison with the evocative portrayal of relationships between black people. The experiences of black women in the Civil Rights movement informs many contemporary novels written by African-American women; but it is often forgotten that these women are also writing in a tradition, until recently almost completely neglected, which includes novelists like Zora Neale Hurston and Ann Petry.

The point of view from which a novel is written has always been an important ideological weapon as well as an aesthetic choice. Harris recognised this in his use of Uncle Remus as did Dixon in his refusal to incorporate the point of view of any black character in his racist novels. The novels looked at in Part Two all use point of view in significant ways. Howard Fast helped to revolutionise the conventional historical novel by deliberately writing from the point of view of an oppressed *group*, and in *The Street* much of the power of the novel derives from the fact that we experience the world Lutie lives in through her thoughts and experiences. We are therefore not allowed to *escape* through the comfortable portrayal of a white romantic relationship as in Tourgee's novel, but are forced to recognise the nature of racism and sexism as it affects a working-class black woman living in Harlem.

In this novel then, using the point of view of a black woman, marginalised and oppressed within the black community, as well as within the wider one, Petry reveals not only the structures of a racist and capitalist society, but concretely portrays a community on the brink of change. The book shares, in its determinism and its detailed realistic description of its social world, a great deal with earlier protest novels. But its real significance lies in its differences with the earlier tradition.

It is through her experiences, not only as a black person, but specifically as a black woman, that Lutie begins to puzzle out the meaning of the world in which she lives. Petry continually stresses that Lutie's relationships cannot be separated from the wider world which has helped to shape them. Through Lutie's memories the reader is shown Lutie's earlier experiences, and in this way is aware of the ways in which her earlier struggles throw light on her present life.

For example, early in the book, Lutie makes the decision to take an apartment in Harlem for herself and her son Bub in an attempt to begin to forge a better life for them both. Returning from signing the lease, she sees an advertisement for a beautiful modern kitchen, in which a woman 'with incredible blonde hair' (Petry, 1986, p. 25), and a 'dark-haired smiling man in a navy uniform' are standing. This triggers off memories of the job as a domestic she once had in a rich woman's house in Connecticut. She had taken this job because her husband could not get work, thus joining the millions of black women with children forced to leave their own families and work for white women and their children. Reflecting later, Lutie herself comes to understand this: 'And she thought, That's what's wrong. We don't have time enough or money enough to live like other people because the women have to work until they become drudges and the men stand by idle' (Petry, 1986, p. 134). Looking at the women coming home from work

She noticed how heavily they walked on feet that obviously hurt despite the wide, cracked shoes they wore. They've been out all day working in the white folks' kitchens, she thought, then they come home and cook and clean for their own families half the night ... here on this street the women trudged along over-burdened, overworked, their own homes neglected while they looked after someone else's while the men on the street swung along empty-handed, well dressed, and carefree. Or they lounged against the sides of the buildings, their hands in their pockets while they stared at the women who walked past, probably deciding which woman they should select to replace the wife who was out working all day. (Petry, 1986, p. 51)

She remembers also that it was during that same job that she learnt how white people had come to view black women:

Apparently it was an automatic reaction of white people – if a girl was col-oured and fairly young, why, it stood to reason she had to be a prostitute. If not that – at least sleeping with her would be just a simple matter, for all one had to do was make the request. In fact, white men wouldn't even have to do the asking because the girl would ask them on sight. (Petry, 1986, p. 37)

While she is working to keep her family together, her husband abandons her for another woman, and Lutie finds herself alone with Bub in Harlem. Lutie, still standing on the train, staring at the advertisement, returns from her memories to the present, and to her determination to fight for herself and her son.

Counterposing this structural movement within the novel is Petry's use of dynamic contrasts which help to illuminate the society in which Lutie is living. The pivotal contrasts which are used are those of ideology – reality, black – white, male – female and poor – rich. Lutie's constant awareness of and attempts to understand the first three of these become the basis of her eventual awareness of the fundamental impor-tance of the last – the significance of class.

The contrast between the ideology of the American Dream and the reality for many Americans, what Malcolm X called the American nightmare, is a fundamental contradiction used by many radical American novelists. It is the awareness of this which enrages Wright's Bigger Thomas who, through advertisements, films, music etc., is taunted by a vision of American society he is not allowed to enter. For Lutie, the kitchen advertisement partially represents this American dream, unattainable for a poor black girl, however hard she is prepared to work and to play by the rules of the system.

For the advertisement she was looking at pictured a girl with incredible blonde hair. The girl leaned close to a dark-haired smiling man in a navy uniform. They were standing in front of a kitchen sink – a sink whose white porcelain surface gleamed under the train lights. The taps looked like silver. The linoleum floor of the kitchen was a crisp black-and-white pattern that pointed up the sparkle of the room. Casement windows. Red geraniums in yellow pots. (Petry, 1986, p. 25)

The dream serves only to emphasise the reality of Lutie's existence. 'It was, she thought, a miracle of a kitchen. Completely different from the kitchen of the 116th Street flat she had moved into just two weeks ago.'

There are hints throughout the book that such exclusion will not be tolerated by black people for ever. As with other devices used by Petry, this contrast is used cumulatively. For example, later in the novel, desperately needing money to free Bub from detention, Lutie goes to see a movie:

And the picture didn't make sense. It concerned a technicolour world of bright lights and vast beautiful rooms; a world where the only worry was whether the heroine in a sequined evening gown would eventually get the hero in a top hat and tails out of the clutches of a red-headed female spy who lolled on wide divans dressed in white velvet dinner suits. (Petry, 1986, p. 295)

Lutie's situation is by now so desperate that

She kept thinking it had nothing to do with her, because there were no dirty little rooms, no narrow, crowded streets, no children with police records, no worries about rent and gas bills. And she had brought that awful creeping silence in here with her. It crouched along the aisles, dragged itself across the rows of empty seats. (Petry, 1986, p. 295)

Petry also shows us a culture which is not allowed to flourish – that of poor black people themselves. Here the feelings of an oppressed people are articulated, but it is still an articulation without faith in the possibility of real change. When Lutie, listening in Junto's bar to a record of 'Darlin' begins to sing along with it,

Her voice had a thin thread of sadness running through it that made the song important, that made it tell a story that wasn't in the words – a story of despair, of loneliness, of frustration. It was a story that all of them knew by heart and had always known because they had learned it soon after they were born and would go on adding to it until the day they died. (Petry, 1986, p. 109)

Lutie is a character who constantly tries to learn from her experiences. Her only experience of the white world is of oppressive employers, and of sexual harassment. White men and women make assumptions about her because she is a black woman, while in the black community black men also oppress women, compensating for their feelings of helplessness in the white world. Lutie recognises this; her bitterness unassuaged by her understanding. She herself is determined not to be mistreated by any man again, black or white.

She struggles against the wall of racism by which she is surrounded. Images of walls and of darkness evoke the claustrophobia of the world in which she is trapped. When her white employer is friendly towards her, 'The wall between them wasn't quite so high. Only it was still there of course' (Petry, 1986, p. 41). Travelling together on a train, they talk almost like friends, but when they reach their destination,

the wall was suddenly there. Just as they got off the train, just as the porter was reaching for Mrs. Chandler's pigskin luggage, the wall suddenly loomed up. It was Mrs. Chandler's voice that erected it. Her voice high, clipped, carrying, as she said, 'I'll see you on Monday, Lutie.'

Later, she feels crushed by her small apartment, 'the walls seemed to come in toward her, to push against her' (Petry, 1986, p. 61). The images accumulate as she moves toward her tragedy, and the claustrophobic rooms in which she lives become a symbol of the narrow, racist world of America:

In the darkness it [the room] seemed to close in on her until it became the sum total of all the things she was afraid of and she drew back nearer the wall because the room grew smaller and the pieces of furniture larger until she felt as though she were suffocating. (Petry, 1986, p. 141)

It is Junto, the powerful and rich white man, who finally seals her fate:

And all the time she was thinking, 'Junto has a brick in his hand, Just one brick. The final one needed to complete the wall that had been building up around her for years, and when that one last brick was shoved in place, she would be completely walled in. (Petry, 1986, p. 303)

Initially, she identifies all white people with this wall: 'It all added up to the same thing, she decided – white people. She hated them. She would always hate them' (Petry, 1986, p. 150). Black – white and poor – rich are for Lutie the same thing. For her, as for many poor blacks, money is white. She learns early on the power of money and associates it with the power of whiteness. While working for the

Chandlers she witnesses a suicide; she witnesses also the way in which the Chandlers' money ensures that there is no scandal. Lutie 'was interested in the way in which money transformed a suicide she had seen committed from start to finish in front of her very eyes into "an accident with a gun"' (Petry, 1986, p. 40). The incident is an ironic contrast to Lutie's later inability to raise just $200 to free Bub. Lack of money and Bub's pathetic attempts to help are the reasons for Lutie's desperate situation.

However, Lutie gradually learns that those black people who do become richer are themselves willing to exploit other blacks. The evil of the white world is no longer enough of an explanation. Boots Smith uses his position and his money to manipulate Lutie. Mrs Hedges lives off the suffering and frustrations of poor blacks. The lawyer who asks Lutie for $200 to get Bub out of the Children's Centre is exploiting Lutie for greed, for he knows that no money is necessary. The rich, white, powerful Junto, who is responsible for the final tragedy, is responsible *not* because he is white, but because he is rich.

It is when Lutie goes to visit Bub at the Centre that she begins to realise that there are also white people who are poor, and that this poverty places them, despite their colour, in a similar position: 'They were sitting in the same shrinking, huddled positions. Perhaps, she thought, we're all here because we're all poor. Maybe it doesn't have anything to do with colour' (Petry, 1986, p. 293).

This recognition, although coming too late to change Lutie's world, creates a perspective ensuring that the complexity of Lutie's experiences in a white, male-dominated world is never simplified. Linked with the theme of a society on the brink of change, it also ensures that the deterministic mode of Lutie's personal tragedy is offset by some feeling of hope for the future.

The hope of future change undercuts the social determinism of the novel. Unlike *Native Son* in which Wright has to resort to long set speeches to put forward his message about racism, Petry builds into the structure of her novel her exploration of racism. Set in the war years, we are constantly reminded of this background, which is changing the world even as Petry describes it. Although the soldiers have not yet returned, there is already a recognition that there must be some change after the war. Boots's determination not to fight a white man's war in a segregated army unit, reflects the wider resentment felt in the black community. The hopeless acceptance of racism by many black people is contrasted with the beginning of a new spirit. In one incident a girl

sees her brother killed in the street; her immediate and passive acceptance of the tragedy is a measure of her defeat:

> It was an expression that said the girl hoped for no more than this from life
> because other things that had happened to her had paved the way so that she
> had lost the ability to protest against anything – even death suddenly like this
> in the spring. (Petry, 1986, p. 43)

But Lutie, watching the people in the street realises

> that it was like a war that hadn't got off to a start yet, though both sides were
> piling up ammunition and reserves and were now waiting for anything, any
> little excuse, a gesture, a word, a sudden loud noise – and pouf! it would start.
> (Petry, 1986, p. 145)

In *The Street* we are shown black people attempting to survive as
individuals within a hostile system, rather than any group resistance
to the racism they face. The words anger and loneliness echo through
the book, and when Lutie breaks down after learning about Bub's
detention, the flat-dwellers in her building pretend not to see her; her
pain is too similar to their own and they also share her feelings of
helplessness.

The sound of Lutie's high-heeled shoes becomes a symbol, not only
of her femininity and vulnerability, but also of her anger and determination not to be defeated. For example, when she first realises that her
job as a singer would depend upon her sleeping with Junto,

> There was a hard sound to her heels clicking aginst the pavement and she tried
> to make it louder. Hard, hard, hard. That was the only way to be – so hard
> that nothing, the street, the house, the people – nothing would be able to touch
> her. (Petry, 1986, p. 220)

Lutie's unbearable anger is finally expressed in an act of individual
violence which leads to her final defeat. But the reader has also seen how
Lutie was driven to this, and it becomes clear that however deterministic
the novel appears to be at first reading, it finally holds out hope for
change and for a real struggle in the future. Partly this is achieved
through the hints supplied by Petry that black people will eventually
fight for their rights, and that things *must* be different after the war, and
also in Lutie's belated, but significant, recognition that there are also
working-class white people who are defeated by the system. For
sympathetic readers at the time it helped to show how great was the need
for action; for readers in the nineteen-eighties the knowledge of the
events of the Civil Rights movements, in which boys like Bub would

have been young and active participants, makes the novel, far from socially deterministic, seem powerfully prophetic.

References

Bigsby, C. W. E. (1980) *The Second Black Renaissance*, Greenwood Press, Westport, Conn.

Davis, A. (1982) *Women, Race and Class*, Women's Press, London

Davis, C. T. (1982) *Black is the Color of the Cosmos, Essays on Afro-American Literature and Culture, 1942–1981*, Garland Publishing, New York and London

Degler, C. N. (1981) *At Odds: Women and the Family in America from the Revolution to the Present*, Oxford University Press, Oxford and New York

Douglass, F. (1982) *Narrative of the Life of Frederick Douglass, an American Slave*, Penguin, Harmondsworth

Evans, M. (ed) (1983) *Black Women Writers (1950–1980): A Critical Evaluation*, Anchor Books, New York

Fast, H. (1972) *Freedom Road*, Futura, London

Gates, H. L. Jr (1987) 'The black person in art: how should s/he be portrayed?', *Black American Literature*, 21, pp. 3-24

Gatlin, R. (1987) *American Women since 1945*, Macmillan Education, Basingstoke and London

Hernton, C. C. (1973) *Sex and Racism*, Paladin, London

Hughes, C. M. (1970) *The Negro Novelist, 1940–1980*, Citadel Press, New York

Lee A. R. (ed) (1980) *Black Fiction: New Studies in the Afro-American Novel Since 1945*, Vision Press, London

Petry, A. (1986) *The Street*, Virago, London

Showalter, E. (ed) (1986) *The New Feminist Criticism: Essays on Women, Literature and Theory*, Virago, London

Towns, S. (1974) 'The black woman as whore: genesis of the myth', *The Black Position*, 3, pp. 39–59

Walker, A. (1983) *In Search of Our Mothers' Gardens*, Harcourt Brace Jovanovich, San Diego, New York and London

Wallace, M. (1979) *Black Macho and the Myth of the Superwoman*, John Calder, London

Wisker, G. (1987) 'Stepping out, speaking out: the personal voice raised against oppression in the work of Alice Walker and Maya Angelou', *Over Here: An American Studies Journal* (University of Nottingham), 7, pp. 35–49

Wright, R. (1972) *Native Son*, Penguin, Harmondsworth

X, Malcolm (1970) *Autobiography*, Penguin, Harmondsworth

9

William Styron: *The Confessions of Nat Turner* (1967)

To understand the significance of Styron's novel, which takes the form of an autobiography of a significant historical figure, it is necessary to look briefly at the history of African-American autobiography as a cultural form.

Autobiography is one of the most significant art forms produced by black Americans. It began with the thousands of slave narratives which kept appearing until the early twentieth century. Autobiographical statements, including novels, remain 'the quintessential literary genre for capturing the cadences of the Afro-American being, revealing its deepest aspirations and tracing the evolution to the Afro-American psyche under the impact of slavery and modern U.S. imperialism' (Cudjoe, 1984, p. 6). For blacks, the autobiographical form is a survival technique adopted in response to their oppression in American society, and 'is one of the ways that black Americans have asserted their right to live and grow' (Butterfield, 1974, p. 6).

Significantly, although autobiography is necessarily written or told from the point of view of one person, within black autobiography this has an unusual function. As Cudjoe (1984, p. 10) points out, African-American autobiography

is objective and realistic in its approach and is presumed generally to be of service to the group. It is never meant to glorify the exploits of the individual, and the concerns of the collective predominate. One's personal experiences are presumed to be an authentic expression of the society, and thus statistical evidences and sociological treatises assume a secondary level of importance. Herein can be found the importance of the autobiographical statement in Afro-American letters.

Mainstream autobiographical writing has different characteristics. The self is central, the community and wider social and political context being merely a backdrop against which the individual plays out her or his fate. Exceptional individuals are shown as struggling to break away from and rise above the confines of the subordinate group, leaving behind the mass of the less fortunate or less determined. The latter are condemned or pitied for their failure to get on. The narrative structure is usually linear and predictable, the writer overcoming various obstacles in order to 'succeed'; the ethos is competitive, the unspoken message being 'how I made it within the system'.

Black autobiography and oral history have played an important part in passing on black traditions of survival and struggle. There is ample evidence that the names of great slave leaders like Gabriel Prosser and Nat Turner were kept alive and their lives used as role models within the black community. Malcolm X refers to Nat Turner as a man who 'wasn't going around preaching pie-in-the-sky and non-violence freedom for the black man'; Maya Angelou describes her resentment when a white visitor at her school graduation ceremony reminds students of their ordained place in a white-dominated society: 'Then I wished that Gabriel Prosser and Nat Turner had killed all white folks in their beds' (Angelou, 1984, p. 176).

The Confessions of Nat Turner can be seen as the response of a white Southern liberal to the events of the Civil Rights movements of the nineteen-fifties and sixties, a response in which he uses and subverts the tradition of the black autobiography to put forward his own views about slavery, the black personality and, by extension, about the activities of black activists at the time at which he was writing.

To do this Styron uses several devices. The first is the use of the first person, the form of the autobiographical novel itself. We have already seen, when looking at novels of the late nineteenth century, that it was a method commonly used by white Southern writers. It was quite usual to put the viewpoint of the white community into the mouth of a black character who thus endorsed his own oppression. In this way it is Uncle Remus who decries the laziness of the freedman, and who cannot understand any black person wishing to leave the South. Styron takes this one step further, for the black character he uses is also a famous historical figure, much revered in black history, and the novel actually takes the form of his 'confessions'.

Secondly, Styron uses a racist theory of the psychological debasement of blacks under slavery, popularised by Stanley Elkins, and conflates this with a new ingredient – that of the existential predicament of modern humanity – through the account Nat Turner gives of his life.

In this way the feelings and actions of the central character, and the novel's tragic theme, are modernised and universalised, thus making it even easier for white liberal readers, ignorant of true black history, to believe that this Nat Turner is the 'true' one. The existential framework also allows him to be portrayed as a modern anti-hero and fulfilling his tragic destiny, so maintaining the emphasis on self that is so important in mainstream autobiography. Nat Turner comes to differ little from the characters of most modern novels with which a liberal middle-class readership would be familiar.

Thirdly, Styron, against all evidence, posits Nat Turner's motivation for leading an uprising against slavery as his sexual obsession with a white woman. Here we come back again to the old myth of the black rapist, being used in a different context to belittle the struggles, both past and present, of black people. In the novel, the myth of the black rapist is expressed in the portrayal of Nat Turner as motivated primarily by sexual obsession, a black rapist who substitutes masturbation and fantasy for the act itself.

These devices are used simultaneously to evoke a general picture of slavery and of Turner and his motivations which is directly contradicted by all historical evidence. Throughout, the use of the first person narrative, interspersed with extracts from the real 'confessions' of the real Nat Turner, give it an apparent authenticity.

The reader is therefore drawn into the novel by identifying with the fictional hero Nat Turner, who is conflated through the text with the real Nat Turner. The motivations expressed, with which we are led to sympathise, in the novel are transformed into the motivations of the real historical figure.

The portrayal of slave society in nineteenth-century Virginia, and of the slave community, is evoked largely through the words and the mind of the fictional character Nat Turner, but based on the work of Elkins and others. Elkins' theory of the black slave personality modified and extended that originally expressed by U. B. Phillips at the end of the nineteenth century. Phillips saw slavery as a benevolent institution, bringing civilisation to a naturally backward race whose members were happy with their lot. He portrayed black people as childlike 'Sambo' figures who looked up to their ever paternalistic owners. Such attitudes were evident in books on Nat Turner's revolt like *The Southampton Insurrection* written by Drewry in 1900. Elkins discarded the notion that blacks were *genetically* inferior, and also rejected the idea of slavery as essentially benign. He argued that the treatment of slaves distorted the personalities of blacks, the resulting psychological damage manifesting itself in Sambo-like characteristics.

Accepting Elkins' description of slave psychology Styron wrote that under slavery, 'total dehumanisation of a race took place, and a systematic attempt, largely successful, was made to reduce an entire people to the status of children' (Styron, 1984, p. 53). This dehumanisation, it appears, only afflicted the victims of oppression, not those whites who ran the system! Although aware of historical evidence, notably that provided by Aptheker, that resistance among slaves was normal and endemic, and that the Nat Turner revolt was the culmination of a particular period of unrest, rather than an historical anomaly, Styron chose to ignore this and to portray blacks in terms of Elkins' theory. He does so by showing that for the vast majority of blacks, slavery produces an inferior person who is passive, coarse, ignorant and clownish. More strikingly, he relies upon neo-Freudian explanations of culture and behaviour to show that in Turner's case the personality distortions are both more complex and more sinister.

Turner himself is shown as distancing himself from his own people, doing so in terms which convey Elkins' thesis of the 'slave personality':

I began more and more to regard the Negroes of the mill and field as creatures beneath contempt, so devoid of the attributes I had come to connect with the sheltered and respectable life that they were worth not even my derision ... Such was the vainglory of a black boy who may have been alone among his race in bondage who had actually read pages from Sir Walter Scott and who knew the product of nine multiplied by nine. (Styron, 1980, pp. 172–3)

This contrasts dramatically with the autobiographical account by ex-slave Frederick Douglass of his attempts to teach fellow-slaves to read:

I had at one time over forty scholars, and those of the right sort, ardently desiring to learn. They were of all ages, though mostly men and women. I look back to those Sundays with an amount of pleasure not to be expressed. They were great days to my soul. The work of instructing my dear fellow-slaves was the sweetest engagement with which I was ever blessed. We loved each other, and to leave them at the close of the Sabbath was a severe cross indeed. When I think that these precious souls are today shut up in the prisonhouse of slavery, my feelings overcome me, and I am almost ready to ask, 'Does a righteous God govern the universe and for what does he hold the thunder in his right hand, if not to smite the oppressors, and deliver the spoiled out of the hand of the spoilers.' (Douglass, 1982, pp. 120–1)

The distance between Nat Turner and other blacks is further emphasised by the way in which the characters express themselves in thought and speech. Nat thinks almost entirely in 'standard American', and rarely lapses into the heavy dialect described (Styron, 1980, p. 137) as the 'thick gluey cornfield accent' and the 'field nigger's tongue' of his fellow slaves.

A glimpse of a Northern white woman who shows pity for another black leads Turner into a

> swift fantasy [in which] I saw myself down on the road beginning to possess her without tenderness, without gratitude for her pity but with abrupt, brutal and rampaging fury, watching the compassion melt from her tear-stained face as I bore her to the earth, my black hands already tearing at the lustrous billowing silk as I drew the dress up round her waist, and forcing apart those soft white thighs exposed the zone of fleecy brown hair into which I drove my black self with stiff merciless thrusts. (Styron, 1980, p. 260)

The slave leader is shown as having a psychological obsession for white women. The myth of the black rapist, expressed in the form of sexual fantasies, becomes his true motivation for leading a revolt against slavery. A subsidiary motivation results from the relatively lenient treatment Turner receives from his white master. Black critics were quick to pick up the lesson to be derived from this thesis in the America of the 1960s. Turner is shown to be driven by a form of Oedipal complex. He venerates his white master, but also hates and wishes to destroy him and his kind. Styron believes that revolutionaries are driven by a 'tormented and complicated relationship' with a father-figure and that 'one cannot help believing' that Nat Turner had such a relationship with his father or with his surrogate father, his master (Styron, 1984, p. 29).

Styron also gives us the myth of the promiscuous black woman. Black women are beneath Nat Turner's contempt, not being 'good enough' for such an exceptional individual as he:

> I was in an unusual position compared to the other Negro boys, who found an easy outlet for their hunger with the available and willing little black girls whom they took during some quick stolen instant at the edge of a cornfield or amid the cool concealing grass of a strand of sorghum down at the edge of the woods.

Turner prefers his vision of the 'golden-haired girl with her lips half open and whispering' (Styron, 1980, p. 176).

Most white literary critics were enthusiastic about the novel, which was to receive the Pulitzer Prize. They welcomed it as a masterpiece:

> there is the selfsame Black Shadow (sic) that has darkened the pages of southern literature from the romances of William Gilmore Sims on through to Mark Twain, George Washington Cable, and Thomas Nelson Page, and more

recently William Faulkner, Robert Penn Warren, and every other southern writer of the twentieth century so far. (Rubin, 1975, p. 232)

White critics were also impressed by the exploration of typically Southern preoccupations in an existential framework. Styron's use of the story of the rebellion as a platform for examining the alienation of modern humanity, and in so doing universalising his theme, receives the greatest praise. For example, Morris and Malin (1981, p. 25) write that *Confessions* is a novel about humanity, an 'archetypal tragedy', while Philip Leon (1981, p. 211) believes that 'the story has a timeless, non-sectarian Christian dimension which one finds over and again in Hawthorn, Melville, Faulkner and Warren'.

The aesthetic devices used by Styron to evoke this world are particularly praised, for it is 'the unique literary gift of poetic descriptive expression which gives his fiction its main strength' (Ratner, 1972, p. 19). His use of symbols, metaphors and elaborately detailed descriptions are particularly singled out. For many critics, his greatest success is his use of the first person narrative, thus enabling the reader to identify with a black protagonist.

For such critics it is the formal text, divorced from its substantive content, which really matters:

it is my belief that when the smoke of controversy blows away and important fiction about a Negro slave leader can be read as fiction and not as either pro- or anti-Negro propaganda, the best critics both white and Negro will recognise how fine a characterisation, and how great a man, William Styron's Nat Turner is. (Rubin, 1975, p. 249)

Styron himself shares this view of art as unsullied by events and ideas in the real world, believing that 'serious' literature is not of this world but somehow above it. He holds that *Confessions* is neither racist nor a tract and that it is the novelist's 'right and privilege to substitute imagination or facts' (Styron, 1984, p. 19). Good novels are not to be considered in ideological terms, either because they carry no such message or because to think of them in this way demeans literary art. The marxist historian Genovese argued that in any case the novel was historically sound, and objected that adverse criticism had been historical and ideological, rather than aesthetic.

In the book *Ten Black Writers Respond*, which caused a furore when it first appeared, the terms of critical debate are dramatically changed. In contrast to the formalistic, ahistorical reaction of many white liberals, the writers in this volume stress the historical distortions in the novel and their ideological effects. Their criticisms centre around three major themes: 1) Turner's relationship with whites and their influence upon him; 2) the deliberate distortion of his sex life; 3) the part played by Turner in the rebellion itself. A further theme we have already identified is Turner's contempt for other blacks. Each set of criticisms is justified. The historical evidence is that Nat Turner was greatly influenced by his father and mother and even by his grandmother, all of whom believed he was meant for some great work. In the novel, his grandmother is dead, his father has run away and his mother is a stereotypic house-servant who looks down on field hands. In one particularly brutal and gratuitous scene the mother is raped by a drunken Irish overseer, but is finally shown to be 'really' enjoying it. Sexism joins double racism (it has to be a drunken *Irish* overseer of course!). This is a particularly vicious twisting of the truth, for one of the worst aspects of slavery for black men was their inability to protect their mothers, wives and daughters from sexual attack, and the inability to enjoy a stable family life because of forcible separation through sale of family members. It was these aspects of their relationships with women that preoccupied black men, not the secret desire they supposedly harboured for white women. Protection of black women is allowed to be a powerful motivation for revolt amongst Nat Turner's most trusted followers, but not for the anti-hero himself.

In reality, Nat Turner was taught to read by his family; in the novel it is his white owners who do so, and who treat him relatively well. In fact, Styron shows this to be their greatest mistake. As Duberman (1969, p. 213) points out:

Styron's particular reconstruction necessarily carries its particular message. He emphasizes that it is the Nat Turners, educated by their masters, given comparatively tender treatment, allowed to sleep an extra hour after their fellow slaves have been driven to the fields, who plot rebellions.

The deliberate distortion of Nat Turner's sex life is the most serious criticism many critics have made of the book. It is known that Nat was married, and probably had two children; his wife lived on another plantation. He would therefore have encountered the problems of family relations described above. In the novel, by contrast, Turner is not married; his only sexual experience is an early homosexual one; otherwise his sexual life consists of fantasies about white women which often occur during lonely masturbating sessions. Gradually, his fantasies about and particular desire for Margaret Whitehead become the *raison d'être* of the uprising. He wants Margaret, as he wants other white women, *because she is white*. This portrayal works ideologically in two ways: it trivialises the rebellion and it supports the Elkins thesis about slavery. Styron shifts the focus of the Turner insurrection, downgrading the main issues, and elevating the white woman to a position of central importance.

The criticisms by black commentators therefore centre upon the ways in which Styron retained certain items from the historical record, rejected others, and introduced particular events, emotions and philosophical frameworks. For them, Styron's judgements in such matters primarily represent ideological and political choices whose impact is ultimately adverse because of their racist implications. However, these choices are the very aspects which Styron and his supporters see primarily as aesthetic, expressing the novelist's 'right and privilege to substitute imagination for facts'. Both groups are correct – the choices made in the creative process are both ideological – political and aesthetic. However, the political message of *Confessions* is not separate from, but is in fact embodied and conveyed through the literary devices and techniques used by Styron.

Some of the more liberal white commentators, while denying that the novel is racist, have recognised that 'Styron's Turner appeared at the most inopportune moment in Afro-American experience'. All the novels previously looked at in this book were written deliberately either from a consciously racist or anti-racist position. All appeared at significant moments in the growth of racist ideology, or a time when that ideology was finally beginning to be questioned. Styron's novel too appeared at a significant moment in the history of racist ideas in America, but Styron himself appears confused about both his intentions and the effects of writing such a book. He always admired, so he says, the historical figure of Nat Turner, and he seemed to believe that he was writing a sympathetic account of his extraordinary life. Many white liberal critics agreed with him, but significantly black critics did not.

Nat Turner's obsession with a white woman confirmed yet again the myth of the black rapist, and implied a motive for racial unrest no different from that of Thomas Dixon in *The Clansman*. It has indeed been suggested that many white Americans liked the novel 'because it legitimatized all of the myths and prejudices about the American black man, and further, because it cut yet another great American black man down to the size of a boy' (Killens, 1968, p. 34).

What Styron stresses repeatedly in the novel is that kind treatment only makes the likelihood of violence greater. Considerate treatment of blacks by whites, and any feeling of pity or guilt expressed by whites, only increase Turner's animosity and rack him with tension:

I was filled with sombre feelings that I was unable to banish, deeply troubled that it was not a white person's abuse or scorn or even indifference which could ignite in me this murderous hatred but his pity, maybe even his tenderest moment of charity. (Styron, 1980, p. 262)

The vehicles he uses most frequently for eliciting such feelings from Nat are of course white women and in particular the character of Margaret Whitehead. The latter character, apart from being the object of Turner's sexual fantasies, is an example of the stereotype of the Southern white belle. She also expresses the kinds of views on slavery that white liberals held from the 1950s on Jim Crow: 'my humble opinion is that the darkies in Virginia should be free' (Styron, 1980, p. 355). As Turner drives Margaret home, her views on slavery and her innocent babbling contrast with his preoccupation with rebellion, his desire to 'take her' and his powerful sense that 'never could I remember having been so unhinged by desire and hatred'.

It appears therefore that Styron himself did not recognise the extent to which his long-held desire to tell his version of Nat Turner's life can be seen as a confused response to the dramatic events of the 1950s and 1960s in American race relations. Many white liberals felt threatened by black assertiveness, by the phenomenon of Black Power, by inner city riots, and by black leaders like Malcolm X. Styron's response was to return to an earlier black leader and rewrite his story in terms of all the fears and myths about black men that ran so deep in the ideology of American racism. Just how deep is underlined by Styron's apparently genuine bewilderment at being called a racist.

A comment which succinctly expresses the thoughts and feelings of blacks about *Confessions* is that by Sherley Anne Williams in an author's note to her novel about slavery, *Dessa Rose* (Williams, 1986, Author's Note). She writes that part of her motivation in writing the novel was

being outraged by a certain, critically acclaimed novel of the early seventies (sic) that travestied the as-told-to memoir of slave revolt leader Nat Turner. Afro-Americans, having survived by word of mouth – and made of that process a high art – remain at the mercy of literature and writing; often, these have betrayed us.

References

Aptheker, H. (1978) *American Negro Slave Revolts*, International Publishers, New York

Aptheker, H. and Styron, W. (1968) 'Truth and Nat Turner; an exchange', *The Nation*, p. 197

Angelou, M. (1984) *I Know Why the Caged Bird Sings*, Virago, London

Blassingame, J. W. (1973) *The Slave Community*, Oxford University Press, Oxford and New York

Butcher, M. J. (1956) *The Negro in American Culture*, New American Library, New York

Bennett, L. Jr (1968) 'Nat's Last White Man', in Clarke (ed), pp. 3–17

Butterfield, S. (1974) *Black Autobiography in America*, University of Massachusetts Press, Cambridge, Mass.

Clarke, J. H. (ed) (1968) *William Styron's Nat Turner: Ten Black Writers Respond*, Beacon Press, Boston

Core, G. (1981) 'The Confessions of Nat Turner and the Burden of the Past', in Morris (ed), pp. 206–36

Cudjoe, S. R. (1984) 'Maya Angelou and the Autobiographical Statement', in Evans (ed), pp. 6–25

Davis, A. (1976) *An Autobiography*, Arrow Books, London

Davis, A. (1982) *Women, Race and Class*, Women's Press, London

Douglass, F. (1982) *Narrative of the Life of Frederick Douglass, An American Slave*, Penguin, Harmondsworth

Dubb, J. B., and Mitchell, P. M. (1971) *The Nat Turner Rebellion: The Historical Event and the Modern Controversy*, Harper and Row, New York

Duberman, M. (1969) *The Uncompleted Past*, Random House, New York

Duberman, M. (1969) 'William Styron's Nat Turner and Ten Black Writers Respond', in Duberman, pp. 203–23

Eaton, M. (1982) 'History to Hollywood – interview with Trevor Griffiths', *Screen* (July–August), pp. 61–71

Elkins, S. M. (1976) *Slavery: A Problem in American Institutional and Intellectual Life*, University of Chicago Press, Chicago

Evans, M. (ed) (1984) *Black Women Writers (1950–1980): A Critical Evaluation*, Anchor Books, New York

Franklin, J. H. (1974) *From Slavery to Freedom: A History of Negro Americans*, Alfred A. Knopf, New York

Geismar, M. (1958) *American Moderns: From Rebellion to Conformity*, New York

Genovese, E. D. (1968) 'The Nat Turner case', *New York Review of Books* (12 Sept.), pp. 34–7

Gilman, R. (1968) 'Nat Turner revisited', *New Republic*, CLVIII, pp. 23–32

Gray, R. (1977) *The Literature of Memory – Modern Writers of the American South*, Edward Arnold, London

Gross, S. and Bender, E. (1971) 'The myth of Nat Turner', *American Quarterly*, pp. 487–518

Hall, S. and Jefferson, T. (eds) (1976) *Resistance Through Rituals*, Hutchinson, London

Killens, J. O. (1968) 'The Confessions of Willie Styron', in Clarke, pp. 34–45

Kirby, J. T. (1986) *Media-Made Dixie: The South in the American Imagination*, Louisiana State University Press, Baton Rouge and London (revised edition)

Lindenmeyer, O. (1970) *Black History: Lost, Stolen or Strayed*, Avon Books, New York

MacKethan, L. H. (1980) *The Dream of Arcady: Place and Time in Southern Literature*, Louisiana State University Press, Baton Rouge

Marable, M. (1983) *How Capitalism Underdeveloped Black America*, Pluto Press, London

Morris, R. K. (ed) (1981) *The Achievement of William Styron*, University of Georgia Press, Athens

Morris, R. K. (1981) 'Interviews With William Styron', in Morris (ed), pp. 29–70

Olsen, T. (1980) *Yonnondio*, Virago, London

Phillips, U. B. (1957) *Life and Labour in the Old South*, Little, Brown & Co., Boston

Ratner, M. L. (1972) *William Styron*, Twayne Publishers, New York

Rubin, L. D. Jr, Jackson, B. J., Moore, R. S., Simpson, L. P. and Young, T. D. (eds) (1985) *The History of Southern Literature*, Louisiana State University Press, Baton Rouge and London

Rubin, L. D. Jr (1975) *William Elliot Shoots A Bear: Essays on the Southern Literary Imagination*, Louisiana State University Press, Baton Rouge

Scott, J. A. (1974) *Hard Trials On My Way: Slavery and the Struggle Against It*, New American Library, New York

Smedley, A. (1979) *Daughter of Earth*, Virago, London

Smith, S. (1974) *Where I'm Bound: Patterns of Slavery and Freedom in Black American Autobiography*, Greenwood Press, Westport, Conn. and London

Strine, M. S. (1981) 'Styron's "Meditation on History" as Rhetorical Art', in Morris, pp. 237–69

Styron, W. (1980) *The Confessions of Nat Turner*, Corgi, London

Styron, W. (1984) *This Quiet Dust*, Black Swan, London

Twelve Southerners (1977) *I'll Take My Stand*, Louisiana State University Press, Baton Rouge and London (originally published in 1930)

Van Deburg, W. L. (1984) 'No mere mortals: black slaves and black power in American literature, 1967–1980', *South Atlantic Quarterly*, 83, pp. 297–311

Williams, S. A. (1986) *Dessa Rose*, Macmillan, London

X., Malcolm (1976) *Autobiography*, Penguin, Harmondsworth

10

Alice Walker: *Meridian* (1977)

It was perhaps inevitable, given the forms which American racism had taken for so long, with its conflation of sexual and racist myths about black people, that the Civil Rights movement of the sixties, a primarily young, black – white movement would find itself torn apart by the legacy of these ideologies. The ways in which racism had developed in America, with the use of the myth of the black rapist, the rape of black women, and the deification of white women, were to mean that when a young inter-racial movement challenged racism in the fifties and sixties many of these ideologies would themselves distort relationships between men and women, black and white. These distorted relationships were an important theme in *The Street*; the antagonisms Petry examined were to surface during the nineteen-sixties.

As the movement developed, both black and white women found that they were always given menial tasks, while at the same time black men often appeared enthusiastic about going out with white women – something that for most of them had always been a dangerous impossibility. White women were confused as black men told them if they did *not* go out with them and have sex with them then they were racist, while black women resented the fact that black men appeared to prefer going out with white women. By 1964 white male volunteers 'were particularly bothered by the rumors that males of the Student National Coordinating Committee (SNCC) forced white women volunteers to have sex with them to prove they were not prejudiced. Black women in the movement, concurrently, grew furious with the female students after hearing the same tales' (Sitkoff, 1981, p.178). Michele Wallace describes her experiences in New York in 1967:

Black men often could not separate their interest in white women from their hostility toward black women ... And black women made no attempt to disguise their anger and disgust, to the point of verbal, if not physical, assaults in the streets – on the white woman or the black man or on both. (Wallace, 1979, p. 10)

On the other hand, white women recognised this 'interest' as a form of hostility. As Rochelle Gatlin writes, 'On SNCC projects, black hostility was directed more at white women than at men. One form it took was that black men tested their 'manhood' by breaking the most potent Southern taboo against sexual access to white women' (Wallace, 1979, p. 83). Unfortunately, many of the sexual encounters were not motivated by love or even desire. White women volunteers were put in a painful double bind, making it almost impossible to pass the 'sexual test'. If they refused black men, they were called 'racists' – the worst epithet of all. They were then more vulnerable to subsequent advances and unlikely to see them as sexual harassment. Women who yielded risked not only being thought 'loose' and 'not serious', but were open to charges of being a 'danger' to the safety of their co-workers. The new white volunteers bore the brunt of male chauvinism, but they were not in a position to combat or even name it.

At the same time, the anger of black women was experienced by white women as a lack of support:

Black women did not support them; instead, interracial jealousy and resentment surfaced. Cynthia Washington contends that she and other black women 'did the same work as men ... But when we finally got back to some town where we could relax and go out, the men went out with other women. Our skills and abilities were recognized and respected, but they seemed to place us in some category other than female.' Or, as another black woman said: 'We became amazons, less than and more than women at the same time.' (Gatlin, 1987, p. 84)

While the experiences of white women in the Civil Rights movement was one factor which led to the Women's Movement of the nineteen seventies, the experiences of black women led to a determination to understand them in terms of their history as black people within America.

Notwithstanding our knowledge of these things, the contradictions between knowledge and action that surfaced in the Civil Rights and Black Power movements forced sensitive and intelligent women to reexamine their own positions vis-a-vis the men and to conclude that they were the victims not only of racial injustice but of a sexual arrogance tantamount to dual colonialism – one from without, the other from within, the Black community. (Henderson, 1983, p. xxiii)

This was one factor which led in the nineteen-seventies to a renaissance of black women's writing, as African-American women came to terms with the significance of the events of the nineteen sixties. This attempt included fiction and poetry written by African-American women like Toni Morrison, Alice Walker, Toni Cade Bambara, Paule Marshall, Maya Angelou etc. It is within many of these novels that we find a clear-eyed determination to explore the meaning of their experiences as black American women, an exploration which often meant returning to their history in order to understand their roots.

If *Confessions* was an early white male response to the upheaval of the Civil Rights movements which used both black history and a well established black art form to implicitly condemn the struggles of black people, *Meridian* is not only a response to the same movement from a black woman writer and poet who had lived through the dramatic events of the fifties and sixties, but it is also a fictional evocation of them. *The Street* was set in a black community on the brink of change; but the forms that the inevitable struggle will take are, as yet, unclear. Lutie is finally destroyed just as was Bigger Thomas in *Native Son* and the last sentence of the novel reminds us that the material conditions which drove Lutie to hopeless violence remain untouched:

The snow fell softly on the street. It muffled sound. It sent people scurrying homeward, so that the street was soon deserted, empty, quiet. And it could have been any street in the city, for the snow laid a delicate film over the pavement, over the brick of the tired, old buildings; gently obscuring the grime and the garbage and the ugliness. (Petry, 1986, p. 312)

Any hope in the novel lies with the next generation, with children like Bub.

It is with this generation that *Meridian* deals. Significantly, in an earlier novel *The Third Life of Grange Copeland*, Alice Walker had already begun to explore the ways in which racism helped to distort relationships between black men and women, as some black men turned, in their frustration, not on their enemies, but on their own families. As a sharecropper Brownfield is as good as a slave.

He prayed for help, for a caring President, for a listening Jesus. He prayed for a decent job in Mem's arms. But like all prayers sent up from there, it turned into another mouth to feed, another body to enslave to pay his debts. He felt himself destined to become no more than an overseer, on the white man's plantation, of his own children. (Walker, 1984, p. 54)

Eventually he turns his frustration upon his wife, 'His rage could and did blame everything, *everything* on her. And she accepted all his burdens along with her own and dealt with them from her own greater heart and greater knowledge' (Walker, 1984, p. 55). The third life of the title is the child of the third generation, Ruth, whose job it will be not only to struggle for change, but to understand the past. It is this burden which Meridian carries in Walker's later novel.

The structure of *Meridian*, like *The Street*, facilitates this exploration, with its movement between past, present and future. This structure is also linked to its pastiche or quilt-like effect. Walker consciously works in this way, evoking the activities of her female ancestors who used so many small pieces of material in order to create a work of art. The triangular relationship between Truman, Lynn and Meridian is the pivot around which this structure is built, and it is also through the presentation of this relationship that many of the problems of the Civil Rights movement and also the sexual relationships between black – white, male – female are examined.

The book is densely packed, and often intense in its effect, using consistent, insistent symbolism to emphasise and link together its thematic preoccupations. Images of death, violence, illness and sex are opposed to those of culture, life and growth. There is, the book hints, an earlier American culture and society, Native American and black, which has been destroyed. The town Chicokema has only its Native American name to remind anyone of its origins. At the old Native American burial ground, and later in Mexico, Meridian has an ecstatic, almost religious experience. This Native American and animistic culture is linked to black culture through the Sojourner tree at Meridian's Southern college: 'This tree filled her with the same sense of minuteness and hugeness, of past and present, of sorrow and ecstasy that she had known at the Sacred Serpent' (Walker, 1982, p. 89).

Meridian is shown to be concerned that the Civil Rights movement may, in its revolutionary violence, destroy not only racism, but the true black culture: 'If they committed murder – and to her even revolutionary murder was murder – what would the music be like?' (Walker, 1982, p. 15). Several incidents are used to show the ways in which black people may unknowingly destroy their own culture. When the black students at Saxon College destroy the Sojourner tree, they are destroying, not the enemy, but their own history. In the same way, when the college gardener kills the memorial shrub to Medger Evers planted by Meridian he is symbolically denying the new culture growing out of the old. When as a child Meridian finds gold in her own backyard, her discovery is ignored by her mother. Throughout the novel there is an awareness of the necessity to understand the past, and preserve what is good. Later, at the appropriately named Saxon College, Meridian finds there is a terrible desire to learn how to fit into white society, together with a lack of awareness of black culture. 'They learned to make French food, English tea and German music.' This is another form of death, and the Dean of Women is appropriately known as the Dead of Women.

Later Meridian discovers by chance the form that the new black church has taken. Religion is no longer associated with death but with life, with music and tradition. Through this recognition Meridian learns her own role as an artist, and also the fact that violence against oppression is possible without necessarily murdering the soul: 'Under a large tree beside the road, crowded now with the cars returning from church, she made a promise to the red-eyed man herself: that yes, indeed she *would* kill, before she allowed anyone to murder his son again' (Walker, 1982, p. 204). Her role, she now sees to be the poet of her people:

> perhaps it will be my part to walk behind the real revolutionaries – those who know they must spill blood in order to help the poor and the black and therefore go right ahead – and when they stop to wash off the blood and find their throats too choked with the smell of murdered flesh to sing, I will come forward and sing from memory songs they will need once more to hear. For it is the song of the people, transformed by the experience of each generation, that holds them together, and if any part of it is lost the people suffer and are without soul. If I can only do that, my role will not have been a useless one after all. (Walker, 1982, p. 208)

The structure of the novel is therefore circular as Meridian finally reaches the point the novelist Walker has already reached, recognising the necessity both to struggle *and* to preserve the 'song of the people.' It is this song – the culture of black people in America – which Styron appeared to black writers and critics to be deliberately destroying, and which writers like Walker are determined to preserve.

The novel opens with a grotesque, almost surreal scene in which Walker sets in motion many of the themes of the novel. In a small Southern town, Chicokema, whose name is the only remnant of its ancient culture, we are introduced to Meridian and to Truman, as Meridian leads some black children to see the mummified remains of Marilene O'Shay, a woman who had 'gone wrong'. Her husband makes money by showing her body, and telling the tale of her unfaithfulness, for which he had first murdered her and then used her body as a sideshow. The scene thus parodies the ways in which men dehumanise women, and it also foreshadows the exploration in the novel of the ways in which men continue to do this. The theme of male violence against women – black and white – is an important one in the novel, and it is linked with the exploration of the kind of violence necessary or permissible in a movement like the Civil Rights movement.

These two themes are conflated early in the novel when Meridian first goes to volunteer her services to the emerging Civil Rights movement. She is immediately asked, 'Can you type?' When she says no, they ask her to learn, and it remains to Meridian to ask 'Don't you want to know my name?' She is shocked to find the same problems she is beginning to be aware of exist also *within* the movement.

One of the ways in which men 'kill' women is to treat them as objects, rather than as real people, and one of the ways in which this is portrayed is by showing how men turn women into art. Racism has used this device; Truman himself is shown as a man who turns black women into art through his sculptures. At one point Truman calls Meridian a 'stone fox'. 'She wondered why, or rather how that term came to be so popular. Surely no one had bothered to analyze it as they said it. In her mind she carried a stone fox. It was heavy, gray and could not move' (Walker, 1982, p. 112 – 13). Later with Lynne:

'Black women let themselves go,' he said, even as he painted them as magnificent giants, breeding forth the warriors of the new universe. 'They are so *fat*,' he would say, even as he sculpted a 'Big Bessie Smith' in solid marble, caressing her monstrous and lovely flanks with an admiring hand. (Walker, 1982, p. 170)

When Truman finally recognises his love for Meridian, she asks, 'is it because I have now become art?' (Walker, 1982, p. 221).

Because of the distorted relationships between men and women, black and white, images of death are associated with sexual relationships throughout the novel, and it is only when Truman and Meridian's relationship is no longer sexual that they can really love one another. Meridian's earliest sexual experiences take place in a funeral home. Motherhood brings only thoughts of suicide and murder:

The thought of murdering her own child eventually frightened her. To suppress it she conceived, quite consciously, methods of killing herself. She found it pleasantly distracting to imagine herself stiff and oblivious, her head stuck in an oven. Or coolly out of it, a hole through the roof of her mouth. It seemed to her that the peace of the dead was truly blessed. (Walker, 1982, p. 63)

This thematic relationship between death and sexual relationships becomes even clearer in the portrayal of inter-racial sexual relationships. For black men, white women are 'a route to Death, pure and simple … They did not even see her as a human being, but as some kind of large mysterious doll' (Walker, 1982, p. 135).

At one level therefore, Walker shows a movement, which, while going through revolutionary change, and challenging the racism of the South, is itself a victim of distorted ideas and is often unaware of its own heritage. The legacy of racism, in particular, has made it almost impossible for good inter-racial sexual relationships, and this is examined most closely in the triangular relationship between Truman, Meridian and Lynne. Truman leaves Meridian for Lynne, whom he marries and with whom he has a daughter. In the days before black pride, everyone thought that Truman was handsome 'because his nose was so keen and his skin was tan and not black; and Meridian, though disliking herself for it, thought him handsome for exactly those reasons, too' (Walker, 1982, p. 95).

Meridian herself rejects automatically any relationship with a white man, 'and though now that she was in college she prided herself on having catholic tastes when it came to men, white farmers were not yet included' (Walker, 1982, p. 101). Truman, on the other hand, goes out with white girls, simply *because* they are white. Meridian is embarrassed by this: 'It was strange and unfair, but the fact that he dated them – and so obviously because their color made them interesting – made *her* ashamed, as if she were less' (Walker, 1982, p. 103).

Her feelings about relationships with whites are part of her heritage:

As far back as she could remember it seemed something *understood*: that while white men would climb on black women old enough to be their mother – for the 'experience' – white women were considered sexless, contemptible and ridiculous by all. They did not even smell like glue or boiled corn; they smelled of nothing since they did not sweat. They were clear, dead water. (Walker, 1982, p. 103)

Meridian finds herself feeling more and more hostile toward white women:

There seemed nothing about white women that was enviable. Perhaps one might covet a length of hair, if it swung long and particularly fine. But that was all. And hair was dead matter that continued – only if oiled – to shine. (Walker, 1982, p. 106)

When Lynne is raped by a black man she thought was her friend, her guilt at racism paralyses her reactions, while Meridian's hostility makes it difficult for her to support her. When she is raped, Lynne thinks, not first of herself, but of the black man who is attacking her:

She lay instead thinking of his feelings, his hardships, of the way he was black and belonged to people who lived without hope; she thought about the loss of his arm. She felt her own guilt. (Walker, 1982, p. 160)

She recognises the way in which she has been dehumanised, in the same way that Meridian had earlier felt humiliated by Truman's attitude towards her:

It was as if Tommy Odds thought she was not a human being, as if her whiteness, the mystique of it, the *danger* of it, the historically *verboten* nature of it, encouraged him to attempt to destroy her without any feelings of guilt. It was so frightening a thought that she shook with it. (Walker, 1982, p. 163)

Tommy Odds himself tells Truman, ' ''Black men get preferential treatment, man, to make up for all we been denied. She ain't been fucking you, she's been atoning for her sins''' (Walker, 1982, p. 165). When Lynne tries to tell Meridian, Meridian responds by saying '''I can't listen to this, I'm sorry, I just can't'' ... ''You wouldn't believe me *either?*'' Lynne asked. ''No,'' Meridian said, coldly.'

This theme is also explored through the ways in which the three characters change and try to make sense of what is happening. They are not seen as simply victims of ideological confusion – they make brave attempts to understand what is happening. For example when talking to Tommy Odds, Truman resists the tendency to blame white women for racism:

He had read in a magazine just the day before that Lamumba Katurim had gotten rid of his. She was his wife, true, but apparently she was even in that disguise perceived as evil, a castoff. And people admired Lamumba for his perception. It proved his love of his own people, they said. But he was not sure. Perhaps it proved only that Lamumba was fickle. That he'd married his bitch in the first place for shallow reasons. Perhaps he was considering marrying a black woman (as the article said he was) for reasons just as shallow. For how could he state so assuredly that he would marry a black woman next when he did not appear to have any *specific* black woman in mind?

If his own sister told him of her upcoming marriage to Lamumba he would have to know some answers before the nuptial celebration. Like, how many times would Lamumba require her to appear on television with him, or how many times would he parade her before his friends as proof of his blackness. (Walker, 1982, pp. 133–4)

Michele Wallace describes the ways in which black men, with the emergence of black power in the nineteen-sixties often turned suddenly against white women – even if these were their own wives. For example, of LeRoi Jones, the black poet, she writes:

LeRoi Jones was the Black Movement's leading intellectual convert, having deserted success in the white world for the uncertainty of the Black Revolution. He had lived in Greenwich Village. His friends were Gregory Corso, Allen Ginsberg, Frank O'Hara, Larry Rivers. His wife was white. His poetry was individualistic, well-crafted, and lauded by the critics. Those who knew him then described him as gentle, 'the nicest man you ever met.'

Then one day – it seemed to happen all of a sudden according to his white friends – he was among the angriest of black voices. His new hatred of whites led him to leave his white wife and his two half-white children to marry a black woman and start a nationalist organization called New Ark in Newark, New Jersey. Now Imamu Amiri Baraka, his poetry – and he was the father of the entire nineteen sixties black poetry movement – advocated violence, the death of all whites, the moral and physical superiority of the black man, Black Macho. (Wallace, 1979, pp. 62–3)

Although Truman and Lynne eventually split up, and to some extent this is because of Truman's hostility toward her as a white woman, by the end of the novel they have managed to create a friendship. In the same way, Meridian and Lynne also manage to find common ground in their awareness of how *all* women, whatever their colour, are oppressed by men, and marginalised within society and its culture.

It is a society also which kills its own children. The novel is full of absent children – they are given away like Meridian's own child, killed accidentally like the Wild Child, murdered like Lynne's daughter. Meridian and Lynne are brought together by this death: 'They knew her suffering did not make her unique; but knowing that crimes of passion or hatred against children are not considered unique in a society where children are not particularly valued, failed to comfort them.'

After Camara's death, Lynne and Meridian spend some time together in New York, and we are told:

As they sat they watched a television program. One of those Southern epics about the relationship of the Southern white man to madness, and the closeness of the Southern black man to the land. It did not delve into the women's problems, black or white. They sat, companionable and still in their bathrobes, watching the green fields of the South and the indestructible (their word) faces of black people much more than they watched the madness. For them, the madness was like a puzzle they had temporarily solved (Meridian would sometimes, in the afternoons, read poems to Lynne by Margaret Walker, and Lynne, in return, would attempt to cornrow Meridian's patchy short hair), they hungered after more intricate and enduring patterns. Sometimes they talked, intimately, like sisters, and when they did not they allowed the television to fill the silences. (Walker, 1982, p. 176)

There is hope therefore in the way the three characters deal with the ways in which relationships between them have been made so difficult by the distortions of years of racism. There is hope also in the way in which Meridian develops throughout the novel towards health and wholeness and a knowledge of what her own role should be. It is partly through images of music and black culture, including the black church, that images of death, numbness and illness are finally defeated. The black church itself is shown as developing in response to the changing times. Meridian's mother's religion, which she remembers from her childhood, is associated with defeat and death; although the music is wonderful, the words are obsessed with awareness of death. Later in the novel, 'The people looked exactly as they had ever since she had known black churchgoing people which was all her life but they had changed the music! She was shocked' (Walker, 1982, p. 199).

'Understand this', they were saying, 'the church', (and Meridian knew they did not mean simply 'church' as in Baptist, Methodist or whatnot, but rather communal spirit, togetherness, righteous convergence), 'the music, the form of worship that has always sustained us, the kind of ritual you share with us, these are the ways to transformation that we know. We want to take this with us as far as we can.' (Walker, 1982, p. 204)

Meridian has taken many years to get to this point. Her long journey has helped her to rediscover her roots. Meridian's physical wanderings echo the journey being made by African-American women as they search for their past in order to understand the present. As Meridian's search progresses, her clothing becomes simpler and simpler and less and less 'feminine'. Towards the end of the novel when Truman comes looking for her 'she'd lost so much of her hair that finally she had shaved her head and begun wearing a striped white and black railroad worker's cap: the cotton was durable and light and the visor shaded her eyes from the sun' (Walker, 1982, p. 143). But for a true understanding of their mutual past, it is necessary that black men too undertake this task. Finally, therefore, it is Truman who dons Meridian's cap:

he pulled it out and put it on his head. He had a vision of Anne-Marion herself arriving, lost, someday, at the door, which would remain open, and wondered if Meridian knew that the sentence of bearing the conflict in her own soul which she had imposed on herself – and lived through – must now be borne in terror by all the rest of them. (Walker, 1982, p. 228)

Meridian is, in some ways an evocation of the struggle which both Ann Petry's *The Street* and Fast's *Freedom Road* showed as inevitable. Petry looked clearly at the distortions imposed by society on the relationships between black men and women, implicitly recognising that any future struggle against racism would also have to address this issue. However, the equally profound differences between the novels are also indicative of the changes which had taken place in the thirty years since Petry's novel appeared.

Firstly, Petry slowly builds up her main character's recognition that it is class as much as race which is responsible for her plight – that there are in fact poor white people who are defeated by American society just as irrevocably as are blacks. Petry's naturalistic and detailed style helps to evoke concretely the material conditions of poverty against which her characters struggle. In one scene in *The Street* Lutie comes home from work and buys hamburger meat, potatoes, peas, butter, hard rolls. Her shopping, her actions, her thoughts, both general and about the meal she has to cook when she gets home, are meticulously realised, as is the description of the street as she trudges home:

> The glow from the sunset was making the street radiant. The street is nice in this light, she thought. It was swarming with children who were playing ball and darting back and forth across the pavement in complicated games of tag. Girls were skipping double dutch rope, going tireless through the exact centre of a pair of ropes, jumping first on one foot and then the other. All the way from the corner she could hear groups of children chanting, 'Down in Mississippi and a bo-bo push! Down in Mississippi and a bo-bo push!' She stopped to watch them, and she wanted to put her packages down and jump with them; she found her foot was patting the pavement in the exact rhythm of their jumping and her hands were ready to push the jumper out of the rope at the word 'push'. (Petry, 1986, p. 50)

With such meticulous detail Petry shows the reader the world in which her protagonist lives and struggles. Socially realistic, the novel shows us a *community* and the relations between people in it; we get to know not only Lutie and her thoughts but her daily life in concrete detail.

The intense, symbolic, almost poetic style used by Walker is more effective in portraying the state of mind of a small number of characters and in foregrounding the significance of *personal* relationships. Because the struggle against racism was itself distorted by the forms these relationships had come to take in American society, in novels like *Meridian* the terms of ideological or cultural discussion are dominated by the necessity of understanding them. Through the triangle black man – white woman – black woman Walker examines the legacy of generations of racism, and through the struggles of these three characters to overcome the ideologies they have inherited she tries to point the way forward. In her determination to tell the truth about the forms racism took in American society in the nineteen-sixties Walker places herself firmly in a tradition of anti-racist writing, which constitutes an important part of oppositional popular culture in American society.

References

Aptheker, H. (ed) (1958) *A Documentary History of the Negro People in the United States*, Citadel Press, New York

Bell, R. P., Parker, B. J. and Guy-Sheftall, B. (eds) (1979) *Sturdy Black Bridges*, Doubleday Anchor, New York

'The black sexism debate' (1979) *The Black Scholar*, 10 (entire issue)

Cambara, T. C. (ed) (1970) *The Black Woman: An Anthology*, New American Library, New York

Christian B. (1980) *Black Women Novelists: The Development of a Tradition, 1892–1976*, Greenwood Press, Westport, Conn.

Davis, A. (1982) *Women, Race and Class*, Women's Press, London

Degler, C. N. (1981) *At Odds: Women and the Family in America from the Revolution to the Present*, Oxford University Press, Oxford and New York

Evans, M. (ed) (1983) *Black Women Writers (1950–1980): A Critical Evaluation*, Anchor Books, New York

Fisher, B. (1984) 'Guilt and shame in the women's movement', *Feminist Studies*, 10, pp. 185–212

Gatlin, R. (1987) *American Women since 1945*, Macmillan Education, Basingstoke and London

Harley S. and Terby, R. (eds) (1978) *The Afro-American Woman: Struggles and Images*, Keenikat Press, Port Washington, NY

Henderson, S. E. (1983) 'Introduction', in Evans (ed), pp. xxiii–xxviii

Hernton, C. C. (1973) *Sex and Racism*, Paladin, London

Hernton, C. C. (1985) 'The sexual mountain and black women writers', *The Black Scholar*, July/August, pp. 2–11

McDowell, D. E. (1981) 'The self in bloom: Alice Walker's *Meridian*', *CLA Journal*, 24, pp. 262–75

McDowell, D. E. (1986) 'New Directions for Black Feminist Criticism', in Showalter (ed), pp. 186–200

McGowan, M. J. (1981) 'Atonement and release in Alice Walker's *Meridian*, *Critique*, 23, pp. 25-36

Parker-Smith, B. J. (1983) 'Alice Walker's Women: In Search of Some Peace of Mind', in Evans (ed), pp. 478–94

Rotschild, M. A. (1979) 'White women volunteers in the freedom summers.'

Their life and work in a movement for social change', *Feminist Studies*, 5, pp. 466–95

Schaufragel, N. (1973) *From Apology to Protest: The Black American Novel*, Everett/ Edwards, Inc., Deland, Fla.

Showalter, E. (ed) (1986) *The New Feminist Criticism: Essays on Women, Literature and Theory*, Virago, London

Sitkoff, H. (1981) *The Struggle for Black Equality, 1954–1980*, Hill and Wang, New York

Smith B. (ed) (1983) *Homegirls: A Black Feminist Anthology*, Persephone Press, New York

Smith, B. (1986) 'Toward a Black Feminist Criticism', in Showalter (ed), pp. 168–86

Stein, K. F. (1986) '*Meridian* – Alice Walker's critique of revolution', *Black American Literature*, 20, pp. 129–41

Towns, S. (1974) 'The black woman as whore: genesis of the myth', *The Black Position*, 3, pp. 39–59

Van Deburg, W. L. (1984) 'No mere mortals: black slaves and black power in American literature, 1967–1980', *South Atlantic Quarterly*, 83, pp. 297-311

Walker, A. (1982) *Meridian*, Women's Press, London

Walker, A. (1983) *In Search of Our Mothers' Gardens*, Harcourt Brace Jovanovich, San Diego, New York and London

Walker, A. (1982) *You Can't Keep a Good Woman Down*, Women's Press, London

Walker, A. (1983) *The Color Purple*, Women's Press, London

Walker, A. (1985) *The Third Life of Grange Copeland*, Women's Press, London

Wallace, M., (1979) *Black Macho and the Myth of the Superwoman*, John Calder, London

Washington, M. H. (ed) (1975) *Black-Eyed Susans*, Anchor Books, New York

Washington, M. H. (1980) *Midnight Birds: Stories of Contemporary Black Women Writers*, Anchor Books, New York

Wisker, G. (1987) 'Stepping out, speaking out: the personal voice raised against oppression in the work of Alice Walker and Maya Angelou', *Over Here: An American Studies Journal* (University of Nottingham), 7, pp. 35-49

PART THREE

Portrayals on film

11

Birth of a Nation and silent film

Racism pervades American film because it is a basic strain in American history.
(Monaco, 1981, p. 225)

The earliest days of commercial cinema from 1895 to 1905 coincided
with the onset of legal attacks on black civil rights, and with American
imperial expansion in the Pacific and the Caribbean involving the
conquest and exploitation of what the *Nation* called 'darker peoples' of
the world. As the century turned, incidents of white violence against
blacks proliferated, both in the Deep South and in Northern cities.

The first films in America were produced for the immigrant working
classes who flooded into American cities from the late nineteenth century
onwards. According to a handbook for motion theatre managers, the
'ideal location... is a densely populated workingmen's residence section'
(Richardson, 1910, p. 160; quoted in Sklar, 1975, p. 16). Audiences
were almost entirely white: 'in some neighbourhoods there were rows
of [nickelodeons] with gaudy fronts and shrill barkers – all largely
unavailable to Negroes' (Cripps, 1977, p. 9). Such arrangements were
yet another expression of the increasing residential segregation by class
and race in American cities after 1890.

Evidence of the roles played by the first blacks to appear on the screen
suggests no systematically racist portrayal (Cripps, 1978, Ch. 1). This
has been attributed in part to the primitive level of early film production
technique. It was difficult to build characterisation and narrative capable
of drawing effectively upon the popular black stereotypes of the Southern
literary tradition.

However, eventually many films began to portray blacks as idiotic
buffoons or 'coons' – as objects of ridicule. For example primitive
eating manners are shown in *The Watermelon Contest* (late 1890s), and

a whole series of releases showed blacks as chicken thieves or crap-shooters. In a few, white violence against blacks is treated in comic fashion (Cripps, 1977, pp. 13–14). *The Wedding and Wooing of a Coon* (1905), described by the producers as a 'genuine Ethiopian comedy' (Mapp, 1972, p. 16), shows the black couple as objects of derision, and in *The Masher* (1907) even a 'lady-killer' draws the line at flirting with a black woman. Two widely distributed series of short comedies also appeared – the 'Rastus' and 'Sambo' films – and in each the central character was a so-called 'coon'.

Another insulting stereotype was the 'tragic mulatto'. All films at this time which dealt with miscegenation and passing, like the *The Octoroon* (n.d.) and *The Nigger* (1915), showed it as shameful and degrading to be at all non-white and implied that it was practically subhuman to be black (Noble, 1948, p. 29). Such portrayals both expressed and reinforced the racism which was by now endemic in American society.

Most blacks on film at this time were in fact played by whites in blackface, thus exacerbating the insult to black people. This was also true of a new cycle of films which drew upon Southern literary sources and were set in the Old South of slavery and during the Civil War. Such portrayals of blacks were to predominate in the cinema until the end of the silent era.

As a hint of what was to come, Edwin Porter's *Uncle Tom's Cabin* (1903) concentrates on the social order of the Old South as essentially benign. Cruel whites are exceptional – and always of lower class origin. The abolitionist sentiment of the ending contrasts uncomfortably with the rest of the film, which includes grinning, singing and dancing blacks who apparently love their masters and are even made to appear grateful when sold.

The wave of Southern films did not develop until after 1905 for technical, economic and political reasons. Technically, movie-makers were now able to make longer films and to shape characterisation and structure narrative through selection, editing and cutting. Production costs rose, turning film-makers' attention to the pockets and desires of middle-class audiences. This encouraged the incorporation of the themes and forms that predominated in the literature read by those groups. Economically, the industry was gradually moving away from a structure based on a very large number of small independent producers. This may have had some influence in leading to greater standardisation of treatment of cinema themes, including the portrayal of blacks. The choice and treatment of themes in these films and the increase in their production and popularity, also owed something to preparation for the commemoration and celebration in 1911 of the fiftieth anniversary of the Civil War. There was a desire to reaffirm North – South reconciliation and national unity. The establishment of a Democratic majority in Congress in 1910 and the election of a Southerner as President of the United States for the first time since 1866 also drew greater attention to Southern traditions and values. For blacks, the corollary of these changes was their abandonment by the Republican party, the encouragement of Jim Crow by the federal government, and the continuation of lynching.

The consensus about race meant that the dominant stereotype at this time was comic, rather than threatening. Since both Northern and Southern whites agreed that black people were inferior, this could be taken for granted and white audiences could laugh as they recognised their favourite stereotypes.

In the period from about 1905 until the late twenties, the portrayal of blacks on film was dominated by stereotypes associated with stories set in the American South during the period of slavery and the Civil War. Their role amounted to 'a black defence of a white world' (Campbell, 1981a, Ch. 2). This apologia for the system of slavery and, by extension, the harsh treatment of blacks in the early twentieth century, was based on two kinds of stereotypes borrowed from the Southern literary tradition (Bogle, 1973, Ch. 1).

A striking feature of the Old South films was their emphasis on black characters. These were usually given passive roles, and portrayed as menials or childlike creatures. One such stereotype was the 'Uncle Tom', who appeared not only as the central character in nine different screen adaptations of *Uncle Tom's Cabin* between 1903 and 1927 but as a socially acceptable 'Good Negro' in other films. The Uncle Tom is a good example of a character who, in the antebellum period, could be employed as an argument against slavery, but whose role by the early twentieth century was to justify the same system. Black audiences despised this caricature, a servile stereotype 'who would not fight against oppression' (Bogle, 1973, Ch. 1; Noble, 1948, p. 32). Another passive stereotype was the 'mammy', a devoted, if at times cantankerous, house servant. The black mammy was a mother and worker, a strong figure who could keep her male counterparts in check if they ever showed any aggressive tendencies, and a necessary counterpart to the Southern white woman who was a mother and wife (Christian, 1985). In literature and film, white women were symbolic mothers of the White race, carrying out few domestic duties in fiction (if not in fact - see Scott (1970), because they could be assigned to the mammy. The 'tom' and 'mammy' stereotypes are also asexual beings. This is a key characteristic, particularly of males, because of the white male pre-occupation with imagined threats to white womanhood.

The aggressive stereotype still made a rare appearance, representing the consequences if servile blacks were not kept in their place. Sexually and physically aggressive, these stereotypes were a threat to white society. However, films normally provided images of contented slaves and loyal house servants who adored their owners and would defend them even if this meant death. Blacks sacrificed themselves for their masters in *The Confederate Spy* (1910), *Hearts and Flags* (1911), and *The Informer* (1912). If rebellion occurs, it is against cruel overseers not against masters, as in *A Slave's Devotion* (n.d.). Among those directing films in this tradition was D.W. Griffith who made a number of Civil War dramas such as *In Old Kentucky* (1910), *His Trust* (1911) and *His Trust Fulfilled* (1911). Although other directors had produced films using similar settings and themes, it was Griffith who made a particularly strong and controversial contribution to a movement that translated literary forms into a mode of cinematic expression. Blacks played a crucial and central role in these films, but as increasingly passive bystanders in the great events of American history.

The first film known to have been made by an African-American was directed by William Foster in 1910, and he produced several films similar to the mainstream Keystone Cops series (Nesteby, 1982, p. 65). Despite the highly demeaning and racist portrayals of blacks that appeared on the cinema screen, blacks themselves seemed indifferent to the new medium until *The Birth of a Nation* was released in 1915. One influence may have been the distaste shown by a fundamentalist black church, and the early ignorance and later disdain shown by the middle classes – black and white – for a new medium regarded as at best frivolous and at worst corrupting.

A second factor was the 'lack of a usable past' (Cripps, 1977, p. 11) that provided substantial and positive roles for blacks in the new medium. Blacks did of course have a usable past; but it was one white movie-makers did not wish to present, as this would immediately destroy popular cultural stereotypes. It would also mean opposing generally accepted racist ideas, in effect making a stand against racism – not something that interested commercial film-makers. Because of the subordinate position of blacks, their own experiences and interpretations of history were hidden. There was an enormous reservoir of common history and experience which could have been drawn upon, including resistance and rebellion under slavery, active and positive roles in the Civil War and Reconstruction and the sheer struggle to survive and preserve institutions like family life. There were also famous leaders, from Nat Turner through Frederick Douglass to Booker T. Washington – the last the personification of the rise from rags to national leadership which has been so important a theme in popular American literature. This is not to mention oral and written black culture and the special strengths of a musical tradition which became one of the original cultural contributions that America has made to the world.

Black leaders and activists in the early nineteen-hundreds were also overwhelmed by more pressing tasks. These included trying to survive under Jim Crow in the South, and coping with discrimination in all walks of life. Much energy was put into the struggle to create and maintain alternative and parallel economic and educational arrangements for blacks.

However interest was raised in the black community when it became known that D. W. Griffith was working on the most ambitious project in cinema history up to that time, a Civil War epic lasting well over three hours which was to become *The Birth of a Nation* (1915). A Southerner from a relatively poor farming family, Griffith believed that the true story of the Civil War had yet to be told from the Southern point of view. To set the record straight, he based *The Birth of A Nation* on two novels by Thomas Dixon – *The Clansman* and *The Leopard's Spots* (see also Chapter 5).

The film is an aberration in terms of the general thematic treatment of blacks based on the Southern literary tradition because it places so much emphasis on violent and sexually aggressive black stereotypes. *Birth* regresses to the race-baiting tradition of Dixon's most virulent outbursts. Its enormous popularity and influence have meant that such stereotypes were strengthened enormously in American popular culture.

The film is organised into three sections – the pre-Civil War period, the Civil War itself, and Reconstruction. As a prelude, a caption informs us that 'the bringing of the African to America planted the first seed of disunion' and briefly shows abolitionist meetings. In the pre-Civil War section members of a Northern family, the Stonemans, visit their friends, the Camerons in the South. It is shown to be a happy place based on an agrarian lifestyle and a social structure characterised both by tradition and by well-to-do, well-mannered whites. The Camerons live in a modest house with classical white columns; caricatured 'uncle toms' and 'mammies' staff the house or work contentedly in the fields. Black workers are shown as buffoons who amuse themselves and white onlookers during the extravagant two-hour lunch break we are told was normally granted to slaves! The Stonemans' arrival sets the scene for shy flirtation or good-natured horseplay between the offspring of both families. Griffith cleverly uses normal family behaviour, together with humour, to enlist the audience's sympathy for the whites. The only cloud on the horizon appears when the action switches to Austin Stoneman's Northern home. Stoneman represents Thaddeus Stevens, long a hate figure for Southern whites. His mulatto mistress is shown as the counterpart at the family level of the unwanted black presence at the national level. The film presents blacks as a threat to the white family and to national unity, but solves the problem by advocating white purity and supremacy. Both are achieved by the end of the film, so giving rise to 'the birth of a nation'.

Griffith's film was unusual therefore for the virulence with which it portrayed active blacks. They were black rapists, petty and vindictive black bureaucrats and politicians, and overbearing black troops, whose only aim was 'negro domination' of the Aryan white race. These stereotypes predominate during the Reconstruction sequences, thus illustrating the dire consequences of giving black people freedom. In contrast, blacks are passive and docile before the war in the Old South sequences, and again after a triumphant Klan defeats Reconstruction. Such race-baiting material was unprecedented on film, despite suggestions of it in some of Griffith's earlier work. It was these portrayals, and particularly that of the Ku Klux Klan as saviours of white women and the white race, that provoked the strongest reactions both for and against the film. Artistically, the most 'cinematic' sequences are those in which such material is combined with masterly editing and cutting to show parallel events leading to a dramatic resolution. Two sequences are particularly memorable for their visual impact.

The first depicts the pursuit of Flora Cameron, the 'little sister' of the Southern family, by Gus, a black initially seen loitering outside the Camerons' home in Piedmont. Eventually he retreats, but only to lie in wait. The camera dwells on his face deep in shadow, a menacing animal gleam in his eyes. Despite warnings, Flora goes to the spring to fetch water. The suggestion of an innocent prey is reinforced by the visual device of cutting between the light-hearted young girl and some squirrels, framed in an iris, that she is watching. Gus appears and proposes marriage. Horrified, she flees. During the chase itself, the camera switches between the terrified young woman, the pursuing Gus, and Flora's distraught brother who tries to rescue her.

Flora is finally cornered on a rock pinnacle. She must choose between death and dishonour. Her position on a pedestal is crucial in furthering the film narrative, but also symbolises that of Southern white womanhood. Flora jumps, and dies in her brother's arms – he tells us that '... she found sweeter the *opal gates of death*'(emphasis in original caption). Meanwhile, Gus scuttles away over the rocks like a misshapen sea creature abandoned by the retreating tide.

The entire sequence lasts over ten minutes, with the minimum of interruptions from captions, and the audience is borne along on waves of visual imagery.

Similar techniques are used a little later in the film in a sequence when the Klan gathers its forces to rescue various whites, both Northern and Southern, together with a few loyal blacks, from ravishment or death at the hands of blacks. 'Civilisation' and white supremacy are restored, and in the closing scenes intersectional marriages confirm the Union – there is a cut to happy crowds wearing classical Greek costume, and we are also given an anti-war message.

The 'tragic mulatto' is also shown as a menace in *Birth*. Thaddeus Stevens, the radical Republican who strongly supported Reconstruction, is thinly disguised as the cold and physically deformed Northern politician Austin Stoneman. He is shown to be under the evil influence of his mulatto housekeeper, Lydia. In South Carolina the new governor, Silas Lynch, also a mulatto, is one of his protégés. Lynch sanctions black aggression against whites and also has designs on Stoneman's daughter. Griffiths shares the basic racist assumption of the time that a mixed-race person was inferior even to a black person, as they would, it was believed, combine the worse characteristics of both races. Only when Stoneman finally realises this does he see the error of his ways, and become a good racist. Whites who support blacks are thus shown as misguided but capable of conversion.

The film had an enormous impact. At a special showing in the White House, President Wilson reportedly said 'It is like writing history with lightning, and one of my regrets is that it is so horribly true' (Campbell, 1981a, pp. 58–9). The film ran for almost a year in New York, Chicago and Boston, and was shown throughout the South for fifteen years. Schools sent entire classes for special showings. At the time the longest and most expensive film ever made – with ticket prices of $2 it was also the most expensive to watch! These features, and its overall theme, were meant to appeal to the American élite, to community leaders and opinion makers (Sklar, 1975, p. 58). It played a part in fostering the growth of the Ku Klux Klan which had been revived as a national, not just a Southern, organisation, in 1915.

Blacks – and some white liberals – were outraged. Normally conservative middle-class leaders did not hesitate to support direct action in protest. Before it was first screened in California, blacks had pressured for cuts and for outright bans. By 1915, the National Association for the Advancement of Colored People (NAACP) was well established as a national organisation with its own newspaper, *Crisis*, and could co-ordinate and publicise opposition.

Cinemas were picketed, and sufficient political pressure exerted to force at least temporary bans in some cities and states. At the end of the war, black veterans picketed in Washington with placards saying, 'We represented America in France. Why should "The Birth of a Nation" misrepresent us here?' The film proved too popular, both North and South, for black protest to succeed (Campbell, 1981a, pp. 59–61). Furthermore, its artistic merits helped to make film respectable as an art form and this meant that many white liberals, abhorring both crude racism and censorship, supported the showing of the film. After all, they were not directly disadvantaged by racism.

The controversy generated by the film ensured that the vicious stereotypes portrayed, although strengthened in popular ideology, were not so crudely presented again in films until the nineteen-sixties. Black characters became once again asexual. The typical black character in the nineteen-twenties was a 'jester' (Bogle, 1973, p. 19) or a servant in films in upper-class settings, and occasionally apeared as a harmless savage in jungle films. When yet another version of *Uncle Tom's Cabin* appeared in 1927, it was significant that the black actor Charles Gilpin was replaced, partly for his 'overly aggressive reading of the script' (Campbell, 1981a, p. 67), while the highly conservative United Sons and Daughters of the American Revolution succeeded in forcing cuts and shifting the emphasis so as to appease Southern white sensibilities (Cripps, 1977, p. 161). The portrayal of blacks as passive and stupid or, more commonly, not including blacks in films at all, continued. Black women and children were less threatening figures, and the popular *Our Gang* series featured a mixed-race group of children. Those supporting the series argued that it favoured black and white children playing together – but so had Southern whites even in the days of slavery(!), whereas those who objected pointed out that the blacks were always the butt of any practical jokes.

There were other reasons for avoiding controversy centred on issues of race or class. In the 'Red Summer' of 1919 blacks fought back in cities like Chicago when attacked by whites, and this pattern was repeated elsewhere over the next few years. Producers had no wish to be accused of inciting public disorder, especially when they were under pressure for other reasons to put their house in order. In 1922, responding to the pressure of middle-class reformers and moralists, they implemented mild self-censorship by establishing the Hays Office. Amongst other things, they prohibited ethnic name-calling and miscegenation, making a gesture towards liberalism and at the same time protecting their takings at the Southern (white) box office. Studio heads consistently used the latter to restrict the range of roles made available to blacks, but this can just as easily be explained by their own conservatism (Cripps, 1977, pp. 110 – 11). Finally, organisation of the industry along oligopolistic lines, in which a few companies controlled production, distribution and exhibition, increased the reliance on outside capital from the banks and reinforced conservative tendencies.

Overall, Hollywood was no more or less racist than most other sections of American society. Despite the presence of liberal whites, 'the air was heavy with casual racism' (Cripps, 1977, p. 98). Because blacks could be selected as types rather than for their talents, no significant cadre of influential black contacts grew up in Hollywood during the silent era. A familiar pattern emerged – blacks who appeared at all regularly in movies kept quiet, grateful for what they could earn on the fringes of the industry.

Partly as a direct response to *The Birth of a Nation*, some African-Americans used the cinema to express a black point of view. The NAACP began an ambitious project to produce an epic on black progress called *Lincoln's Dream*. Scaled down because of confusion over aims, and failure to obtain substantial backing from the business community, whether black or white, it floundered when issued as *The Birth of a Race* in 1919.

The Noble brothers had greater success at a more modest level with *The Realisation of a Negro's Ambition* (1916) and *The Trooper of Company K* (1916). Both aimed to show positive contributions made by blacks to American life, the former in terms of a rags-to-riches story and the latter as a patriotic tale – it showed blacks fighting the Mexicans at

Carrizal in 1916. Both films reflected the burning desire of middle-class blacks to be accepted just like any other Americans.

Early efforts to develop a cinema by blacks for blacks depended upon a growing black ghetto audience in the cities, particularly in the North and West, as labour moved off the land into services and manufacturing. One of the traditional responses of the black *petite bourgeoisie* to racism was to establish a parallel economy to serve black needs. This was therefore adopted in the production of 'race movies'. Lack of capital, hectic competition, insufficient black spending power and the post-war depression killed off many companies, but over a hundred appeared during the nineteen-twenties to serve more than 700 ghetto cinemas. The enormous costs of conversion to sound, and the Depression, liquidated most black independents in the nineteen-thirties, although Oscar Micheaux, an exceptionally determined director, made films until 1948. From the early nineteen-thirties, however, most 'race movies' were made almost entirely by whites (Bogle, 1973, pp. 107–8).

With rare exceptions, the plots of most 'race movies' did little to bolster a strong black self-image. Few dealt with the specific problems in the ghetto or in the South. There was a strong middle-class pre-occupation with passing, and the general emphasis on 'the lighter the better' encouraged an interest in hair straightening and skin lightening liable to promote a negative self-image amongst most blacks. Another important feature of many films was the boosting of conventional American values through the portrayal of black rags-to-riches characters.

Oscar Micheaux was more willing to tackle controversial issues and look at the less palatable aspects of ghetto life at the risk offending the black middle-classes (Cripps, 1977, pp. 26–9). The only one of his silent films to survive is *Body and Soul* (1924). Many of his films, including his first *The Homesteader* (1919), expressed the conflict between urban and rural ways and values encountered by the great wave of Southern black migrants to the city (see also Lauter, 1985, p. 36). *Body and Soul* keeps to this theme and examines black preachers who, in the style of Sinclair Lewis's Elmer Gantry, exploited the religious fervour of poor blacks who had settled in the Northern ghettos. In the initial version, Paul Robeson plays such a preacher who enters a black community in Georgia which is totally unable or unwilling to counter bootleggers and gamblers (Cripps, 1977, pp. 191–2). The New York censors found the portrayals of both preacher and community unacceptable, and the film was modified. It touches on a dilemma – either blacks strive for middle-class respectability according to the rules of white capitalist society, or they escape to a life of hustling. This presentation of 'two sides' to black culture, and the strong religious emphasis, has occasionally been tapped since in *Hearts in Dixie* (1929), *Hallelujah* (1929), and *The Green Pastures* (1936) (Chapter 12), *Nothing But a Man* (Chapter 13) and *The Color Purple* (1985) (Chapter 14). Micheaux also looks at the ambivalent attitude of the black community to the numbers racket in *Spider's Web* (1926) and the stresses of urban life on a black family in *Wages of Sin* (1929).

The portrayal of blacks in the early cinema was highly demeaning. Black people were shown as crude stereotypes, either as objects of derision or as poor passive creatures. Sometimes they were given major roles but only as apologia for slavery and segregation. Many of these parts were in fact acted by whites in blackface. Virulent racism on the screen was exceptional, but its impact was startling when it came with *The Birth of a Nation*. Blacks and some whites realised after *Birth* the enormous potential of film to affect or at least confirm predominant trends in public opinion and behaviour. In particular, many blacks realised what a powerful anti-racist medium film could potentially be. The economic power of the major studios and the enormous size of the white audience ensured that portrayals of blacks on film seen by most people to the end of the silent era were those that Hollywood chose to depict. This is a pattern that, with rare exception, has continued to the present day. Anxious to avoid controversy that might reduce box-office takings, the studios expressed racism either by ignoring blacks completely or assigning them peripheral and demeaning roles. Black actors now normally played these parts and there was an ambivalence in the black community about Hollywood that has not yet disappeared. Those who got parts were thankful for the work, while many others were dismayed by the results. The black response in terms of 'race movies' was limited by the meagre resources available to the black community. Attempts to make 'message movies' in direct response to *The Birth of a Nation* failed. However, black film-makers serving the cinemas of a rapidly growing urban ghetto population began to explore black concerns, occasionally dealing with controversial aspects of ghetto life, the contrasting rural and urban aspects of black culture and issues like lynching.

References

Aitken, R. E. (1965) *The Birth of a Nation Story*, Denlinger, Middleburg, Va.
Armour, R. A. (1981) 'History written in jagged lightning: realistic South vs. romantic South in "The Birth of a Nation"', in W. French (ed), *The South on Film*, University Press of Mississippi, Jackson (special issue of *Southern Quarterly*, 19 (3/4), pp. 14-22
Bogle, D. (1973) *Toms, Coons, Mulattoes, Mammies and Bucks: An Interpretive History of Blacks in American Films*, Viking Press, New York
Boskin, J. (1970) 'Sambo: the national jester in the popular culture', in G. B. Nash and R. Weiss (eds), *The Great Fear: Race in the American Mind*, Holt, Rinehart & Winston, New York, pp. 165 – 85
Campbell, E. D. T. Jr (1981) *The Celluloid South*, University of Tennessee Press, Knoxville
Carter, E. (1960) 'Cultural history written with lightning: the significance of "The Birth of a Nation"', *American Quarterly*, 12, pp. 347 – 57
Christian, B. (1985) 'Shadows uplifted', in J. Newton and D. Rosenfelt (eds), *Feminist Criticism and Social Change: Sex, Class and Race in Literature and Culture*, Methuen, New York and London, pp. 181-215
Cripps, T. S. (1974) ' "The Birth of a Race" company: an early stride toward a black cinema', *Journal of Negro History*, 59, pp. 28-37
Cripps, T. S. (1977) *Slow Fade to Black: The Negro in American Film*, Oxford University Press, New York
Cripps, T. S. (1979) ' "Race movies" as voices of the black bourgeoisie: *The Scar of Shame*', in J. O'Connor and M. Jackson (eds), *American History/ American Film: Interpreting the Hollywood Image*, Frederick Ungar, New York, pp. 39 – 55
Ehrlich, E, (1981) 'The Civil War in early film: origin and development of a genre', in W. French (ed), *The South on Film*, University of Mississippi Press, Jackson (special issue of *Southern Quarterly*, 19 (3/4), pp. 70 – 82
Gallagher, B. (1982) 'Racist ideology and black abnormality in the "Birth of a Nation"', *Phylon*, 43, pp. 68 – 76
Lauter, P. (1985) 'Race and gender in the American literary canon: a case study from the twenties', in J. Newton and D. Rosenfelt (eds), *Feminist Criticism and Social Change: Sex, Class and Race in Literature and Culture*, Methuen, London and New York, pp. 19 – 44
Leab, D. J. (1973) 'The gamut from A to B: the image of the black in pre-1915 movies', *Political Science Quarterly*, 88, pp. 53 – 70
Leab, D. J. (1975) *From Sambo to Superspade: The Black Experience in Motion Pictures*, Houghton Mifflin, Boston, Mass.
Leab, D. J. (1975) ' "All-Colored" – but not much different: films made for negro ghetto audiences, 1913 – 1928', *Phylon*, 36, pp. 345 – 56
Lemons, J. S. (1977) 'Black stereotypes as reflected in popular culture, 1880 – 1920', *American Quarterly*, 29, pp. 102 – 16

Mapp, E. (1972) *Blacks in American Films: Today and Yesterday*, The Scarecrow Press, Inc., Metuchen, NJ

Monaco, J. (1981) *How to Read a Film*, Oxford University Press, Oxford and New York

Nesteby, J. R. (1982) *Black Images in American Films, 1896 – 1954: The Interplay between Civil Rights and Film Culture*, University Presses of America, Washington, DC

Noble, P. (1948) *The Negro in Films*, Skelton Robinson, London

Pines, J. (1975) *Blacks in Films: A Survey of Racial Themes and Images in the American Film*, Studio Vista, London

Richardson, F. H. (1910) *Motion Picture Handbook: A Guide for Managers and Operators of Motion Picture Theatres*, The Moving Picture World, New York

Rogin, M. (1985) 'The sword became a flashing vision: D. W. Griffiths' *The Birth of a Nation*', *Representations*, Winter 1985, pp. 150 – 95

Scott, A. F. (1970) *The Southern Lady: From Pedestal to Politics, 1830 – 1930*, University of Chicago Press, Chicago

Silk, J. A. (1987) 'Racism and Anti-racism in Films of the American South', in P. Jackson (ed), *Race and Racism: Essays in Social Geography*, Unwin Hyman, London, pp. 324 – 44

Silverman, J. (1981) '"The Birth of a Nation": Prohibition propaganda', *Southern Quarterly*, 19, pp. 23 – 30

Sklar, R. (1975) *Movie-Made America*, Chappell & Co., London

12

Hollywood's Golden Age and
Gone With the Wind

The costs of conversion to sound were enormous – $500 million in capital expenditure, and a doubling of production expenses. The great financial empires like those of the Morgans and the Rockefellers exercised influence through some of the largest American corporations who now had a stake in the industry. The Crash meant that all the major studios except Warner had handed financial control to their backers by 1933: 'Sound and the Crash had attached the film industry irretrievably to the bastions of American capitalism' (Maltby, 1981, p. 47). Before the Crash, the coming of sound seemed to present a major opportunity for blacks to increase their participation and improve their image in films. There had been a vogue for black musical stage artists and for black culture generally among East Coast liberals from the early nineteen-twenties. The achievements of the Harlem Renaissance in the arts might, it was hoped, make a comparable impact on the screen. There was a new assertiveness among Northern urban blacks, shown in increased litigation over civil rights, and short-lived optimism about the future of blacks in film.

Such hopes were strengthened as it was rumoured that black voices sounded superior to those of whites in the expanded medium: 'it may be that the talking movies must be participated in exclusively by Negroes, but, if so, then so be it ... There is a quality in the Negro voice, an ease in its delivery, and a sense of timing in reading the lines that make it an ideal medium for the talking picture' (Benchley, 1975, pp. 84 – 5). However, hopes were soon dashed; parts for blacks remained small, and sound was more often than not used to film minstrel and other musical entertainments for predominantly white audiences.

Black vaudeville, dancing and 'commercial' jazz also became popular, usually being produced as short two-reel films (Cripps, 1978,

Ch. 9). Unfortunately, the artistry of performers like Billie Holliday, Louis Armstrong and Jimmy Rushing was mostly confined to the production of these 'shorts', few of which had definite plots, and which were merely entertaining fillers or prefaces to the main films. Some – more by accident than design – gave an idea of the flavour of black life in Northern urban ghettos. Another distinctive trend was very conservative and depicted crooning slaves in the Old South. Short films of this kind continued to be produced until the early nineteen-forties. Cheap to make, they were chiefly used – like cartoons – as lightweight diversions. Technical and financial aspects of such film production remained in white hands.

Films that initially raised black hopes were *Hallelujah* at MGM and *Hearts in Dixie* at Fox, two musicals with all black casts that came out in 1929. Both were set in the New South and praised by black and white critics for their attempts to make black characters and life central to the narrative. Black people are presented as ordinary people who need to make a living, as people who fall in and out of love, marry, and have children, for whom they nurture hopes of a better future. The nobility of Clarence Muse's Nappus in *Hearts in Dixie* is unfortunately countered by the idiotic antics of Stepin Fetchit as Gummy. Significantly, both films avoided controversial issues, and neither heralded the long hoped for breakthrough for blacks in the movie industry.

Both also incorporated ideas of the 'exotic primitive' which had become popular among white intellectuals in the nineteen-twenties. This was a relatively new stereotype, having its roots in the racist idea that blacks were more primitive and less civilised than whites. In the nineteen-twenties version we see a particularly subtle form of racism in this image, one which has survived in some form to this day, as white writers and artists 'praised' blacks for their 'exoticism', and for 'primitive' qualities which, they imply, whites have unfortunately lost by becoming 'over-civilised'. The new interest in Freud and the discoveries of previously unknown primitive societies, romanticised in the work of painters like Gauguin, strengthened these ideas in respectable intellectual circles.

In *Hallelujah*, for example, its director King Vidor hoped to explore the rich life of the 'pristine Southern Negro' in order to understand how 'the polished [urban] Negro ... possesses, under the surface, the rhythm and abandon, the love song and laughter of those in a primitive state' (Cripps, 1978, p. 243). The patronising racism of many North-east liberals in the nineteen-twenties had, briefly, found its way on to the screen.

Black and white film critics were enthusiastic about both films. They did well at the box office, despite the initial timidity of many exhibitors. The shabby and seedy urban scenes in *Hallelujah* caused some unease among both working-class and middle-class blacks who wished to see more positive black images on the screen, and suspected the motives of white film-makers.

Whatever the intentions and views of film-makers and critics, evidence from advertising of the time suggests that it was romantic views of a happy Dixie and its equally happy black workers, supported by lively musical interludes, that attracted the average cinema-goer (Campbell, 1981, pp. 89–91). Because the films concentrated on blacks with virtually no reference to white influence, it was possible for disturbing features of the wider social context not to impinge on audiences. It would not be long before even such films were superceded by the revival of romantic, escapist films set in the South. Hopes, therefore, that *Hearts in Dixie* and *Hallelujah* would trigger off a cycle of similar movies were misplaced. The impact of the Depression on the film industry was, for blacks, to be almost entirely negative. As in most sectors of the American economy, racism meant blacks were the first to be laid off by the studios. Given the long tradition of blackface in the American cinema, the dictum, 'the last to be hired, the first to be fired' (Foner, 1974, p. 188), was particularly apt. By the time 1930 began there were no longer any roles for black actors as central figures – even Stepin Fetchit, one of the few black stars, was released from his contract. So desperate was the situation that any black role came to be regarded as 'progress' (Cripps, 1978, p. 106), and it is little wonder that black actors and actresses were so willing to play stereotypic roles later in the nineteen-thirties – they needed the work.

The Depression had contradictory effects on the movie industry; the thirties are perhaps best known for escapist movies, screwball comedies and expensive musicals which were meant to help people forget their troubles. But for various reasons, sometimes in an attempt to combat loss of profits in their own industry, sometimes because there was some questioning and criticism of the social order thrown up by the Depression that not everyone in Hollywood wanted to ignore, there were a few important socially critical, or at the least liberal, films made during the period. Warner Brothers is particularly known for films of this kind like *I Am a Fugitive from a Chain Gang* (1932).

At the same time there was a growing body of literary material advancing revisionist views of the South. Mythical views of the region had been increasingly questioned during the nineteen-twenties, and the entire social mores of the region ridiculed by commentators like H. L. Mencken and by reaction to the 'Monkey Trial' in Tennessee in 1925 (Tindall, 1980, Ch. 3). More attention was being paid to the poverty and racism of the 'embarrassing New South' (Kirby, 1986, Ch. 3) in both serious and popular literature. 'Sharecropper realism' and the 'Southern Gothic School', the latter including works by Faulkner and Caldwell, exploited these themes. During the nineteen-thirties novels critical of Southern racism, many of them by whites, appeared (Butcher, 1956, Ch. 11). Southern scholars like Odum (1936) and Vance (1932, Ch. 17) supported the contention that the region's colonial status persisted and that the Southern states propped up the American league table on virtually all measures of economic health and social welfare.

For all these reasons, there were throughout the thirties exceptional films which examined important social issues, including occasionally, though more obliquely, the problem of racism. *Cabin in the Cotton* (1932) was based on a novel of the same name written by a sharecropper's son. It deals with the class battle between sharecroppers and the merchants to whom their crops are in lien. Again, nearly all those suffering from this system in the film are white, although in reality most sharecroppers were black. As Kirby (1986, pp. 46–7) remarks, treatment of class militancy was daring enough for Hollywood, let alone battles based on class and race.

I Am a Fugitive from a Chain Gang (1932) concentrated its attack on the convict lease system, still common in the Southern States. It attracted great attention because of strong protest from the South, especially from Georgia, as the film was based on events which had occurred there. A memorable scene shows how the black convict helps the unjustly imprisoned white hero, James Allen, to escape. In this, and other reformist prison films like *The Last Mile* (1930) and *The Big House* (1930) a form of equality was suggested by portraying black convicts among whites. However, once again Hollywood only dared obliquely to attack racism, by criticising the ways in which blacks were particularly oppressed – sharecropping, lynching, convict-lease system – in films in which the characters are predominantly or completely white.

One problem for the film industry during this period was the reaction of pressure groups like the Catholic League of Decency. Many films ignored the new production code of 1930 and relied increasingly on sexual titillation and gangster violence. Fears of possible government intervention led the industry to set up its own stiffer Production Code

Administration, overseen by a conservative Catholic journalist, Joseph
Breen. This code operated until well into the nineteen-fifties. It worked
to limit strictly the treatment of sexual issues, including miscegenation,
and politically it worked as an extremely conservative force within the
industry. Many social and political issues fully debated in all other
American media in the late nineteen-thirties were now rarely treated
on the screen.

As we have already seen, social issues as they related to race had
always been treated very conservatively, and therefore the new stricter
Production Code had very little effect upon the portrayal of blacks in
movies. Films continued to be made which implicitly condemned
racism, but the tradition continued of doing this with all-white films
which only hinted that the real victims of oppression were black.

The Green Pastures (1936) is to some extent exceptional. In an all-black
version of the Old Testament, good is identified with Southern rural
values and evil with the 'New Negro' of the North. For blacks, the story
of the Israelites, as told in the film, was a symbolic representation of
their own history and struggles. The title *The Green Pastures* itself is
presumably taken from the twenty-third psalm, 'The Lord is my
shepherd; I shall not want. He maketh me to lie down in green pastures:
he leadeth me beside the still waters'. Black audiences could appreciate
the various levels of meaning within the film, where all characters,
including God, are black; while whites could enjoy familiar biblical
stories presented in a strikingly different way.

They Won't Forget (1937), also from Warner Brothers, is a film which
attacks lynching, and the tendency for the South to live in the past; hence
the title, the Civil War being what Southerners refuse to forget.
However, the film does not take as its central theme the lynching of a
black man; no studio was prepared to tackle that issue head-on. The
subject is approached by having the man who is lynched a white
Northerner, who represents the person who is different – the outsider.
It is, however, a powerful film which condemns lynching unequivocally,
strengthening its case by not allowing the audience ever to find out if
the man lynched committed the murder or not.

Fury (1936), Fritz Lang's second film made in the United States,
strongly condemns mob rule leading to lynching. MGM were reluctant
to produce it, and every important reference to race was deleted in the
cutting room. Lang also misunderstood the social implications of the
black rapist myth as he originally intended to centre the plot on the rape
of a white woman by a black man (Cripps, 1978, p. 295). In the final

version, any connection to the Southern treatment of blacks is so oblique as to be virtually non-existent, the action being set in the Mid-west. There are just four black characters in the film, all minor, and two appear fleetingly, visually suggesting their peripheral role in a white-dominated world. Otherwise, the clearest reference to the maltreatment of blacks is the district attorney's statement that 'American democracy is on trial here today' and his assertion that 'in the last forty nine years, mobs have lynched 6010 human beings by hanging, burning and cutting in this proud land of ours.' These and other comments suggest that Lang is also using the lynching as a warning of the need for eternal vigilance to defend any democracy against the dangers of fascism.

Showboat (1936) is unusual in that it gives prominent and sympathetic treatment to a sub-plot dealing with inter-racial marriage and allows Paul Robeson to express black anger against white dominance in 'Old Man River'.

Even these films which indirectly criticised racism were the exceptions; the transition from the all-black casts of *Hearts in Dixie* and *Hallelujah* to the 'mammies' and 'toms' of most later films was a rapid one. In many films parts given to blacks were so peripheral that if you blinked you could miss them. When they did gain parts they tended to exist only in relationship to whites. As 'mammies' and 'toms' they could be seen counselling, scolding and supervising the activities of white characters; they appear to have no existence when they are not with white people and when they live it is vicariously, through the activities of their white employers. This is particularly true in the relationships depicted between mammy and young girl, as played for example by Hattie McDaniel and Vivien Leigh in *Gone With the Wind* (1939). Ms McDaniel plays an equally effective mother substitute to the son of the eponymous *Judge Priest* (1934).

In *So Red The Rose* (1935), the planter's daughter, Vallette, stops a slave rebellion – just about the only suspicion of such an event in nineteen-thirties Hollywood films – by slapping one slave across the face and reminding their leader how he had cared for her as a child. A slave leader can thus be transformed into an Uncle Remus figure by a few words from his white mistress. Other films emphasising the essential docility and loyalty of black slaves, or simply failing to mention slavery, ranged from *Slave Days* (1929), *Dixiana* (1930) and *Cotton Pickin' Days* (1930) in the earlier years of sound through *Mississippi* (1935) to *Rainbow on the River* (1936) and *Way Down South* (1939).

Young black male actors got even fewer parts, as it was difficult to portray them as 'uncles' and any assertive behaviour on their part would be seen as threatening. As servants they passed the occasional comment or raised an eyebrow over the master's or mistress's behaviour, as in *Jezebel* (1938). Bill 'Bojangles' Robinson was an important example of an extremely talented black artist, being forced always to play the harmless old uncle figure, entertaining the audience and fellow characters with his dancing skills as 'uncle' to Shirley Temple in *The Littlest Rebel* (1935) and *The Little Colonel* (1935). As language-mangling, chicken-stealing and crafty 'coons', a few male actors were sometimes allowed to provide light relief, functioning as foils to major white characters and adding a touch of Southern local colour as Stepin Fetchit did in *Judge Priest* (1934).

These roles were integral to escapist films which temporarily insulated audiences from Depression conditions by portraying a pre-industrial South characterised by wealth, ease and stability. The Old South – often confused with the New – was shown to be a relatively simple and unproblematic society in which the only groups appeared to be white planters and black slaves living in intimate conditions, almost like extended families, in and around great white-columned houses.

The best-known and financially most successful of these films was *Gone with the Wind*. A 'woman's film', it focuses on the life of a Southern belle, Scarlett O'Hara, and her ill-fated relationship with Rhett Butler – the latter being played by the cinema's greatest male heart-throb of the time, Clark Gable. There were important supporting roles for Hattie McDaniel as Scarlett's personal maid (she hardly seems to be a slave at all!), for which she received an Oscar, and for Butterfly McQueen as Prissy, a silly and incompetent young black female – McQueen later regretted playing the role.

A significant feature of the film is its repetition of the sequence of Old South, Civil War and Reconstruction shown in *The Birth of a Nation*, but with significant variations. The most provocative forms of Griffith's racism are toned down, as is the virulent racism which is so clear in the Reconstruction section of Margaret Mitchell's (1936) novel. This was partly because Selznick, the producer, wanted to avoid controversy, but also because the NAACP and other groups fought to get the most offensive scenes removed or softened (Reddick, 1975, p. 15).

In one scene, Sam, the loyal ex-slave, rescues Scarlett from attack by a free black, thus encapsulating the age-old stereotypes of docile 'good' black and 'uppity bad' black. Earlier, Scarlett is jostled and subjected to derogatory remarks as she walks down a street crowded with

Northern carpetbaggers and credulous blacks who, in laughably exaggerated accents, recite the slogan 'forty acres and a mule'. There is no explicit reference to the Ku Klux Klan in the film, but the organisation which the respectable Ashley Wilkes is forced to join after this incident, and for which the women, including the virtuous Mrs Wilkes, are sewing uniforms, is of course none other.

There are some suggestions of the embarrassing New South when Scarlett joins the scallawags and runs her husband's lumber mill using convict labour, despite the protestations of other Southerners who had fallen on hard times but who 'kept their honour and their kindness' – they are fated to live up to the title of the film.

The survival of the mythical South of the film is symbolised by Scarlett's eventual return to Tara. Just before the Second World War the film was praised for its depiction of the regenerative spirit of the American character, and was seen as 'a national epic of contemporary meaning' (Campbell, 1981, p. 119).

However, the meaning to many blacks and left-wing radicals was only too clear. Black leaders condemned the film, and in *The New Masses* an article criticised *Gone with the Wind* as 'vicious', 'reactionary', 'inciting to race hatred', 'slander of the Negro people' and 'justifying the Ku Klux Klan' (Reddick, 1975, p. 16). Like *The Birth of a Nation* over twenty years before, *Gone with the Wind* was a regression compared with Southern 'talkies', with its strong hints of the mythical black rapist and the honourable and defensive role of the Ku Klux Klan during Reconstruction.

The publicity and general ballyhoo surrounding the making of the film, as well as its content, ensured eager anticipation by audiences which turned into a rapturous reception, not only in the South, but throughout the nation. The success of revisionist novels was insufficient to counter the impact of the mass medium of the time. Caldwell's *Tobacco Road* may have sold more copies than Mitchell's *Gone with the Wind* by 1966 (Campbell, 1981, p. 84), but more people could watch *Mississippi* or *Gone with the Wind* in one night in the nation's cinemas. It was possible, therefore, in the nineteen-thirties for the most popular films, like *Gone With The Wind*, to put forward racist portrayals of blacks which had not changed since the late nineteenth century.

Although we have been concentrating on the ways in which blacks were portrayed in films, most nineteen-thirties movies ignored black people completely, and most histories of the American cinema discuss the decade without even mentioning black artists and actors. Within the dominant genres of the period such as escapist films, screwball comedies, and gangster movies, there was a steady stream of very minor parts for blacks playing bellhops, lift operators, janitors and railway car porters. Black actors made the most of these roles; occasionally the role of servant was given some structural significance in the narrative. Often female servants in particular were allowed to represent the voice of common sense and to counsel their employers. Hattie McDaniel for example developed this side of her roles to such an extent that there were some complaints from Southern movie goers that black servants were being portrayed as 'uppity', and as not always reflecting the white characters in a positive way.

There are excellent examples of such roles in *Jezebel* (1938) and also in *Judge Priest* (1934), the judge's black housekeeper slyly making derogatory remarks about Yankee ways to the son of the house. An especially memorable performance is that by Hattie McDaniel as the maid who comments contemptuously upon the disastrous dinner party given by her snobbish mistress in *Alice Adams* (1935).

Such comments on the mores of white people are allowed; they function also to stress the peripheral role of black people both in the movies and in society. None of these characters exists at all except in relation to whites; they are not developed as characters in their own right, and therefore while their comments on the action are narratively useful, they are not seen to present any threat.

One or two films rose above this. *Imitation of Life* (1934) was a woman's film that incorporated sympathetic and melodramatic treatment of passing – presumably the film was released before the new Breen Code became effective. Louise Beavers plays Aunt Delilah, a black cook whose flapjack recipes make a fortune for her white mistress. However, Delilah's daughter finds she can pass for white, rejecting both her mother and her race, and this story becomes an important and tragic sub-plot within the film. It did surprisingly well financially – white magazines and audiences were enthusiastic. Although perpetuating the stereotype of the tragic mulatto, and removing much of the daring observation of racism in Fannie Hurst's original novel, the film 'was a high notch of Hollywood racial vision' (Cripps, 1978, p. 303). *Arrowsmith* (1931) was a 'first', and for a long time a 'last' in showing Clarence Brooks as a black doctor who plays a key role in working out the moral dilemma posed by a choice between western medicine and voodooism in the West Indies.

In his portrayal of black foils the actor Stepin Fetchit became more controversial. He repeated his role as a 'coon' many times, being paired with Will Rogers in films like *Judge Priest* (1934), *David Harum* (1934) and *Steamboat 'Round the Bend* (1935). His portrayals attracted public condemnation from white liberals and organised blacks at the time, because of the way they took to almost parodic lengths the obsequious, stupid, Uncle Tom stereotype. Watching his portrayal in *Judge Priest* is to say the least an uncomfortable experience and black audiences at the time were understandably upset. In her autobiography, Maya Angelou describes what it was like for a black child to go to the movies in the nineteen-thirties:

It was a gay light comedy, and Kay Francis wore long-sleeved white silk shirts with big cuff links. Her bedroom was all satin and flowers in vases, and her maid, who was Black, went around saying, 'Lawsy, missy' all the time. There was a Negro chauffeur too, who rolled his eyes and scratched his head, and I wondered how on earth an idiot like that could be trusted with her beautiful cars. (Angelou, 1984, p. 115)

After the Civil Rights movement of the nineteen-sixties Stepin Fetchit felt compelled to take out a law suit in order to defend himself against the accusations of the black community (McBride, 1971; Perry, 1973).

Black responses at the time were more conflict-ridden, as it was recognised that black film stars were highly-talented performers, but blacks were unhappy with the roles that had to be played to achieve success. In Hollywood itself, black criticism was muted as experience showed that significant protest would lead to parts being cut or, more likely, reallocated. Debate within the NAACP during the nineteen-thirties over the respective merits of black economic solidarity and integration, a phenomenon paralleled by the political dilemma facing members of Roosevelt's 'Black Cabinet', had little resonance in Hollywood. There was constant debate about the issue in black circles, but ultimately if black actors wished to work at all, they were forced into playing stereotypes. Hattie McDaniel herself once asked why she should be a maid for $25 a week, when she could *play* one for $25,000 a week.

In most Hollywood feature films of this period, before or after 1934, there is rarely any treatment of the ordinary lives and concerns of black eople, nor is there any reference to black history or achievement.

Outside the mainstream cinema there were some attempts to rectify this, but lack of finance, and an inability to get their films widely shown, guaranteed failure. Independent white producers like Dudley Murphy, produced films such as *St. Louis Blues* (1929), a two-reeler in which Bessie Smith gave a memorable performance as a sexually oppressed black woman. The film was set in the ghetto, like *Black and Tan* (1930) that followed it. Both failed financially, even in black areas, because widespread exhibition depended upon the big Hollywood studios that controlled most outlets. In 1933, things looked more promising when Murphy joined forces with Eugene O'Neill, adapting his play *The Emperor Jones* with Paul Robeson in the title role. It did well in Harlem and, surprisingly, in the South, but patchily elsewhere.

Black entrepreneurs turned briefly to Europe, attempting an international project in 1930 – *Borderline* (1930) with Paul Robeson – but the hostility of American exhibitors to any foreign film meant that it could not be distributed in the United States. There was also an abortive attempt to make an anti-racist film in Russia, but production was halted when Stalin was persuaded by the United States government to cancel the project.

Paul Robeson continued to attempt to make anti-racist films in Europe from the mid nineteen-thirties; unfortunately, he was unable to exercise much control over the form of the final product and in films like *Saunders of the River* (1936) found himself unwittingly justifying British imperialism, much to his own outrage and that of the black press in America. Most of these are now forgotten, but his career shows the enormous difficulties in combating racist stereotypes when an actor of Robeson's stature never found a suitable vehicle for this, either at home or abroad.

The 'race movies' of the silent era continued in sound as a strand of film-making, providing many parts for blacks and producing movies aimed at the all-black ghetto cinemas. As in Hollywood itself, commercial considerations predominated and there were few attempts to counter demeaning racist portrayals or even to deal, as had some of the silents, with issues like passing or miscegenation. This was largely because production, direction and distribution were almost entirely in white hands, although it made little difference if the film-makers were black (Leab, 1975, p. 173). A leading white producer of such films was patronising about black artists – 'there's never a downcast moment when a Negro film is in production' – and about black audiences, seeing them as unsophisticated since 'all they know is that they want plenty of singing and dancing or drama depicting Negro life in a Negro spirit' (quoted in Leab, 1975, p. 188).

These films attracted black audiences on their own account but were designed to run in tandem with Hollywood products, so increasing the latter's acceptability. It was estimated that in 1937 there were 232 cinemas, North and South, catering almost exclusively for African – Americans, rising to 684 by 1947.

In the new race movies 'good English' was added to the light skins and straight hair of the leading characters, while bad or comic characters were more Negroid in appearance, darker-skinned and tended to speak in dialect.

The most common form was the all-black musical such as *Harlem is Heaven* (1932), starring Bill Robinson, and *The Duke is Tops* (1938) in which Lena Horne made her screen debut. Imitations of major Hollywood genres appeared, including gangster movies like *Moon Over Harlem* (1937) which inadvertently provided social comment on the protection racket, Westerns like *The Bronze Buckaroo* and *Harlem Rides the Range*, and even features in which actors such as Mantan Moreland played demeaning parts as eye-rolling stooges. Black athletes were also enlisted to boost audience interest, Joe Louis being used in this way in *The Spirit of Youth* (1938).

Micheaux was one of the few black directors to continue in the nineteen-thirties, making ten films in that decade. He was criticised for portraying blacks as gullible gamblers or simply as stupid. *God's Step Children* (1938) was picketed in New York because it showed lighter-skinned blacks as contemptuous of those with darker skins. Unfortunately, as several black autobiographies show, it was one of the tragedies of the black community that such attitudes were not uncommon at the time (see for example Malcolm X, 1968, pp. 82 – 3).

All-black films for ghetto audiences finally disappeared in the fifties as blacks began to get better parts in Hollywood films and integration became an important issue in American society.

With rare exceptions, therefore, the portrayal of blacks in mainstream American movies during this period was either non-existent, patronising, or downright racist. If a director like Lang, or an actor like Robeson attempted to change this, it was made impossible for them to do so. Malcolm X in his autobiography describes how humiliating it was to watch black stereotypes being played in films. Little compensation could be found in films produced solely for the ghetto cinemas. In other media, there were significant changes in the ways blacks were portrayed during this period, and in literature black artists were slowly beginning to find their own voices to tell of the African-American experience in America. But in movies, the world stood still, Northern urban life was ignored and black actors, if they wanted to work had to play Uncle Remus and Aunt Jemima to an endless cast of white superstars. As the Second World War started hopes were raised once again that the position might change.

References

Angelou, M. (1984) *I Know Why the Caged Bird Sings*, Virago, London
Benchley, R. (1975) 'Hearts in Dixie (The First Real Talking Picture)', in Patterson (ed), pp. 84–7 (originally published in *Opportunity Magazine*, 7, 1929, pp. 122-3)
Bogle, D. (1973) *Toms, Coons, Mulattoes, Mammies and Bucks: An Interpretive History of Blacks in American Fiction*, Viking Press, New York
Butcher, M.J. (1956) *The Negro in American Culture*, New American Library, New York
Campbell, E. D. T. Jr (1981) *The Celluloid South,* University of Tennessee Press, Knoxville
Cripps, T. S. (1970) 'Paul Robeson and black identity in American movies', *Massachusetts Review*, 11, pp. 468–85
Cripps, T. S. (1977) *Slow Fade to Black: The Negro in American Film, 1900–1947*, Oxford University Press, New York
Curran, T. (1981) ' "Gone With the Wind": an American tragedy', in French (ed), pp. 47–57
Dyer, R. (1983) *Heavenly Bodies: Film Stars and Society*, BFI/Macmillan, London
Flamini, R. (1975) *Scarlett, Rhett, and a Cast of Thousands: The Filming of Gone With the Wind*, Macmillan, New York
Foner, P. S. (1976) *Organized Labor and the Black Worker: 1619–1973*, International Publishers, New York
French, W. (ed) (1981) *The South on Film*, University Press of Mississippi, Jackson (special issue of *Southern Quarterly*, 19 (3/4))
Harwell, R. (ed) (1983) *Gone With the Wind as Book and Film*, University of South Carolina Press, Columbia
Jeter, I. (1981) ' "Jezebel" and the emergence of the Hollywood tradition of a decadent South', in French (ed), pp. 31-46
Kirby, J. T. (1986) *Media Made Dixie: The South in the American Imagination*, Louisiana State University Press, Baton Rouge and London (revised edition)
Koppes, C. R., and Black, G. D. (1987) *Hollywood Goes to War: How Politics, Profits and Propaganda Shaped World War II Movies*, I. B. Tauris & Co. Ltd, London
Leab, D.J. (1975) *From Sambo to Superspade: The Black Experience in Motion Pictures*, Houghton Mifflin, Boston
Locke, A. (ed) (1968) *The New Negro*, Johnson Reprint, New York (originally published in 1925)
McBride, J. (1971) 'Stepin' Fetchit talks back', *Film Quarterly*, 24, pp. 20–6
Maltby, R. (1981) 'The political economy of Hollywood: the studio system',

in P. Davies and B. Neve (eds), *Cinema, Politics and Society in America*, Manchester University Press, Manchester, pp. 42–58

Mitchell, M. (1936) *Gone With the Wind*, Macmillan, London

Murray, J. P. (1973) *To Find an Image: Black Films from Uncle Tom to Superfly*, Bobbs-Merrill Co., Indianapolis

Noble, P. (1948) *The Negro in Films*, Skelton Robinson, London

Odum, H. (1936) *Southern Regions of the United States*, University of North Carolina Press, Chapel Hill

Patterson, L. (ed) (1975) *Black Films and Film-makers: A Comprehensive Anthology from Stereotype to Superhero*, Dodd, Mead & Co., New York

[Perry, Lincoln] (1973) "'I'm no derogatory black image'': Stepin' Fetchit', *Jet*, 3 May, p. 61

Pyron, D. A. (ed) (1983) *Recasting: Gone With the Wind in American Culture*, University Presses of Florida, Miami

Reddick, L. (1975) 'Of motion pictures', in Patterson (ed), pp. 3-44

Rollins, P. C. (1979) 'Will Rogers and the Relevance of nostalgia: "Steamboat 'Round the Bend"'', in J. O'Connor and M. Jackson (eds), *American History/American Film: Interpreting the Hollywood Image*, Frederick Ungar, New York, pp. 77–96

Tindall, G. B. (1976) *The Ethnic Southerners*, Louisiana State University Press, Baton Rouge

Van Deburg, W. L. (1984) *Slavery and Race in American Popular Culture*, University of Wisconsin Press, Madison

Vance, R. B. (1932) *Human Geography of the South*, University of North Carolina Press, Chapel Hill

Woll, A. L., and Miller, R. M. (1987) *Ethnic and Racial Images in American Film and Television: Historical Essays and Bibliography*, Garland Publishing, Inc., New York and London

X, Malcolm (1970) *Autobiography*, Penguin, Harmondsworth

13

'The Death of Uncle Tom' (1941 – 1969)

The Second World War marked a turning point in black – white relations in the United States (see Chapter 6). The Office of War Information (OWI) became the arbiter and censor of racial themes in the cinema when set up in 1942. It issued a guidebook on the subject of racial content and exerted pressure to increase opportunities for blacks in the film industry. NAACP leaders and the studio heads met and the latter promised to liberalise their depiction of blacks. The studios, with the notable exception of Warners, had been worried about portraying the war in Europe too sympathetically before the United States itself became involved. This was partly because they feared a loss of foreign markets which provided forty per cent of their revenue and also adverse reaction from isolationists at home. In the end, sheer force of world events was too much even for them!

Popular culture during the war stressed American unity; despite racism and poverty what Americans had in common outweighed anything which divided them. Patronising portrayals of black people became more muted therefore during the war, and a few liberal portrayals of blacks appeared in which black people are treated with some dignity. For example, *Casablanca* (1942) shows Sam as a sidekick character, but he plays an integral part in the early unfolding of the plot. There is no hint of patronage in his relationships with other characters, and Rick can even take out his frustration on him in one scene without it being demeaning. Only in the latter part of the film is Sam absent, left to the tender mercies of Ferrari to whom Rick/Bogart has sold his café, while the self-sacrifice of the whites as lovers and as symbols of a Euro – American partnership against fascism comes to the fore. *In This Our Life* (1942) features a non-stereotyped black role. Parry Clay is a hard-working ambitious young man studying to be a law student in

his spare time, receiving full support from his mother. The role is structurally important to the film, and in the denouement it is shown that
a spoilt rich white woman's attempt to use racism to escape blame for
a fatal car accident does not pay. Leigh Whipper plays a black preacher
in *The Ox-Bow Incident* (1943) who has the coolness and courage to try
and dissuade a posse from a lynching, declaring that he comes from a
race which has had to bear the brunt of lynch law, and lynching is no
way to settle things for either black or white people (Noble, 1948, p. 195).

The most radical departure from the normal portrayal of blacks was
The Negro Soldier (1942), produced as a training film for the army. It was
non-patronising and highly successful. Hollywood then decided it was
safe to produce three feature-length rivals – *Crash Dive* (1943), *Sahara*
(1943) and *Bataan* (1943) – showing blacks in non-stereotypic if token
roles. Such portrayals were highly satisfactory to OWI, as they depicted
racial integration and racial tolerance on the screen although this did
not exist in actuality. In most war films, however, blacks did not appear
at all. Films in which blacks did appear therefore, although mildly
encouraging, were exceptional. Generally, Hollywood took few chances
and for the most part would rather write blacks out of scripts than depart
radically from the established stereotypes. Membership of the black
actors' union fell by fifty per cent during the war, suggesting that
opportunities had fallen, rather than risen. OWI representatives wanted
to see nothing that challenged the vision of a united democratic America,
and would not countenance realistic portrayals of black life or history
any more than the studio heads. These they believed would be inevitably
controversial and divisive (Koppes and Black, 1987, p. 184). *Tennessee
Johnson* (1943), initially conceived as a white supremacist apologia for
Andrew Johnson's presidency from 1865 to 1869, went too far in the
other direction, but the changes negotiated between MGM and OWI
achieved a point of 'balance' that cut nearly all reference to slavery and
reduced black roles to the depiction of four servants in Washington DC.
On the other hand, a *Roots*-style proposal for a history of blacks from
African origins to contemporary professional success got nowhere.

The studios felt safe in producing two all-black musicals in 1943,
Cabin in the Sky and *Stormy Weather*, which were packed with stereotypes
and reverted to the notion of black primitivism. Ethel Waters, Duke
Ellington, and Louis Armstrong were 'forced to grin' (Mapp, 1972,
p. 31), the films being partially redeemed only by the skill and vitality
of the performers. Lena Horne expressed her general outrage by asking
'that the Negro be portrayed as a normal person. Let's see the Negro

as a worker at union meetings, as a civil service worker or elected official'
(quoted in Ellison, 1981, p. 181). Films like *Dixie* (1943), in which
crooning stevedores accompany Bing Crosby and in which black
minstrels appear, and *Song of the South* (1946), Disney's version of the
Uncle Remus tales, showed the continuing profitability of Old South
themes. The latter, together with *Tales of Manhattan* (1946) caused protest
and a major split amongst organised blacks. It was a continuation of
the conflict between those who were more impressed by major roles and
studio employment for blacks, and others more concerned with film
content.

Because of the wartime rhetoric, and despite the continued appearance of stereotypes, black expectations of Hollywood rose. Although
not fulfilled, some roles had been offered which moved distinctly away
from the old stereotypes and it was these which were to be built upon
and extended after the war.

American film audiences peaked in 1946, but research showed that
competition from radio and newspapers was growing. The mass movement of many white households to the suburbs brought about new
leisure patterns that kept many former patrons away from downtown
cinemas. Audiences fell in 1947 and the decline was accelerated by the
impact of television from the early nineteen-fifties. Harassment by the
House Un-American Activities Committee, a major anti-trust suit, and
economic retaliation against the industry by foreign governments, added
to their troubles. Surveys also showed that increases in filmgoing between 1935 and 1945 were mainly among the middle- and higher-income
groups.

Thus it was primarily business reasons, the hope of increasing
middle-class patronage, rather than any desire to promote revisionist
or enlightened views, that caused studio heads to go for 'good pictures'.
These moved sharply away from the escapist themes of the nineteen-
thirties, and made some attempt to deal with the problems facing racial
and religious minorities in quality 'problem movies'.

A small number of these examined racism *and* provided non-
stereotypic roles for blacks. *Intruder in the Dust* (1949), adapted from a
novel by Faulkner, provided a strong comment on Southern racism.
It was the first major Hollywood feature film to be critical of lynching
and show blacks as its victims. Lucas Beauchamp, a black farmer, is held
for the murder of a poor white. He is shown as a dignified man who
has spent his life coping with racism by refusing to acknowledge its
existence. For example, when he rescues the white boy from the creek

and takes him home and gives him a meal, the boy, as is the Southern custom, attempts to pay him, thus emphasising Lucas's inferiority in white society. Lucas refuses the money, which the boy then petulantly throws on the floor, recognising that by his actions, Lucas is determined to treat him as a guest in his house, in other words as an equal. The film also emphasises, realistically, the true helplessness of blacks in Southern society. Salvation for Lucas can come only through the actions of whites, and the device of using a boy and an old woman as its agents is highly effective. As a young boy not yet 'cluttered' with ideas, as Lucas puts it, together with a very old woman, they are themselves marginal-ised and so can act in ways in which no white man could. They therefore drive off in the middle of the night and dig up the body of the man Lucas is supposed to have killed, and eventually prove his innocence. The film, however, does not put fundamental change on the agenda, as Beau-champ's white lawyer is allowed the final word, that it 'depends on people like us' to safeguard Beauchamp – the latter is no more than 'the keeper of our conscience'! This was the only film about blacks in the nineteen-forties to be uncut by Southern censorship (Cripps, 1978, p. 58), perhaps because of respect for Faulkner. The film was not a financial success, as Beauchamp was too 'uppity' a character of which most white Americans at that time would not approve (Nesteby, 1982, p. 236).

Home of the Brave (1948) explores a black soldier's hysterical paralysis as a guilt-ridden reaction to the death of his white best friend killed in battle in the Pacific. The army psychiatrist uses his knowledge of racism to heal Moss by saying, 'You dirty nigger get up and walk!' This shocking scene is meant to illustrate the depths of racism in American society. *No Way Out* (1949) marks the screen debut of Sidney Poitier and shows how a black medical intern, Luther Brooks, is thought to be an easy target for an accusation of professional malpractice because of his colour. He is vindicated but only after an attempt on his life and a near race riot – a warning perhaps of the possible consequences of continued racial discrimination.

'Problem movies' died out by the early nineteen-fifties. Enormous increases in production costs and the breakup of the studio system after anti-trust proceedings against the industry, led to layoffs and to a reduction in the number of blacks employed. The industry concentrated on gimmicks, like 3-D, and epic blockbusters which afforded few opportunities for black actors and black-related subjects.

One strand of film production that continued yielded a cycle of

Southern Gothic movies that lagged fifteen to twenty years behind its literary counterpart. This policy unintentionally produced Southern films whose characteristics were in total contrast to the romantic portrayals of the region that had predominated in the cinema before the Second World War. The contrast was heightened because blacks were virtually absent from these films. It was this feature, combined with the increasing momentum of the Civil Rights movement in the late nineteen-fifties and early sixties, which ensured 'the death of Rastus' (Cripps, 1975, p.59), for it became increasingly difficult to portray blacks as contented, docile and loyal to whites (see Chapter 6).

The grotesque characters and grim plots also provided an indirect critique of the South. Such portrayals of the region were an implicit criticism of it and helped to undermine earlier romantic portrayals. The effect was heightened because the studios, desperate to attract the widest possible audience for the new films and counter television competition, reshaped the plots, using the more shocking and lurid scenes simply to thrill. Advertising material emphasised corruption and decadence (Campbell, 1981a, p.159). Up to 1962, more than twenty works by Southern writers were so adapted, including Tennessee Williams' *A Streetcar Named Desire* (1951) and *Suddenly Last Summer* (1959), Erskine Caldwell's *God's Little Acre* (1958), and Robert Penn Warren's *Band of Angels* (1957). In the last-named, set in the slavery era, there is no portrayal of the mythical Old South. Instead, the cruelty and lust of a slave-owner, and tensions between him, the overseer, and slave are highlighted. Such trends were in line with the gradual easing of Hollywood's period of self-censorship after 1954, aided by a series of Supreme Court decisions in obscenity cases and by liberalisation of views on such issues in the Catholic Church (Sklar, 1975, pp.295–6).

Throughout the late nineteen-fifties and early sixties, the Civil Rights campaign gathered increasing momentum in the Southern states, attracting not only nationwide but world-wide media coverage. By contrast, integration was still taboo on film and Hollywood mostly avoided dealing openly with such controversy. Johnson (1975, pp. 167–8) says the industry 'would hesitate to release a fiction film based upon the true life horrors experienced by white and Negro civil rights workers in the backward counties of Mississippi, Georgia and Alabama. To make such films today would be inflammatory and raise cries of anarchy.' In the North, discontent among blacks led to major riots during much of the sixties, and the cinema was even less willing to deal with these.

Even on issues like inter-racial sex and romance, Hollywood film-makers still tended to approach the subject primarily in terms of passing and the associated stereotype of the tragic mulatto. *Pinky* (1948) and *Lost Boundaries* (1949) were 'problem movies' dealing with these themes. Both contain strong scenes showing the problems and dangers to blacks posed by racism in the United States, but each avoids portraying inter-racial romance. Nevertheless, they suffered at the hands of Southern censors. In Atlanta cuts were ordered in *Pinky* and *Lost Boundaries* was banned as 'likely to have an adverse effect on the peace, morals and good order of the city' (quoted in Mapp, 1972, p. 39).

Film-makers and audiences then showed less interest in the impact of racism on black – white romance until the late nineteen-fifties. By this time the theme had been profitably used in foreign films, and was seen by Hollywood as another way of countering the continuing decline in cinema earnings in the United States. This, and shifts in the overall climate of opinion, led American film-makers to exert pressure to end the Production Code ban on portraying miscegenation. Darryl F. Zanuck's *Island in the Sun* (1957) treated the subject with sympathy, and confirmed the director's own statement that 'controversial pictures ... can be pretty good box office' (quoted in Leab, 1975, p. 210) by gross-ing over $8,000,000. The film showed two mixed romances but allowed no physical contact between the black man (Harry Belafonte) and the white woman (Joan Fontaine), a state of affairs that lasted well into the nineteen-sixties.

Other films were made to exploit the more titillating aspects of inter-racial sex, and also included (for the time) violent and sensational scenes as in *Band of Angels* (1958), *Kings Go Forth* (1958) and the remake of *Imitation of Life* (1959). Apart from all-black films like *Carmen Jones* (1953), these films usually starred white actresses in the pivotal role of tragic mulatto.

Three highly successful films dealt with inter-racial romance and sex by 'displacing' the issue – setting the films far from America so that any anti-racist message was implicit, and not too controversial. Of the three – *Love is a Many Splendored Thing* (1955), *Sayonara* (1957), and *South Pacific* (1958) – only *South Pacific* portrayed inter-racial relationships at all positively. Set in the Second World War, Ensign Nellie Forbush, from Little Rock(!), falls in love with a Frenchman who, unknown to her, has two mixed-race children by a previous marriage. (His wife is now dead.) On discovering this, she struggles to overcome her own race prejudice. In this she eventually succeeds, and agrees to marry him.

A parallel relationship involves a young white soldier and a Polynesian girl. Again, he finally overcomes his prejudice but is stopped from marrying her by his death in action. The film strongly implies that there is hope for integration and tolerance from the younger generation. Anti-fascist and anti-racist messages are skilfully woven into the narrative to give a moving and strikingly cumulative impact which avoids didacticism.

Apart from this, Hollywood could offer only the protagonists of *Guess Who's Coming to Dinner?* (1967), discussed later. For any daring or different explorations of racism and black life on film, the cinema goer had to turn to independent producers whose works were confined to small urban cinemas and the college rental market – the 'art movie' circuit.

The first American film to portray inter-racial marriage between a black man and a white woman was *One Potato, Two Potato* (1964). A white divorcee, Julie, who already has a small daughter, falls in love with and marries a black man, Frank. There are telling indicators of racism throughout the film – a policeman assumes that Julie is a prostitute because she is accompanied by Frank, and her ex-husband tells her 'You know how *they* feel about white women', and tries to rape her, confirming Frank's earlier comment, 'You know what's between us? Hate, riots, lynching, prejudice. It won't work.' He is wrong, but a high price is paid when a court awards custody of Julie's daughter to her biological father. Although tragic and at times melodramatic, the film implies that prejudice is social, not natural, and can therefore be changed. Critically acclaimed, it reached only a limited audience as an 'art movie'.

The same is true of *Shadows* (1960), produced on a tiny budget provided by John Cassavetes, and *Nothing But a Man* (1964). In the latter film, set in Alabama, Duff and Josie are a black married couple 'from opposite sides of the tracks'. The film sharply contrasts blacks and whites from the point of view of a black male, Duff. White employer power is underlined when Duff, refusing to be a 'white man's nigger' is sacked and blacklisted for trying to organise his black co-workers in a protest against unfair working conditions. The responses of two generations of blacks to white racism are explored in the relationships between Duff and his father-in-law, a minister, and between Duff and his own father. Josie's father counsels accommodation, telling Duff that if he would 'try living in a town like this instead of running free and easy you'd soon change your tune', while Duff in a later scene responds, 'You been stoopin' so long, Reverend, that you don't even know how to stand up straight no more. You just half a man.' Under the pressure of despair, Duff leaves Josie for the city and discovers his father, whom he thought dead, is alive. He finds him an unemployed, uneducated alcoholic taking out his frustrations upon a strong black woman. After his father's death, Duff returns to small-town married life with Josie, rejecting the city as a possible solution to the problems posed by racism. In the process, he rescues his illegitimate son from an urban nightmare – the fate of whose mother remains unknown.

The Cool World (1963) mostly employed non-professional actors to obtain greater realism. It depicted the seamier aspects of ghetto life and includes drug addiction, dope pushing, communal sex and gang killings. The film excited intellectuals and critics, but the overwhelmingly negative portrayals of blacks worried some commentators (for example, Mapp, 1972, pp. 94 – 6).

There were more parts for blacks in Hollywood films in the nineteen-sixties as pressure was exerted by the NAACP and the federal government (Cripps, 1978, p. 48), pushed by the force of events generated by the Civil Rights movement.

Directors could make indirect comments on the Civil Rights movement by incorporating blacks, or non-whites, in films displaced in time or space from the geographical area of current conflict. This approach was used in *South Pacific*, but the Western was more widely employed to explore white racism and black reactions to it. In some cases the historical record on film was also rectified to show that blacks played a role in 'winning the West'. John Ford's *Sergeant Rutledge* (1960), set in the eighteen-seventies, shows how whites who apparently respect Rutledge can turn and assume him to be guilty of rape and murder, simply because he is black. Rutledge is vindicated and white racism condemned, although this can be achieved only by depicting Rutledge, not only as innocent, but as superhuman in character.

Black characters symbolise the awakening of white liberal conscience over the treatment of Native Americans as well as of black people in *Rio Conchos* (1964), *Duel at Diablo* (1966), and *100 Rifles* (1969). Ralph Nelson directs with more daring in *Dual at Diablo*, where Toller, played by Poitier, is not preoccupied with the lot of whites, but leaves the army to be a successful horse trader 'who gives rather than takes orders' (Ellison, 1981, p. 185). In *The Scalphunters* (1968), Lee, a fugitive slave, is depicted as non-servile and although initially non-violent becomes militant because of his dealings with a number of captors. However, this growing militancy is undermined by the necessary happy ending in which black and white are reconciled. *Shenandoah* (1965), although set in Virginia during the Civil War, is structured like a Western. A farming family oppose what they see as the planters' war and in one incident, when Union troops overrun the area, they tell a black lad he is now free. Unlike many earlier stereotypes, he immediately runs off without a thought for his white master. Another romantic Old South formula is also neatly reversed when, after a tortuous set of events, the same black, now a Union soldier, encounters his former white friend on the battle ground and saves his life. The film was one of the top box office attractions of 1965.

Some mainstream films made more direct comments upon racism, although they tended to be heavily laced with liberal fantasy in order to spare the sensitivities of white audiences. Otto Preminger's *The Cardinal* (1963) shows Ossie Davis as a black Catholic priest, Father Gillis, who takes on the Ku Klux Klan when trying to desegregate a white Catholic school in Georgia. He receives threatening phone calls and hate mail before his church is burnt down. After a beating from the Klan, he testifies against them. The ending, although improbable, is highly satisfying for blacks and liberal whites because Klan members are convicted – although only of 'disorderly conduct ' – on the basis of a black's testimony.

To Kill a Mockingbird (1963) and *In the Heat of the Night* (1967) are both anti-racist films set in small Southern towns. *Mockingbird* has a powerful opening evoking the lost innocence of childhood, as the narrator, Jean Louise Finch – better known as Scout – recalls events in Alabama in 1935, as she pours over her box of mementoes. The imagined terrors of childhood and the real ones of white rural poverty and racism are so intimately blended in her memory that nostalgia triumphs over anti-racism. The film skilfully uses the device of seeing events through the eyes of children. Like Boo Radley, the simpleton, the children are shown to be able to differentiate clearly between right and wrong, especially when tutored by a liberal white middle-class adult. In a dramatically superb, but totally unrealistic, scene they shame a lynch mob into disbanding, and (for a while) save Tom Robinson, a black unjustly accused by a poor white teenage girl, Mayella Ewell, of rape. No reason is given in the film for the unjust and irrational behaviour of most whites, including the existence of a segregated courthouse and a mockery of a trial. The implication yet again is given that all would be well if only all whites were educated and enlightened like the judge, the sheriff, and Scout's father, Atticus, who defends Robinson! Like many liberal films of the period the narrative is structured entirely from a white point of view, and Atticus, not Tom Robinson, is the hero of the film. Like earlier more stereotypic films, black characters appear to have no existence apart from their relationships with whites. One of the film's strengths is its evocation of everyday life in a small Southern town in the thirties, but it is the life of white people only. Black people live literally on the periphery in shacks on the edge of town as Jem discovers when he visits Tom Robinson's wife with Atticus, but it is what the discovery means to *him* which is stressed. The problem of racism is portrayed as one which liberal whites can solve; blacks are shown as completely passive. Nevertheless, it is an important film with a consciously anti-racist message.

In the Heat of the Night provides a strong plot in which Tibbs, a black homicide detective from Philadelphia is unwittingly drawn into a murder investigation in Mississippi. Until his identity is revealed, Tibbs is automatically suspected of the murder because he is the only strange black in town. The lips of an otherwise inoffensive patrolman twist in hatred and contempt when he apprehends Tibbs. We are given a gallery of Southern white racists including ambushing rednecks and a landowner who only knows how to speak patronisingly to black people; he cannot cope with being questioned by Tibbs. Much of the film is in fact an answer to the question of a local white, 'What's that coloured boy doing in white man's clothes?' The murdered man, Colbert, was a Northern industrialist who plans to build a factory in the town. It is only because Tibbs takes the case that Colbert's widow agrees to go ahead, as she distrusts the locals and, it is implied, because she is a Northerner she is not prejudiced. This portrayal of the North, personified by the Colberts and Tibbs, as rational and forward-looking, and as an example to the backward-looking South, once again confirms the death of the traditional romantic portrayals of the region. This applies also to Southern white women. Both in this film, and in *Mockingbird*, it is 'poor white trash women' who are the immediate source of the problems to be resolved, not glamorous Scarletts or Jezebels!

In a New York setting, the major feature film *Madigan* (1968) incorporates police brutality against the son of a black minister in a subplot, and a black reaction of overwhelming reasonableness. As the police are reluctant to investigate, the minister begins to question his own earlier moderate attitudes, wondering if blacks had been right to call him 'an Uncle Tom, for using whatever influence I had to bring about peace and understanding'.

One aspect of many of the black roles in these films was the major new black stereotype to appear in the nineteen-fifties and sixties, that of the impossibly noble and virtuous superhero – the 'ebony saint'. To ensure acceptance of a black male lead the character must be 'whiter than white'. Reconciliation of equals can occur only if the black characters are 'more equal than equal'. It is true of the main black characters in Westerns like *Sergeant Rutledge* and *Rio Conchos*, and epitomised by many of the roles played by Sidney Poitier in which he is impeccably dressed, sincere, honest, engagingly self-sacrificing and sexually abstinent.

In *The Defiant Ones* (1958), Poitier and Tony Curtis play two fugitives chained together. Eventually, the chains are broken, and the black succeeds in leaping aboard a freight train – but Poitier sacrifices his chance of freedom by going back for a man who has scorned him. The idea of the two convicts chained together is effective dramatically; the fate of black and white in America is inextricably linked, and it is impossible to escape the consequences of racism. However, the stereotypic ending of the superhuman black being prepared to sacrifice his life for a white, tends to undermine any power the film might have had.

To Sir, With Love (1967) provides a totally different setting. Poitier plays Mark Thackeray, a middle-class professional who tames a class of unruly schoolchildren in London's East End through compassion, reason, firmness and consistency. He is shown as having no life of his own, and the inter-racial romance described in the book upon which the film is based disappears. When he finally gets a job for which he has been trained as an engineer, he tears up the acceptance letter, preferring to continue with his true vocation as an inspiring teacher cum social worker. By sheer force of character he is shown to wean a teaching colleague and the white pupils in his class from racism. Poitier brilliantly plays a powerful role within the limits imposed by an industry that was indifferent or hostile to black concerns (Baldwin, 1968). He conveys a feeling of repressed resentment and, at times, of repressed rage. But all is channelled into highly acceptable behaviour, and again he sacrifices himself for others – this time young white racists. It appears that many liberals were now ready to portray blacks in positive roles, but only if they became superhuman and self-sacrificing.

Other films which are variants on the same theme are *All the Young Men* (1960), *Lilies of the Field* (1963), *A Patch of Blue* (1965) and *In the Heat of the Night* (1967). In the highly popular *Guess Who's Coming to Dinner?* (1967), Dr John Prentice (Poitier) is the epitome of academic and social perfection and engaged to an educated white woman, Joanna Drayton. One commentator summarised the film's theme as 'whoever thought that nice young man was a Negro?' (Mapp, 1972, p. 165.) We are allowed one glimpse of the couple kissing in the rear view mirror of a taxi at the start of the film – apparently other love scenes were cut (Mapp, 1972, p. 161) – and we are later assured that *he* doesn't make love before marriage. Fears about the 'black buck' image apparently die hard, but rapidly if the circumstances dictate, as we see in the next chapter!

With all its faults and timidity, *Guess Who's Coming to Dinner?* was the only film up to the late nineteen-sixties to use inter-racial romance and sex to symbolise hopes for integration between black and white. So coolly does Poitier play the role that he hardly seems involved with his fiancée at times, distancing Prentice from the absurd behaviour that racism produces.

Poitier had misgivings about some of the roles he had to play – after making a *Patch of Blue* which required him to conceal his racial identity and deny his sexuality, he said that he was 'at his wit's end' (Mapp, 1972, p. 114). Nevertheless he believed that, as one of the few black stars, he had a duty to portray only positive images (Cripps, 1978, p. 49). He was increasingly attacked by black commentators for this position as the nineteen-sixties drew on and blacks looked for less accommodating roles. Victories in the Civil Rights movement and the emergence of 'Black Power' made many blacks impatient with what Poitier was trying to do.

Later reappraisals of Poitier's career acknowledged that he made whites take black characters seriously, at least while they were in the cinema (Bogle, 1988), and provided a model for later black dramatic roles: 'a broad spectrum of black performers ... owed [him] debts of style, manner, business, stifled smiles, flashes of silent anger, rhetorical pauses, and standing up to whites with more at his disposal than mere empty rage' (Cripps, 1980, quoted in Woll and Miller, 1987, pp. 59–60). Thus his roles broke with previous racist stereotypes. although 'empty rage', and worse, predominated in the short-lived 'blax-ploitation' film cycle of the early seventies.

Perhaps this is why Poitier accepted a totally different role in the *The Lost Man* (1969) – he is a war veteran, the 'lost man', who carries out a robbery to get money to support the families of imprisoned 'black brothers'. He also kisses the white leading lady but the inter-racial relationship ends with their deaths! The film did poorly at the box office. It followed *Uptight* (1968), produced and directed by Jules Dassin, in dealing with black revolution in the United States.

The period from the outbreak of the Second World War to the late nineteen-sixties was marked by a number of shifts in the portrayal of blacks in cinema. Despite much tokenism, Hollywood produced a number of films during and immediately after the war which portrayed black characters with dignity and sometimes in non-stereotyped roles. This wave of liberal and 'problem' movies died out in the early nineteen-fifties and the number of films with significant parts for blacks was extremely low during this decade. However, there were a few films, other than those with all-black casts, which featured blacks like Sidney Poitier and Harry Belafonte in leading roles. Uncertain how to proceed when departing from the pre-war stereotypes, screenwriters and directors produced yet another – black characters so selfless that no one could object to them on the grounds that they were demeaning, or accuse the film-makers of racism! The number of films dealing directly with racism was relatively small and many sought refuge in other times and places. Nevertheless, the overall tenor of films dealing with blacks and black concerns was clearly anti-racist, portraying African-Americans sympathetically. A small number of films made by independents explored the complex and differing responses of blacks to racism in depth but, although critically acclaimed in some cases, reached a relatively limited audience.

References

Alvarez, M. (1970) '*No Way Out* and *The Defiant Ones*', in E. Cortes and L. G. Campbell (eds), *Race and Ethnicity in the History of the Americas: A Filmic Approach*, University of California, Riverside (Latin American Studies Program Film Series No. 4), pp. 45–6

Baldwin, J. (1968) 'Sidney Poitier', *Look*, 32, pp. 50–4

Bogle, D. (1988) *Toms, Coons, Mulattoes: Blacks in US Films*, Crossroads, New York

Campbell, E. D. T. Jr (1981) *The Celluloid South*, University of Tennessee Press, Knoxville

Cawelti, J. G. (1973) 'Reflections on the new Western films: the Jewish cowboy, the black avengers, and the return of the vanishing American', *The University of Chicago Magazine*, Jan.–Feb., pp. 25–32

Couch, W. Jr (1950) 'The problem of negro character and dramatic incident', *Phylon*, 11, pp. 127-33

Cripps, T. S. (1975) 'The death of Rastus: negroes in American films since 1945', in Patterson (ed), pp. 53–64 (originally in *Phylon*, 28, 1967, pp. 267–75)

Cripps, T. S. (1977) *Slow Fade to Black: The Negro in American Film, 1900–1947*, Oxford University Press, New York

Cripps, T. S. (1978) *Black Film as Genre*, Indiana University Press, Bloomington and London

Cripps, T. S. (1980) 'The dark spot in the kaleidoscope: black images in American film', in R. M. Miller (ed), *The Kaleidoscope Lens: How Hollywood Views Ethnic Groups*, Jerome S. Ozer, Englewood Cliffs, NJ, pp. 15–35

Cripps, T. S. (1981) '*Casablanca, Tennessee Johnson* and *The Negro Soldier* – Hollywood liberals and World War II', in K. R. M. Short (ed), *Feature Films as History*, University of Tennessee Press, Knoxville, pp. 138–56

Cripps, T. S. and Culbert, D. (1979) '*The Negro Soldier* (1944): film propaganda in black and white', *American Quarterly*, 31, pp. 616–40

Ellison, M. (1981) 'Blacks in American Film', in Davies and Neve (eds), pp. 176–94

Jerome, V. J. (1950) 'The negro in American films', *Political Affairs*, 29, pp. 58–92

Johnson, A. (1965) 'The negro in American films: some recent works', in Patterson (ed), pp. 153–81 (originally in *Film Quarterly*, 18, pp. 14–30)

Jones, C. J. (1981) 'Image and ideology in Kazan's *Pinky*', *Literature/Film Quarterly*, 9, pp. 110–20

Koppes, C. R., and Black, G. D. (1987) *Hollywood Goes To War: How Politics, Profits and Propaganda Shaped World War II Movies*, I. B. Tauris & Co. Ltd, London

Leab, D. (1975) *From Sambo to Superspade: The Black Experience in Motion Pictures*, Houghton Mifflin, Boston

Mapp, E. (1972) *Blacks in American Films: Today and Yesterday*, The Scarecrow Press, Inc., Metuchen, NJ

Murray, J. P. (1973) *To Find an Image: Black Films from Uncle Tom to Superfly*, Bobbs-Merrill Co., Indianapolis

Nesteby, J. R. (1982) *Black Images in American Films, 1896–1954: The Interplay Between Civil Rights and Film Culture*, University Presses of America, Washington, DC

Noble, P. (1948) *The Negro in Films*, Skelton Robinson, London

Patterson, L. (ed) (1975) *Black Films and Film-makers: A Comprehensive Anthology from Stereotype to Superhero*, Dodd, Mead & Co., New York

Pines, J. (1975) *Blacks in Films: A Survey of Racial Themes and Images in the American Film*, Studio Vista, London

Poitier, S. (1981) *This Life*, Ballantine Books, New York

Roffman, P., and Purdy, J. (1981) *The Hollywood Social Problem Film: Madness, Despair, and Politics from the Depression to the Fifties*, Indiana University Press, Bloomington

Sklar, R. (1975) *Movie-Made America*, Chappell & Co., London

Warner, V. (1971) '*The Negro Soldier*: a challenge to Hollywood', in L. Jacobs (ed), *The Documentary Tradition: From Nanook to Woodstock*, Hopkinson and Blake, New York, pp. 224–5

Woll, A. L., and Miller, R. M. (1987) *Ethnic and Racial Images in American Film and Television: Historical Essays and Bibliography*, Garland Publishing, Inc., New York and London

14

From Blaxploitation to *The Color Purple*

The hints of black militancy and nationalism in films at the end of the sixties found full expression in movies of the early seventies, albeit in distorted forms. After victory in the battle for Civil Rights in the South, the urban riots which occurred in many Northern American cities in the latter half of the nineteen-sixties, and the rise of the Black Power movement, blacks turned increasingly to the promotion of positive self-images. These, apart from rejecting traditional racial stereotypes, also moved towards a rejection of white culture and mores. 'Black is beautiful' was the cry and Afro hairstyles became popular as hair straighteners and skin lighteners were thrown away. There was no longer any attempt to discourage an emphasis on black values and attitudes. Young blacks in particular became highly receptive to the expression of positive ideas about black culture in films.

The recession that Hollywood suffered in the mid nineteen-sixties provided an opportunity for many black producers, performers and technicians (Murray, 1973, p. 118). A number of independent companies sprang up to fill the gap as the major studios drastically cut back production. Some of these were run by black film-makers like Melvin Van Peebles, who made *Sweet Sweetback's Baadasssss Song* (1971) and Gordon Parks who made *Shaft* (1971). By Hollywood standards, both films were made on extremely low budgets but grossed $11 million and $18 million respectively in box office receipts. This achievement was all the more remarkable in the case of *Sweetback* as it was produced and distributed entirely outside established industry channels.

In *Sweetback* the hero is no cool, superior black who channels his resentment into acceptable behaviour, but a full-blown ghetto outlaw who is the natural product of 'whitey's' unjust laws. According to the credits, the stars are the 'Black Community of Los Angeles' and the

film is for 'all the black brothers and sisters who have had enough of
the Man [representing white police specifically, white society
generally]'. The film is episodic in structure, and often slides from a
political position that recommends being a 'bad-ass nigger' opposing
all things white, into a fantasy in which racist oppression is compensated for by superior black sexual performance. *Shaft* was hailed by some
as featuring the first true black counterpart of characters like Philip
Marlowe and James Bond. Richard Roundtree in the title role is cool
and invincible when handling the Mafia, the police and black militants
– and a great lover too, all in a style and setting reminiscent of nineteen-
forties *film noir*.

Hollywood finally seemed to realise the potential of black audiences,
particularly among the young. In this it was anticipating the more
general 'juvenilisation' of the medium. Many talented blacks and ex-
athletes were suddenly offered roles in what became known as 'blaxploitation' films. The highly profitable *Superfly* (1972) features a dope
pusher who outwits white police and black hoods while satisfying the
sexual needs of both black and white women. In all, there were nearly
two hundred imitations in which 'a string of witless, brutal black heroes
smashed the empires and fortunes of a succession of grotesque, boorish
white villains and their sexually unsatisfied white women.' (Cripps,
1978, p. 130.) The new black superhero had arrived on the scene and
with him the stereotypic 'black buck' in a new guise. Many of the films
were white action genres – urban private eye, cop, drug and caper
movies – reworked to include blacks.

Some black critics were disturbed by what they saw as a perpetuation
of portrayals of blacks as 'violent criminal, sexy savages' (Poussaint,
1974). Black leadership and the struggle for freedom were no longer
clothed in biblical imagery. In fact, Bennett (1971) condemned *Sweetback* as reactionary for its implication that black people were 'going to
be able to sc*** their way across the Red Sea ... If f***ing freed, black
people would have celebrated the millenium 400 years ago.' The
NAACP and other civil rights groups objected to blaxploitation films
as 'a rip-off ... potentially far more dangerous than Stepin Fetchit and
his lot' (quoted in Woll and Miller, 1987, p.63), and tried to get the
films censored. Mapp (1975) was troubled by the sexist portrayals of
black women in these films – although apparently not by similar
portrayals of white women. Large and mainly young black audiences
did not see it that way – they wanted, and got, blacks who won,
preferably at the expense of whites. Predictably, the response of

black performers was mixed – at least blaxploitation films meant work.

Monaco (1984, p. 187) points out that the 'Hollywood Renaissance' of 1968–70, was based to a significant extent on black films – not only blaxploitation movies – written, produced and acted by blacks, and sometimes even directed and financed by them as well. This success had also been made possible by continued black migration to Northern and Western cities, and the white flight to the suburbs, so that large downtown cinemas were increasingly patronised by blacks.

Films set in the Old South were not immune to the new portrayals of blacks. *Slaves* (1969) shows black families being split up, and slaves being maltreated and auctioned. Luke, played by Ossie Davis, resists and is transformed from an Uncle Tom to a new type superhero. Dionne Warwick made her first film appearance symbolising the stereotype of superior black sexual performance, playing the mistress of the white slave-owner. This feature was exploited in advertising for *Slaves* which declared 'he bought me for $650 but I own him'! (Campbell, 1981a, p. 185.) *Mandingo* (1975), together with its sequel *Drum* (1976), was a blaxploitation crossover film, i.e. it used 'uppity' blacks, inter-racial sex and violence to attract young black and white film goers. Both were financially very successful. *Mandingo* results from a strange mixture of apparently liberal attempts to correct stereotypes of the Old South, gestures to greater black self-awareness and pride, and the hunger for profits. Many incidents in the film are based on historically accurate facts, for example it is true that blacks surreptitiously learned to read and that they consistently tried to escape. White slave-owners and overseers did inspect slaves for purchase like livestock, and frequently raped black women. However, the inter-racial sex scenes are clearly meant to titillate, and the demeanour and language of defiant blacks owe more to (supposed?) ghetto behaviour of the seventies than to the realities of the slave plantation. The trappings of the Falconhurst plantation, and the social atmosphere are seedy and depressing – no great civilisation of ladies and gentlemen here! The film is a grotesque parody of the plantation myth and of a grotesque society. Old stereotypes recur as black sexuality, whether male or female, is shown to be superior to that of whites. Perhaps anti-racist in intent, the film's 'message' is conveyed by means of crude caricatures of all those involved.

There was, however, a broad split between the types of film portraying blacks, depending upon whether they were aimed at black inner-city or white suburban audiences. As we have seen, blaxploitation dominated the urban market. For the middle-brow group *Gone With the Wind* was re-released in 1971 and *Song of the South* in 1972, both doing well and the latter earning $5.9 million and placed sixteenth in the earnings table for its year (Campbell, 1981a, p. 175). The romantic South was revisited in two films promoted for family viewing by *Reader's Digest*. *Tom Sawyer*, ranking 25th at the box office in 1973, was produced as a musical comedy and described as a 'unique work of local history and folklore'. *Huckleberry Finn* (1974), although more serious in tone, marginalised slavery, and smoothed away the complexities of Twain's original novel. The black musical tradition was also a good standby and, suitably modified for white audiences, featured the artistry of black musicians in *Soul to Soul* (1971) and *Wattsax* (1973), and in 'biopics' like *Lady Sings the Blues* (1972) and *Leadbelly* (1975).

For the better educated, there were re-releases of Poitier's films, and new productions examining social issues and offering dramatic roles.

Production of these films depended upon the commitment of individuals and small groups whose notions of what cinema might do ran counter to the values of those who have always dominated the industry. Little had changed in this respect since Will Hays had consistently opposed films dealing with serious social and political themes in the nineteen-thirties and nineteen-forties, and Sam Goldwyn had made his much quoted remark to the effect that anyone looking for messages should go to Western Union. The prospects for a film project put together by committed stars, directors and promoters were poor unless one of the major distributors was prepared to back it – the latter were not obliged to handle any film and needed a financial incentive to do so (Davies, 1981, pp. 129–30). Distributors disliked 'political movies' because this was thought to jeopardise box office receipts, and their influence over the kinds of theme tackled was considerable.

Stars and 'bankable' directors were among the very few who got the opportunity to explore racism and highlight black issues outside the blaxploitation trend. Poitier directed himself in *Buck and the Preacher* (1972), a black Western in which Native Americans support blacks escaping from Southern peonage after the Civil War. The film is both tense and witty, and employed an unusually large number of blacks as technicians. Ossie Davis, who made his reputation as a black actor in the seventies, formed the Third World Cinema Corporation in 1970. It was designed to use the talents of, and provide jobs for, blacks, Puerto Ricans and other minority groups in New York (Monaco, 1984, pp. 194 – 6). The Corporation produced *Claudine* (1974) and *Greased Lightning* (1977) and Davis's idea for *Lady Sings the Blues* (1972) was 'stolen' by Motown Productions and finally by Hollywood in the guise of Paramount. Parks directed *Leadbelly* (1975), but Paramount failed to promote it.

Martin Ritt, a white, and for many years a 'bankable' director who consistently tackled contentious social and political issues, found that 'it's a problem to get money to make anything, particularly serious work' (Davies, 1981, p. 129). Nevertheless he made four films in the nineteen-seventies that dealt with race and racism and which did quite well at the box office.

The first of these, *The Great White Hope* (1970), based on a Pulitzer prize-winning play, is a 'biopic' of Jack Johnson – renamed Jefferson in the film – who became world heavyweight champion in 1910. In a significant early exchange Jefferson denies a black preacher's contention that he is fighting for his race – it is, he says, just a fight that will change nothing for the mass of blacks. He defeats a white fighter, but is himself finally defeated by the system because of his sexual relationship with a white woman. The couple are harassed by the FBI and flee to England. The film shows how the social pressures of racism destroy their relationship. She has an abortion because they are so poor, and he is driven to playing humiliating versions of Uncle Tom in Paris theatres. Eventually she commits suicide and it is only over her body that Jefferson gives voice to his realisation that racism has destroyed both his career and their relationship. Like *One Potato, Two Potato* it is one of the few films which shows how racism causes personal tragedy in inter-racial relationships.

Sounder (1972) and *Conrack* (1974) are both what Cripps (1978, p. 116) describes as black pastoral films in Southern rural settings. *Sounder* is set in Louisiana during the Depression. It is a low-key and moving film which shows how a black woman and her children cope when her husband has been jailed for stealing food to feed his family. The injustice of the situation is understated, as is the love of family members, being conveyed by exchange of glances and their willingness to do things for one another. Such patience and dignity functions to elicit sympathy from the audience and gives 'a rich and fully realised portrait of the black family in America' (Bogle, 1973, p. 240) that had not been achieved before. The portrait of the mother suggests the 'strong black women' who have so often held black American families together in reality, in contrast to Hollywood portrayals of them either as 'superstitious and grotesque crones' (Trumbo, quoted in Koppes and Black, 1987, p. 179) or as substitute mothers – mammies – for spoilt white people. The film was generally praised by critics, partly because it was a r lief from the surfeit of sex and violence elsewhere, but some attacked it for perpetuating the 'good nigger' stereotype through characters who were too good to be true (Mapp, 1975, p. 119) or for historical inaccuracy (Patterson, 1975).

Conrack is adapted from Pat Conroy's account of his own experiences as a white Southerner who spent several months in 1969 teaching black children on Dafuskie Island, South Carolina. The children mispronounce his name *Conrack*. It is a lightweight and enjoyable film, but irritating for its concern with how much better Conrack feels because he is no longer a racist rather than with the feelings of black people. It may have made some white liberals feel good, but it has a strongly patronising and missionary feel about it in terms of both race and class. The point of view we are forced to adopt is that of the white Conrack. As long as the children are fascinated by his trendy new teaching methods in class, Conrack is satisfied and takes no interest in other aspects of their lives or of any activities on the island. After a dispute over his teaching methods with the black principal and a racist white superintendent, he is sacked and, according to the film, leaves the children with no prospects for the future. The other characters in the film are only foils for a white outsider who can take risks because he can leave at any time. Civil rights groups boycotted the film (Nesteby, 1982, p. 243).

Some films took a different approach to attack black stereotypes and racism, successfully using the weapon of humour as *Claudine* (1974) and *Blazing Saddles* (1974) did in very different settings and in contrasting ways.

Claudine (1974) examines a situation which is the experience of many American black women, that of a ghetto mother raising children in the father's absence. It cleverly and wittily explores some of the issues and relationships involved. The mother, Claudine, and her children devise various stratagems to outwit the white social worker who represents patronising white bureaucracy, concealing 'unauthorised' earnings which include gifts from a new boyfriend. In a gentle play on black family life, it pokes fun at the stereotype of the unreliable black male and at various forms of teenage rebelliousness, all of which centre on the mother's response. It also manages a sly but affectionate dig at local Black Power supporters. Throughout, the film adopts the viewpoint of the black woman, and shows that Claudine's main concerns are – in order of priority – keeping her family together, finding a decent job, and maintaining the relationship with her boyfriend. It is refreshing to find a film that deals with matters of basic importance to many black families without a hint of condescension. Critics noticed the film but it did not earn outstanding profits. *Blazing Saddles* is set in the days of the 'Old West' and gets an anti-racist viewpoint across by parodying racist behaviour and racist stereotypes.

By the mid-seventies Hollywood realised that black audiences also watched many non-black films like *The Godfather* (1972), *The Exorcist* (1973) and *Chinatown* (1974), and that whites might therefore be attracted to films starring blacks in black stories, but directed and written by whites. Martial arts or 'kung fu' films which depended on violent revenge themes set in the Far East also began to attract young black audiences. The *Sweetback*-inspired fantasies of lust and power were replaced by metaphors of African-American experience in another culture (Cripps, 1978, p. 54). Apart from a few independent productions, the 'crossover' film, designed to attract both black and white audiences, replaced the black film by the mid-seventies.

A parallel development was that more blacks had jobs in the film industry than ever before, but with little participation in the production process and virtually no control over film content. Studios satisfied the letter of affirmative action guidelines by hiring more blacks in clerical and administrative positions but allowed little control either before or behind the camera (Monaco, 1984, pp. 187–8). Very few blacks worked regularly during the nineteen-seventies and the early eighties (Dempsey and Gupta, 1982).

Television also attracted and absorbed the small number of nationally-known black actors and actresses for television films like *The Autobiography of Miss Jane Pitman* (1974) and mini-series like *King* (1977), *Roots* (1977) and its sequel *Roots: The Next Generations* (1979). All were highly successful, partly because of the presence of well-known black actors. However, *Roots* appeared to be an aberration that had surprisingly little impact on subsequent television programming. Douglas (1978) suggests that treatments of black history in historical and rural settings are more acceptable to a general audience because the problems with which they deal – slavery and Southern Jim Crow – can be regarded as solved. The contemporary plight of blacks in the ghetto is not confronted. Another reason for the enormous viewing figures for *Roots* may be the general awakening of interest among all ethnic groups – including Italians, Germans, Puerto Ricans and Chicanos – in their cultural heritage in the early nineteen-seventies (Polenberg, 1980, pp. 243 – 50). Other films about black history or experience have been few and far between – *I Know Why the Caged Bird Sings* (1978), *Booker* (1983), *Crisis at Central High* (1981) – and many of the old stereotypes returned to the screen in a series, *North and South* (1985), that commanded an enormous audience.

Monaco (1984, pp. 187 – 8) summarises the position when he comments that 'the virtual disappearance of Black film in the mid-seventies has been the greatest feature of the American film business in recent years ... Blacks in film, as elsewhere, have in a way been co-opted, as Black aspirations have been trimmed, modified and channelled by the industry to serve its own ends.'

This change expressed itself in various ways. There has been little scope for black directors either within the Hollywood system or as independents. Occasionally a white director has been attracted, following Martin Ritt, by a novel or a script that gives blacks a prominent role or addresses black concerns, but black stars like Richard Pryor and Eddie Murphy seem to be more acceptable as comics than in dramatic roles. Black actors, and especially black actresses, had little opportunity to appear in films, let alone influence film content.

Most black directors have struggled in obscurity as independents, some making action films for the inner-city market, a few moving into television. Monaco (1984, pp. 205 – 7) cites the case of Bill Gunn, who made *Ganja and Hess* (1973), a film received with enormous enthusiasm at the Cannes film festival and which is an 'underground black classic' in the United States – it has only ever been seen by a few thousand people. However, the Black Film-Makers Federation of New York, founded in the late seventies, has increasing confidence in the prospects for black independents in the eighties, particularly because of the work of Spike Lee and Robert Townsend. Lee directed *She's Gotta Have It* (1986), an all-black comedy dealing with sexual politics using male characters representing a cross-section of the black community. The film was noticed by the critics, has done relatively well in the video rental market, and Lee subsequently got studio backing to make *School Daze* (1988).

Otherwise, the only black director to have worked regularly and to have been reasonably successful since 1974 is Michael Schultz. He made *Cooley High* (1975) and *Carwash* (1976), *Which Way Is Up?* (1977) and *Greased Lightning* (1977).

Greased Lightning is a 'biopic' based on the life of Wendell Scott, played by Richard Pryor. The film shows how Scott combats opposition, including racism, to become the first black stock car racing champion of America in 1970. Scott returns from fighting in Europe and uses his driving skills initially as a bootlegger, an occupation in which apparently whites and blacks work together. He does this in order to save the money to buy a garage. In these sequences the film plays upon Southern hillbilly stereotypes usually asociated solely with whites – moonshine, car chases, bumbling cops, the fat, frustrated redneck sheriff – but gives Scott and his friend Peewee an integral role in events. Southern racism is always clearly portrayed through humour. Eventually caught, Scott has to choose between jail and becoming 'black bait' as a stock car driver at the local track – the owner wants to increase the gate, attracting blacks to see Scott take on whites, and whites to see him humiliated, or worse. Scott turns the tables, finds a white friend, and even has time to desegregate a restaurant on his way to becoming champion. The film also portrays changes in attitudes and behaviour as the Civil Rights movement progresses without labouring the point – for example there are 'colored only' signs at the small-town racetrack and rigid segregation of crowd in the late forties compared with their complete absence by 1970, and contempt and hatred at the track turn to mutual respect.

Since the early seventies and the demise of the blaxploitation movie, the situation for blacks in and behind movies is again bleak. The old stereotypes have largely disappeared, but the number of movies in which blacks and their history and lives are treated seriously is still minute, and there are still no mainstream commercial films in which the hero/heroine *happens* to be black – a black *Jagged Edge* or *Fatal Attraction*. In many mainstream commercial films, blacks are still non-existent, token, or treated with subtle racism.

For example there is unintentional racism in films like *The Deep* (1977), and racist attitudes pervade films like *Rocky* (1976) in which a white fighter knocks down a parody of Muhammed Ali. In *Star Wars* (1977) and *The Empire Strikes Back* (1980) evil is black or foreign and sinister, although balance is contrived by making a good rebel black in the latter. In films like *Angel Heart* (1986), black people are again presented as both sinister and exotic, and involved in practices like black magic and voodooism.

Parts for blacks are therefore still rare; when Spielberg was casting *The Color Purple* (1985) he commented on the wealth of black acting talent available which is rarely used. This situation is even worse for black women; the NAACP became so disgusted with the paucity of roles for women that it suspended its image award for best film actress in 1981.

Those mainstream films which do feature blacks or black history tend to be unusually good; and some of them have even become popular! In 1979 Martin Ritt directed *Norma Rae* about the unionisation of a textile factory in the South. Black – white relationships are portrayed in a positive way, and part of the fight to unionise the factory is to overcome racism among the workers so that they can fight back together. Blacks are shown therefore in an extremely sympathetic light, but they are not very important in the narrative structure of the film, which is really about a white woman, Norma Rae, and her politicisation. However, there are some significant scenes in which she and the other white workers are shown either as overcoming racism or as being anti-racist.

In the modern *film-noir*, *Remember My Name* (1979), about a falsely imprisoned woman seeking revenge on her ex-husband, black – white relationships are similarly portrayed. Several blacks have minor roles, and Moses Gunn as the janitor has a significant one. All are allowed to function as characters in the narrative without condescension or subtle racism. This is a striking feature of the film, because it is still so rare.

Sympathetic films in which blacks have important or even central parts, although rare, are among some of the best films of the past decade. Among these are *A Gathering of Old Men* (1987), *A Soldier's Story* (1984), *The Killing Floor* (1984), *Freedom Road* (1979) and *The Color Purple* (1985).

A Gathering of Old Men is based on the powerful novel about racism in Louisiana by Ernest Gaines. A black man shoots and kills a viciously racist white man in the nineteen-seventies. A group of old black men all claim to have committed the crime, each giving excellent reasons why he might have done so. Any black man, it seems, would have had reason to kill him. The humiliations and disappointments of their lives as black people living in the heart of Louisiana are gradually unfolded as they tell their tales. The young white girl, who genuinely wishes to help, is finally seen as suffering from racism herself – however subtle, it is just as poisonous.

The Killing Floor (1984), which took the producer over ten years to finance, is arguably the most powerful film made about black – white relationships within the organised working class. Set in the 'Red Summer' of 1919 in Chicago, the year of the worst race riots ever seen in the city, it explores the divisive effect of racism among workers in the meat-packing factories. It succeeds in portraying seminal events, the migration from the South of black rural workers, the effects of the

Hollywood realised that black films could be modified and directed at a wider audience, and that blacks would watch many films with few or no black characters, most film directors have ignored black actors and actresses. The old stereotypes can no longer be used, but the industry is still unwilling to treat black characters in any other way. Nor does it address the particular issues and problems of blacks and rarely focuses on any aspects of black history – it is usually left to the very small number of committed independent producers to make films of this kind.

References

Adams, M. (1981) 'How come everybody down here has three names?', in French (ed), pp. 143–55

Bennett, L. Jr (1971) 'The emancipation orgasm: sweetback in wonderland', *Ebony*, 26, p. 106ff

Bogle, D. (1973) *Toms, Coons, Mulattoes, Mammies and Bucks: An Interpretive History of Blacks in American Films*, Viking Press, New York

Bogle, D. (1988) *Toms, Coons, Mulattoes: Blacks in US Films*, Crossroads, New York

Campbell, E. D. T. Jr (1981a) *The Celluloid South*, University of Tennessee Press, Knoxville

Campbell, E. D. T. Jr (1981b) '"Burn Mandingo Burn": the plantation South in film', in French (ed), pp. 107–16

Chappell, F. (1978) 'The image of the South in film', *Southern Humanities Review*, 12, pp. 303–11

Cripps, T. S. (1978) *Black Film as Genre*, Indiana University Press, Bloomington and London

Cripps, T. S. (1980) 'The dark spot in the kaleidoscope: black images in American film', in R. M. Miller (ed), *The Kaleidoscope Lens: How Hollywood Views Ethnic Groups*, Jerome S. Ozer, Englewood Cliffs, NJ, pp. 15-35

Davies, P. (1981) 'A growing independence', in Davies and Neve (eds), pp. 119–35

Davies, P., and Neve, B. (eds) (1981) *Cinema, Politics and Society in America*, Manchester University Press, Manchester

Dempsey, M. and Gupta, U. (1982) 'Hollywood's color problem', *American Film*, 7, pp. 67–70

Douglas, P. (1978) 'The bleached world of black TV', *Human Behaviour*, 7, pp. 63–6

Ellison, M. (1981) 'Blacks in American Film', in Davies and Neve (eds), pp. 176–94

Fiedler, L. A. (1979) *The Inadvertent Epic: From Uncle Tom's Cabin to Roots*, Simon and Schuster, New York

French, W. (ed) (1981) *The South on Film*, University Press of Mississippi, Jackson (special issue of *Southern Quarterly*, 19 (3/4))

Gulliver, A. C. (ed) (1974) *Black Images in Films: Stereotyping and Self-Perception as Viewed by Black Actresses*, Afro-American Studies Program, Boston University, Boston

Koppes, C. R., and Black, G. D. (1987) *Hollywood Goes To War: How Politics, Profits and Propaganda Shaped World War II Movies*, I. B. Tauris & Co. Ltd, London

Leab, D. J. (1975) *From Sambo to Superspade: The Black Experience in Motion Pictures*, Houghton Mifflin, Boston

Mapp, E. (1972) *Blacks in American Films: Today and Yesterday*, The Scarecrow Press, Inc., Metuchen, NJ

Mapp, E. (1975) 'Black women in films: a mixed bag of tricks', in Patterson (ed), pp.196–205

Monaco, J. (1984) *American Film Now*, Plume/New American Library, New York and London

Murray, J. P. (1973) *To Find an Image: Black Films from Uncle Tom to Superfly*, Bobbs-Merrill Co., Indianapolis

Nesteby, J. R. (1982) *Black Images in American Films, 1896–1954: The Interplay Betwwen Civil Rights and Film Culture*, University Presses of America, Washington, DC

Patterson, L. (1975) '*Sounder* – a Hollywood fantasy?', in Patterson (ed), pp. 106–8

Patterson, L. (ed) (1975) *Black Films and Film-makers: A Comprehensive Anthology from Stereotype to Superhero*, Dodd, Mead & Co., New York

Polenberg, R. (1981) *One Nation Divisible: Class, Race and Ethnicity in the United States since 1938*, Penguin, Harmondsworth

Poussaint, A. F. (1974) 'Blaxploitation movies: cheap thrills that degrade blacks', *Psychology Today*, 7, p. 26ff

Stephens, L. C. (1981) 'Black women in film', in French (ed), pp. 164–70

Walton, B. (1981) 'Black culture in films' *Phylon*, 42, pp. 194–203

Woll, A. L., and Miller, R. M. (1987) *Ethnic and Racial Images in American Film and Television: Historical Essays and Bibliography*, Garland Publishing, Inc., New York and London

Index

abolitionists, 6–7
African nations, new, 64
African-Americans, 8
  discrimination against in Second
    World War, 64
  disfranchisement of, 36, 38–9,
    49, 72
  early attitudes to film, 124–5
  enslavement of, 3–4
  resistance under slavery, 6–7
  treatment after Civil War, 27–9,
    36
African-American autobiography,
  32, 52, 86, 95–6
African-American film directors
  and producers, 124, 129–31,
  144–5, 163–4, 170–1
African-American literature,
  women writers, 112, 174
African-American men
  in fiction, 15, 23, 31–2, 41–2,
    63, 78–9, 97, 115; *see also*
    interracial romance; stereotype
  in film, 23, 123, 124, 125–7,
    128, 139–40, 142–3, 148–9,
    150–1, 158, 163–4; *see also*
    interracial romance; stereotype
African-American women
  in fiction, 15, 42, 43, 53, 87–94,
    99, 101, 106–17; *see also* inter-
    racial romance; stereotype
  in film, 122, 123–4, 127, 128,
    139, 140, 156, 157, 165, 167,

168–9, 173–4; *see also* inter-
  racial romance; stereotype
  myth of promiscuity in, 99; *see*
    also stereotype
African-American women's writing,
  70, 108
aggressive black stereotypes; *see*
  stereotype
Ali, Muhammad, 173
American Socialist Workers' Party,
  75
American War of Independence, 4
Angelou, Maya, 86, 96, 108, 143
anti-Communism, 65
Anti-Slavery League, 6
anti-slavery movement, 5
Aptheker, Herbert, 98
Armstrong, Louis 135, 149
art movie circuit, 154
Atlanta Constitution, 13, 14
audiences, fiction
  changing, 45–6
  for Fast's work, 81
  for Tourgee's work, 36, 37
  for Uncle Remus stories, 21–2,
    23
  Northern 31, 38, 49
audiences, film, 121, 122, 128, 130
  black, 130, 138, 144–5, 163–5,
    166–7
  differences in, 165–6
  ghetto, 130, 145, 164

backlash, white, 66, 67
Bakke decision, 68–9
Baldwin, James, 68
Bambara, Toni Cade, 108
Barnett, Neema, 70
Baskette, James, 23
Beavers, Louise, 143
Belafonte, Harry, 153, 160
Birth of a Nation, The
  black protest against, 128
  white liberal attitudes to, 128
Black actors' union, 149
Black Aesthetic movement, 68
'Black Cabinet', 143
black church, attitude to film, 124
Black Codes, 27
Black Film-Makers Federation of
  New York, 170
black film musicals, 145, 149, 153,
  166
Black Panther Party, 68
Black Power, 68, 103, 159, 163
black rapist, myth of, 21, 49, 86,
  97, 99, 102, 126–7, 138
blackface in film, 122
blacklisting, 65
blaxploitation films, 164–6, 171
blockbuster films, 151
Bond, James, 164
Breen Code, 137–8; *see also* Prod-
  uction Code Administration of
  1934
Breen, Joseph, 138
Bricks Without Straw, 26–37
Brooks, Clarence, 142
Brotherhood of Sleeping Car
  Porters, 75
Brown, John, 9

Cable, George Washington, 31, 40,
  72
Caldwell, Erskine, 137, 141, 152
Catholic Church, liberalisation of,
  152
Catholic League of Decency, 137
censorship, film
  easing of, 153, 174
  Hays office, 129

  in South, 129, 151, 153
  Production Code of 1930, 137
  Production Code Administration
    of 1934, 137–8
Chesnutt, Charles, 22, 38–47, 72,
  84 76, 116, 134
civil rights
  attacks upon, 121
  litigation over in thirties, 134
Civil Rights Act, 1875, 38
Civil Rights Act, 1964, 67
Civil Rights Movement, 23, 37,
  65–7, 152, 163, 171
  and Stepin Fetchit, 143
  effect on film, 152, 156
  effects of racism in, 106–8
  experience of black women in,
    87–8, 106, 108
  experience of white women in,
    67, 106–7
  gains of, 67
  influence in North, 67–8
  splits within, 67, 106–7
Civil War 5, 9, 123
Clansman, The, 48–57, 102, 125
Cleaver, Eldridge, 66
Cold War, 65
Colonel's Dream, The, 45
colonial status, of South, 137
Comunist Party of the USA
  (CPUSA), 73, 74–5
communists, 65
Confessions of Nat Turner, The, 76,
  95–105, 108, 161, 175
Congress of Racial Equality
  (CORE), 66
  expulsion of whites from, 67
Conjure Woman, The, 38–47
Constitutional Convention, 5
convict lease system, 29, 39
'coon' stereotypes; *see* stereotype
Cooper, James Fenimore, 30
CORE; *see* Congress of Racial
  Equality
cotton gin, and slavery, 5
CPUSA; *see* Communist Party of
  the United States
Crisis, The, 128

Crosby, Bing, 150
crossover films, 165, 169
Cullen, Countee, 63
Curtis, Tony, 158

Davis, Ossie, 156, 166–7
Debs, Eugene, 61
Depression of 1930s, 62
   and film industry, 136
   and escapist films, 140
discrimination, racial, vii, 2, 29,
   38, 61, 62, 64, 65, 72, 75, 121
disfranchisement, 38–9, 49, 72
Dixon, Thomas, 48–58, 88, 102,
   125
Douglass, Frederick, 6, 85, 98, 125

Ebony, 69
education
   and desegregation, 65, 66, 68–9
   desire for by blacks, 86
Eisinger, Charles, 76, 80
Elkins, Stanley, theories of slavery,
   96, 97
Ellington, Duke, 149
Ellis, Trey, 70
exotic primitive stereotype; *see*
   stereotype

Fast, Howard, 29–30, 33, 72–83,
   84, 85–6, 116
Faulkner, William, 137, 151
Fetchit, Stepin, 136, 140, 142–3
film censorship; *see* censorship, film
First World War, 61
Fontaine, Joan, 153
Fool's Errand, A, 31
Ford, John, 155
Foster, William, 124
Freedom Rides, 66–7
Freedom Road (novel), 33, 72–83,
   85–6, 116
Freud, Sigmund, 135

Gaines, Ernest, 172
gangster films, black, 145
Garvey Movement, 62
Genovese, Eugene, 100

ghetto cinemas, 130, 145
ghetto life on film, 130–1, 135,
   155, 157, 159, 163–4, 168–9
Gilpin, Charles, 128
Goldwyn, Sam, 166
Gone With the Wind (novel), 63, 141
Green, Paul, 63
Griffith, D.W., 124, 125–6
   and racism, 127
Gunn, Bill, 170

Hardwick, Leon, 23
Hardy, Thomas, 78
Harlem Renaissance, 63, 134
Harris, Joel Chandler, 3–25, 30,
   36, 46, 54, 88
Hayes–Tilden compromise, 28, 38
Hays, Will, 166
Hays Office, *see* censorship, film
Hicks, Granville, 74
Holliday, Billie, 135
Hollywood
   and anti-racism, 149–50
   and racism, 127–9
   black expectations of, 150–1
   recession in 1960s, 163
Horne, Lena, 145, 149
House Un-American Activities
   Committee (HUAC), 150
Hubbell, Jay, 80
Hughes, Langston, 63
Hurst, Fannie, 142
Hurston, Zora Neale, 70, 87

immigrant working classes, and
   film, 121
imperialism, 21, 39, 49, 55, 144
indentured labour, 3
Industrial Workers of the World
   (the Wobblies), 73

Jackson, Jesse, 69–70
jester stereotype; *see* stereotype
Jim Crow, 86, 123, 125, 169
Johnson, James Weldon, 63
Johnson, Lyndon, 67
Jones, LeRoi, 114
Joyce, James, 78

180 *Index*

Kansas – Nebraska Act, 8
Kennedy, William, 8
Kerouac, Jack, 78
Keystone Cops series, 124
King, Martin Luther, 66, 67
  assassination of, 68
KKK, *see* Ku Klux Klan
Knights of the White Camellia,
  48
Kristofferson, Kris, 173
Ku Klux Klan, 28, 29, 31 – 2, 48,
  50
  and Federal Election Acts, 28
  composition of, 33
  in fiction, 48 – 50, 55 – 6
  in film, 126, 128, 141, 156
  re-emergence of, 61 – 2
Kung Fu films, 169

Lang, Fritz, 138, 145
Lee, Spike, 70, 170
Leopard's Spots, The, 125
Lewis, Sinclair, 63, 130
Lincoln's Dream, 129
Little Rock, Arkansas, 66, 153
local colour, 8, 13, 20
  in Chesnutt, 40
  novels, 26, 30, 49
  stories, 20
London, Jack, 21
Louis, Joe, 145
lynching, 21, 39, 49, 62, 86
  on film, 138 – 9, 150

macho stereotype; *see* stereotype
McCullers, Carson, 76
McDaniel, Hattie, 17, 140, 142,
  143
McKay, Claude, 63
McMillan, Terry, 70
McQueen, Butterfly, 140
magazines, Northern, 13, 30
mainstream films, and anti-racism,
  156 – 9
'mammy' stereotype; *see* stereotype
Man in the Grey Flannel Suit, The, 81

Manifest destiny, 49
maroons, 7
Marshall, Paule, 108
men, black; *see* African-American
  men
Mencken, H. L., 137
Meridian, 106 – 18
'message' films, 166 – 8
MGM, 149
Micheaux, Oscar, 130, 131, 145
miscegenation 122, 129, 139
Mississippi Freedom Summer, 69
Mitchell, Margaret, 56, 141
'Monkey Trial', 137
Montgomery bus boycott, 66
Moreland, Mantan 145
Morrison, Toni, 108
Murphy, Dudley, 143
Murphy, Eddie, 170, 174
Muse, Clarence, 215

National Association for the
  Advancement of Colored
  People (NAACP), 61, 62, 65,
  66, 72, 128, 129, 143, 148, 164
Native Americans, 109, 155
Native Son, 87, 92, 108
Nazi-Soviet Non-Aggression Pact,
  74
Nelson, Ralph, 155
New Criticism, 76
New Deal, 62 – 3
New England Anti-Slavery Society,
  6
New Masses, The, 74
New South, The, portrayals on
  film, 135, 136 – 7, 138, 150 – 1,
  152, 156 – 7, 167 – 8
newspaper competition with film,
  150
Nixon, Richard, 68
Noble brothers, 129
Norris, Frank, 21
Northwest Ordinance, 5
novels, oppositional, 26, 36, 84; *see
  also* proletarian novel; socialist
  novel

Office of War Information (OWI), 148, 149
O'Hara, Scarlett, 140–1
O'Neill, Eugene, 63, 144

Page, Thomas Nelson, 13, 30
Page, Walter Hines, 45
Parks, Gordon, 163
Parks, Rosa, 66
passing, in film, 122, 130, 142, 153
peonage, economic, 27, 29, 39, 49
People's Party, The, 73
Petry, Ann, 84–94, 116
Phillips, U. B., 97
plantation stereotype; *see* stereotype; Old South, The
Poitier, Sidney, 151, 155, 158–9, 160, 265
popular culture, definition of, ix
Populist movement, 39, 73
Preminger, Otto, 156
'problem movies', 150, 151, 153
Production Code Administration of 1934; *see* censorship
Progressive movement, 61
proletarian literature, 74
Prosser, Gabriel, 96
Pryor, Richard, 170, 171, 174

race, debate on, vii–viii
'race movies', 130–1, 144–5
race riots, 129, 151, 152, 163
racism, definition of, vii–viii
radio competition with film, 150
Rainbow Coalition, 69–70
Randolph, A. Philip, 64, 75
Ransom, John Crowe, 76
Rastus films, 122
Reade, Charles, 30
Reagan administration, 69
Reconstruction, 26, 28–9, 38, 49, 82, 85–6
  in fiction, 31–7, 55, 77
  in film, 125–7, 140–1, 173
Reconstruction Acts of 1867, 27–8
Reconstruction, Radical; *see* Reconstruction
Reconstruction, Second, vii, 65, 82;

  see also Civil Rights Movement
'Red Summer', 62, 129, 172
registration of black voters, 65, 66–7
Rena Walden, 45
Republican Party, 28, 29, 123
Rideout, Walter, 73, 80
Ritt, Martin, 167, 170
Robeson, Paul, 130, 139, 144, 145
Robinson, Bill, 140, 145
Rogers, Will, 143
Rollins, Howard, 173
romance, interracial
  in fiction, 106–7, 112–16
  in film, 153–4, 159, 164, 165, 167
Roosevelt, Franklin D., 62, 64
Roundtree, Richard, 164
Rushing, Jimmy, 135

Sambo films, 122
Schultz, Michael, 170
SCLC; *see* Southern Christian Leadership Conference
Scott, Sir Walter, 30
screwball comedies, 136
Scriven, Abream, 85
Second World War, 63–4, 75–6, 92
  and individual liberties, 74–5
segregation, viii, 2, 38, 61, 64, 65, 72, 75
servants, black, in film, 123–4, 128, 139, 140, 142
'sharecropper realism', 137
sharecropping, 39, 137
slave culture, vii, 8
slave labour, 3–4
slave narratives, 6, 95
slave revolts, 14
slavery
  arguments to justify, viii, 6, 8
  family under, 84–85, 101
  in fiction, 14, 15–20, 40–45, 55, 97–102
  in film, 123, 124, 126, 139, 140, 152, 165
Smith Act, 1941, 75

Smith, Bessie, 143
SNCC; *see* Student Nonviolent
    Coordinating Committee
Social Darwinism, 21, 39
Socialist Party, 73
Solid South, The, 72
sound, conversion in cinema, 134
South, The Old (*see also* slavery)
    portrayals in fiction, 8, 13, 22,
    26, 96–7; *see also* stereotype
    portrayals in film, 123–4, 125–6,
    139, 150, 152, 165–6, 172;
    see also stereotype
South, 'embarrassing New', 136–7
Southern Christian Leadership
    Conference (SCLC), 66
Southern film censorship; *see*
    censorship
Southern Gothic films, 151–2
Southern Gothic school of
    literature, 137
Spielberg, Steven, 171
Stalin, Joseph, 144
stereotype
    aggressive black, 49, 124, 125–7,
    163–5
    'coon', 121–2, 140, 142–3
    exotic primitive, 63, 72, 135, 149
    jester, 128
    macho, 164, 174
    'mammy', 123, 139, 168
    plantation, 8, 13
    tragic mulatto, 122, 127, 142,
    153
    Uncle Tom, 123, 128, 139, 143
Stevens, Thaddeus, 126
Street, The, 84–94, 106, 109, 116
Stribling, T.S., 63
Student Nonviolent Coordinating
    Committee (SNCC), 60
Styron, William, 95–105
suburbanisation, 105
    and segregation, 65
    impact on cinema audiences,
    150, 165
superhero stereotype
    of fifties and sixties, 158–9, 160
    of seventies, 163–4

Supreme Court
    1954 decision, 65
    1956 decision, 66
    reverses civil rights decisions, 68
    revokes protection after Recon-
    struction, 38

Taft–Hartley Act, 65
television
    competition with film, 150
    roles for blacks, 169–70
Temple, Shirley, 140
Ten Black Writers Respond, 100
Third Life of Grange Copeland, The,
    108–9
Third World Cinema Corporation,
    166
Tobacco Road, 141
Toomer, Jean, 63
Tourgee, Albion, 26–37, 49–50,
    72, 84, 88
Townsend, Robert, 170
Turner, Nat, 7, 96–103
Twain, Mark, 31, 166

Ulysses, 78
Uncle Tom stereotypes; *see* stereo-
    type
Uncle Tom's Cabin (novel), 8
United Sons and Daughters of the
    American Revolution, 128

Van Peebles, Melvin, 163
Van Tilburg Clark, Walter, 76
Vesey uprising, 7
Vidor, King, 135
Vietnam War, 68
Voting Rights Act, 1965, 67

Walker, Alice, 15, 84, 106–18,
    173–4
Wallace, George, 68, 69
Wallace, Michele, 106, 114
Warren, Robert Penn, 76, 152
Warwick, Dionne, 165
Washington, Booker T., 125
Washington, George, 4
Waters, Ethel, 149

Watson, Tom, 38–9
Westerns, and anti-racism, 155–6
  black, 145, 155–6, 166
Whipper, Leigh, 149
Williams, Sherley Anne, 103
Williams, Tennessee, 152
Wilson, Woodrow, 61, 127
Wister, Owen, 21
women, African-American; *see*
  African-American women
women, African-American and
  white, in Civil Rights move-
  ment, 87–8, 106–17
women, white

in fiction, 41, 44–5, 51, 54, 99,
  101–2, 110–11, 112; *see also*
  romance, interracial
in film, 126–7, 139, 140–1,
  153–5, 156, 157, 159, 164,
  165, 167, 172; *see also* romance,
  interracial
Women's Movement, 107
Wood, Clement, 63
Wright, Richard, 32, 74, 86, 87

X, Malcolm, 32, 67–8, 86, 89, 96,
  103, 145

Zanuck, Darryl F., 153

Filmography

100 Rifles (1969), 155

Alice Adams (1935), 142
All the Young Men (1960), 158
Angel Heart (1986), 171
Arrowsmith (1931), 142
*Autobiography of Miss Jane Pitman,
   The* (1974), 169

Band of Angels (1957), 152, 153
Bataan (1943), 149
Beverley Hills Cop (1984), 174
Big House, The (1930), 137
Birth of a Nation, The (1915), 48, 49,
   61, 76, 124, 125–8, 129, 131,
   153, 160
Birth of a Race, The (1919), 129
Black and Tan (1930), 144
Blazing Saddles (1974), 168, 169
Body and Soul (1924), 130
Booker (1983), 170
Borderline (1930), 144
Bronze Buckaroo, The (1936), 145
Buck and the Preacher (1972), 137

Cabin in the Cotton (1932), 137
Cabin in the Sky (1943), 149
Cardinal, The (1963), 156
Carmen Jones (1958), 153
Carwash (1976), 170
Casablanca (1942), 148
Chinatown (1974), 169
Claudine (1974), 168–9

Color Purple, The (1985), 15, 131,
   171–2, 173–4
Confederate Spy, The (1910), 124
Conrack (1974), 167, 168
Cool World, The (1963), 155
Cooley High (1975), 272
Cotton Pickin' Days (1930), 139
Crash Dive (1943), 149
Crisis at Central High (1981), 170

David Harum (1934), 143
Deep, The (1977), 171
Defiant Ones, The (1958), 158
Dixiana (1930), 139
Dixie (1943), 150
Drum (1976), 165
Duel at Diablo (1958), 155
Duke is Tops, The (1938), 145

Emperor Jones, The (1933), 144
Empire Strikes Back, The (1980),
   171
Exorcist, The (1973), 169

Fatal Attraction (1988), 171
Freedom Road (1979), 173
Fury (1936), 138

Ganja and Hess (1973), 170
Gathering of Old Men, A (1987), 172
Godfather, The (1972), 169
God's Little Acre (1958), 152
God's Step Children (1938), 145

Gone With the Wind (1939), 17, 140–1, 166
Greased Lightning (1977), 170–1
Great White Hope, The (1970), 167
Green Pastures (1936), 131, 138
Guess Who's Coming to Dinner? (1967), 154, 159

Hallelujah (1929), 131, 135–6, 139
Harlem is Heaven (1932), 145
Harlem Rides the Range (1935), 145
Hearts and Flags (1911), 124
Hearts in Dixie (1929), 131, 135, 139
His Trust (1911), 124
His Trust Fulfilled (1911), 124
Home of the Brave (1948), 151
Homesteader, The (1919), 130
Huckleberry Finn (1974), 166

I Am a Fugitive from a Chain Gang (1932), 136, 137
I Know Why the Caged Bird Sings (1978), 170
Imitation of Life (1934), 142
Imitation of Life (1959), 153
In Old Kentucky (1910), 124
In the Heat of the Night (1967), 156, 157, 158
In This Our Life (1942), 148–9
Informer, The (1912), 124
Intruder in the Dust (1949), 150–1
Island in the Sun (1957), 153

Jagged Edge (1985), 171
Jezebel (1938), 140, 142
Judge Priest (1934), 139, 140, 142

Killing Floor, The (1984), 172–3
King (1977), 169
Kings Go Forth (1958), 153

Lady Sings the Blues (1972), 166, 167
Last Mile, The (1930), 137
Leadbelly (1975), 166, 167
Lilies of the Field (1963), 158
Little Colonel, The (1935), 140
Littlest Rebel, The (1935), 140
Lost Boundaries (1949), 153

Lost Man, The (1969), 159
Love is a Many Splendored Thing (1955), 153

Madigan (1968), 157
Mandingo (1975), 165
Masher, The (1907), 122
Mississippi (1935), 139, 141
Moon Over Harlem (1937), 145

Negro Soldier, The (1942), 149
Nigger, The (1915), 122
No Way Out (1949), 151
Norma Rae (1979), 172
North and South (1985), 170
Nothing But a Man (1964), 154–5

Octoroon, The (n.d.), 122
One Potato, Two Potato (1964), 154
Our Gang series, 128
Ox-Bow Incident, The (1943), 149

Patch of Blue, A (1965), 158, 159
Pinky (1948), 153

Rainbow on the River (1936), 139
Realisation of a Negro's Ambition, The (1916), 129
Remember My Name (1979), 172
Rio Conchos (1964), 155, 158
Rocky (1976), 171
Roots (1977), 149, 169–70
Roots: The Next Generations (1979), 169

Sahara (1943), 149
St Louis Blues (1929), 143
Saunders of the River (1936), 144
Sayonara (1957), 153
Scalphunters, The (1968), 155–6
School Daze (1988), 170
Sergeant Rutledge (1960), 155, 158
Shadows (1960), 154
Shaft (1971), 163, 164
She's Gotta Have It (1986), 170
Shenandoah (1965), 156
Showboat (1936), 139
Slave Days (1929), 139

Slave's Devotion, A (n.d.), 124
Slaves (1969), 165
So Red The Rose (1935), 139
Soldier's Story, A (1984), 172, 173
Song of the South (1946), 23, 150, 166
Soul to Soul (1971), 166
Sounder (1972), 167–8
South Pacific (1958), 153–4, 155
Spider's Web (1926), 131
Spirit of Youth, The (1938), 145
Star Wars (1977), 171
Steamboat 'Round the Bend (1935), 143
Stormy Weather (1943), 149
Streetcar Named Desire, A (1951), 152
Suddenly Last Summer (1959), 152
Superfly (1972), 164
Sweet Sweetback's Baadasssss Song (1971), 163–4

Tales of Manhattan (1946), 150

Tennessee Johnson (1943), 149
They Won't Forget (1937), 138
To Kill a Mocking Bird (1963), 156–7
To Sir, With Love (1967), 158
Tom Sawyer (1973), 166
Toy, The (1978), 174
Trooper of Company K, The (1916), 129

Uncle Tom's Cabin (1903), 123
Uncle Tom's Cabin (1927), 123, 128
Uptight (1968), 159

Wages of Sin (1929), 131
Watermelon Contest, The (1890s), 121
Wattsax (1973), 166
Way Down South (1939), 139
Wedding and Wooing of a Coon, The (1905), 195
Which Way Is Up? (1977), 170